TWENTIETH CENTURY VIEWS

The aim of this series is to present the best in contemporary critical opinion on major authors, providing a twentieth century perspective on their changing status in an era of profound revaluation.

Maynard Mack, *Series Editor*
Yale University

BLAKE

A COLLECTION OF CRITICAL ESSAYS

Edited by
Northrop Frye

Prentice-Hall, Inc. *Englewood Cliffs, N.J.*

To the memory of
PETER F. FISHER

The starry floor,
The wat'ry shore,
Is giv'n thee till the break of day.

Table of Contents

Introduction

by Northrop Frye

This book offers what it is hoped is a representative collection of contemporary critical essays on Blake. I have found it very difficult to make, and I still feel like apologizing to the reader, not for anything I have included, but for what I have been compelled to leave out. Apart from restrictions of space, what I have left out that I might have included was left out mainly in the interest of trying to get some distribution over the whole of Blake's output and outlook, while avoiding topics too impossibly specialized. Some of the best and most important criticism on Blake today is editorial and bibliographical, and such things as G. E. Bentley's recent edition of *The Four Zoas*, Foster Damon's *Blake Dictionary*, or David V. Erdman's reconstruction of obliterated passages in *Jerusalem*, however brilliant in themselves and fascinating as well as necessary to the Blake expert, do not lend themselves to a collection of critical essays for the general reader. On the other hand, Blake's total range of interests is so enormous that nobody can cover more than a small corner of it: there will never be any such person as the world's greatest authority on Blake. The kind of general comment represented by T. S. Eliot's essay in *The Sacred Wood* (1920) already belongs to a vanished world. All Blake criticism today that is worth reading is specialized to some degree, and in the nature of things has to be.

In this situation the best I can do is to give the sense of a busy and widespread body of criticism *in process*. Blake criticism today is moving ahead rapidly after a very slow start; new editions, bibliographies, reproduction of the illuminated books, are providing the apparatus his students need. The lack of such apparatus forty years ago makes Foster Damon's great pioneering study, *William Blake: His Philosophy and Symbols* (1924), almost unbelievable. But a good deal of dust has still to settle. One of the contributors to this book remarked to me in a letter that in his opinion such a collection was premature: that it would be another twenty years at least before the full impact of Blake had consolidated and clarified itself. He is also one of half a dozen contributors who,

1

even since I made the selection, have done more and, as they consider, better work on Blake. Again, the reader will notice that all the essays in this book are by academic scholars. Blake makes an immense appeal to a great variety of people outside the academic profession: poets, novelists, painters, philosophers, psychologists, theologians, students of everything from mathematics to ballet. But there is little written on Blake outside the academic world: there is still too great a gap between the private possession of Blake and the public declaration of that possession. The main reason for this, of course, is the one just glanced at: the great variety of things Blake could do and the complexity of what he did.

The largest single section of this book is concerned with commentary on some of the well known lyrics from *Songs of Innocence* and *Songs of Experience*. These explicatory essays deal with poems which make a vivid impact on the reader at once, and it is only after we turn to the secondary matter of trying to understand what they "say" that complications arise. Mr. Gleckner and Mr. Grant, in particular, deal with these. There are two main elements of complication. One is context: most of Blake's best known lyrics are expressions either of what he called innocence or of what he called experience, and as these are "two contrary states of the soul," one should know which of these contraries any given poem represents. The other is what Mr. Gleckner calls point of view and what some critics call *persona:* just who is speaking in the poem? "Blake himself" is an answer that tells us nothing: a poet speaks in many moods and states of mind. Blake in particular thought of the individual as a bundle of these moods or states which are far more articulate than he is, and over which he has only the most limited control. The longer poems or "prophecies" are full of monologues by such states—in the standard edition of Sir Geoffrey Keynes these monologues are put in quotation marks, but Blake himself rarely provides any helpful punctuation, and in the lyrics it is often an intricate matter to decide just what should be thought of as the "point of view." In Mr. Grant's article one may see something of the critical disagreements provoked by what looks at first sight one of the world's least complicated poems.

Mr. Nurmi and Mr. Erdman are concerned with a different type of interpretation, showing how Blake's poems recorded the life of his time as Blake saw it. They show too how concrete and specific his reactions were, and how little truth there is in the popular picture of him as a mystic with his gaze fixed on eternity and turned away from his neighbor. In reading about child labor and slavery in Blake's time (or their equivalents in our time) we hardly know which is more detestable: the cruelty involved or the complacency with which that cruelty was rationalized in pamphlets, Parliamentary debates, newspapers, and sermons. Blake was struck with this too, and never failed to see the rationalizing of evil as an essential part of the evil itself, if not its actual essence. That is why he gave so much attention to what he thought of as intellectual errors, to abstraction and Deism and natural religion, which he violently attacked, not because he thought they were bad arguments, but because he thought they were arguments designed to defend bad things. That is, abstraction and the like are states of mind resulting from what we should now call anxiety, and anxiety is the state of mind that contemplates the horror of war or the suppression of freedom and says "Oh yes, but. . . ." Blake does not react in this way, and so he can establish a direct human contact with readers however remote in time or space from his world.

Mrs. Chayes and Mr. Keith follow up a third critical approach, the one now called archetypal. Blake's use of imagery and symbolism, in the lyrics at least, is simple but haunting, drawing many of the reader's previous literary associations together into a focus. This is because Blake himself was an intensive rather than an extensive reader. He studied the Bible and Ovid's *Metamorphoses* with great concentration, and struck his roots directly into the central mythical heritage of our culture. His lyrics are in the tradition of the "emblem books" which used a great deal of mythological and allegorical material from Christian and Classical sources. Blake's technique, without being allegorical, nevertheless unobtrusively stirs echoes in our mind of Narcissus, of Persephone, of Eve, of the sky-god Jupiter, and of the kind of significance that modern psychologists and anthropologists help us attach to such myths. For the same reason Blake can, unexpectedly, throw light on the imagery of other poets who came after him and did not know him or thought of him as mad. An increasing number of scholars in English Romanticism find that Blake, simply because of the concentration and accuracy of his imagery, enlightens their understanding of Wordsworth, Coleridge, Shelley, Keats, in spite of his lack of influence in his own time.

Many readers of Blake know only the lyrics, and are unaware, or only vaguely aware, that Blake also wrote a number of longer poems, usually called "prophecies," the title he occasionally gave them himself. One of the shorter and clearer prophecies, *Visions of the Daughters of Albion,* is the subject of Mr. Erdman's commentary, already referred to. To the general reader the later prophecies are apt to look formidable at first, but to anyone who will approach them without prejudice they can be an inexhaustible source of profit and delight. My article on the "Introduction" to the *Songs of Experience* attempts to show how one may proceed from the simpler to the more complex poetry of Blake. I have strictly limited the amount of commentary on the prophecies for this book, as most of it belongs in critical studies that need to be read by themselves. Some of the later lyrics, very simple in language but very difficult in thought, form a transition from lyric to prophecy, and are studied by Mr. Adams. For the longer prophecies I have selected Mr. Bloom's brief but extremely lucid guide to *The Four Zoas*. This poem was left in manuscript, exists in several layers of revision, and is divided into nine sections, called "Nights," there being two complete versions of the seventh Night. Which one is closer to Blake's final intentions about the poem (though of course even the phrase "final intentions" is special pleading) is still disputed. But the reader will, with Mr. Bloom's help, find it an extremely lovely and profound poem for all its incompleteness.

Mr. Adams' essay indicates that there is a tough skeleton of ideas behind Blake's lyrics which criticism could, to some extent, reconstruct even if we did not have the prophecies. The prophecies themselves are not merely mythical poems: they are guides to the process of poetical myth-making, and can be used as a key to poetic mythology just as the lyrics can be used as a key to Romanticism.

For all his greatness as a poet, Blake was an amateur in literature: what he was professional in was painting and engraving. His poetry is unique in English literature in that it was not (except for a volume of early lyrics) published, but was etched on copper plate with accompanying designs, stamped on paper, and colored by hand. Blake was one of England's greatest painters as well as poets, and his poetry was produced in a form which combined the two arts. My second article is an attempt to introduce the reader to this combination of the two arts in his work. The complicated engraving process he invented has been reconstructed, as summarized by Sir Anthony Blunt. (None of Blake's original plates survives except one small corner of a plate of the poem *America*.) Sir Anthony also deals with some of the paintings that, as much as the poetry, tell us about Blake's thought and attitudes. Mr. Grant's essay on "The Fly," already referred to, also deals to some extent with the pictorial impression the poem makes and with some problems in Blake's iconography.

In spite of the specialization of scholarship that Blake's versatility makes necessary, certain aspects of it have become simpler. Formerly, allusions to Blake often used to assume that he was a timeless mystic who was dazed all his life by having been born in a definite place at a definite time; that he influenced no one and that no one influenced him; that his interests were occult and esoteric, with few parallels west of India. Gradually this notion is giving place to a figure who is a much more credible product of eighteenth century, middle-class, Nonconformist England, whose religious views were Christian, whose philosophical views were derived from a negative reaction to Bacon, Newton, and Locke, whose political and social views were close to a large body of contemporary liberal opinion, and whose poetry and painting were strongly influenced by his own cultural environment.

The two final articles in the book deal with some of Blake's intellectual reactions to his milieu. Blake belongs, not to the half of the eighteenth century that we characterize by the daytime metaphor of "Enlightenment," but to the darker, *Sturm-und-Drang* half, to the enthusiasm for the sublime and the "Gothic," for graveyard meditations and evangelical enthusiasm, to the emphasis on feeling and sensibility, the cult of the primitive, and allied developments that had gathered strength by mid-century and had modulated to "Romanticism" by 1800. Mr. Hagstrum deals with the critical, negative aspect of Blake's intellectual position, with his repudiation of the more "Augustan" and "Neo-Classical" values that we attach, with some oversimplification, to the names of Pope and Samuel Johnson. Mr. Fisher explores Blake's interest in the extraordinary eighteenth century myth of the "Druids." The books about the Druids were, at their best, primitive attempts at essays in comparative religion and the language of symbolism. As such, they would naturally interest a poet—poets of all ages, including our own, have used such books. They are generally written by cranks, but that does not detract from their value to poets, most cranks of this type being essentially frustrated poets. Blake made a surprisingly restrained and sensible use of such material—surprisingly in view of what seems his uninhibited tendency to myth-making and of his popular reputation for off-beat thinking. One hopes that some younger scholar will carry on Mr. Fisher's work, especially in Blake's reading of British historians and antiquarians: Rapin, Holinshed, and, above all, Camden's *Britannia*.

The reader will notice that the contributors to this book read Blake as they would read any other poet. There are disagreements over how a given poem is to be read, as there are with all poets, but there is general agreement on Blake's general meaning, and a common feeling that some readings of him are obviously right and others obviously wrong. This simple fact represents a considerable critical achievement. There have been many books asserting that Blake was mad, that his prophecies were unintelligible, that what he said was too private or emotionally colored to have any meaning except what the reader chose to give it. Such sentiments are supported by others who wish to find that Blake was a precocious discoverer of their own views, or who wish to believe in something chaotic or elusive at the center of creative power that will make criticism look foolish. The real reason for this resistance to the normality of Blake's mind is hard to express, because it is a phenomenon unknown (I think) to psychology and only vaguely understood even by critics.

What I am referring to is the sense of panic engendered by lucidity. It is a well known principle in science and philosophy that the simplest questions are those that only great genius can answer, because it takes great genius to become aware of them as questions. The situation is much the same in literature. The great poets, who say something definitive about the human situation, are resisted for a long time as mad, obscure, obscene, or what not, until their revelation seems less dazzling. I said that this phenomenon is unknown to psychology: it is, of course, the central psychological principle of resistance, but the area in which it operates is unexplored. The instinct to call Blake mad was the same instinct that insisted, for well over a century, that Shakespeare was a wild and undisciplined genius with no knowledge of the "rules" of dramatic structure. Similarly, Dickens and D. H. Lawrence were long regarded as flawed and imperfect novelists compared to Thackeray or Galsworthy; torrents of scorn were heaped on Swift in the nineteenth century and on Milton in the twentieth. Our own time has become more cautious: it has happened too often that the thundering denouncer of one generation has sounded like a noisy fool in the next. There are still various devices, such as inventing literary *isms* or selecting a central tradition, that will rationalize our resistance to literature, or to most of it. But a really definitive poet, such as Blake was, makes his way in spite of all resistance.

It is the peculiar quality of a definitive poet that he always seems to have a special relevance to the preoccupations of one's own age, whatever they are. Blake's early critics found him especially eloquent on the sense of the infinity of experience, which they found more fully expressed in Whitman. *Symbolisme* filtered in from France, and Blake's lyrics became poems that presented more than they said. When Nietzsche was better understood, Blake's doctrine that reality is what man creates and not what he studies was better understood too. Freud became a part of our understanding of life, and *The Marriage of Heaven and Hell,* with such aphorisms as "He who desires but acts not, breeds pestilence," took on a new meaning. Frazer joined Freud and the symbolism of "Druidism" in *Jerusalem* became clarified; revolutionary doctrines began to trouble the West and the character of Orc in the prophecies seemed charged with an immediate significance. At present, one may notice that the character in *Jerusalem* called the Spectre of Urthona is a pure existentialist, and a very articulate one. And whatever the cultural interests of the year 2000 may be, it will be discovered in that year that Blake had them particularly in mind, and wrote his poems primarily to illustrate them. In the nature of poetry it cannot be otherwise: poets who are for all time are also for all ages. Naturally, anything that assists the reader to understand such poets is to be welcomed, and it is hoped that the present book will therefore be welcomed too.

Point of View and Context
in Blake's Songs

by Robert F. Gleckner

A flower was offerd to me;
Such a flower as May never bore.
But I said I've a Pretty Rose-tree,
And I passed the sweet flower o'er.

Then I went to my Pretty Rose-tree:
To tend her by day and by night.
But my Rose turnd away with jealousy:
And her thorns were my only delight.

Joseph Wicksteed, the only critic to devote an entire book to Blake's songs, said this about Blake's poem, "My Pretty Rose Tree": it "shows how virtue itself is rewarded only by suspicion and unkindness." And Thomas Wright, Blake's early biographer, commented on the poem as follows: " 'My Pretty Rose Tree,' Blake's nearest approach to humour, may be paraphrased thus: 'I was much taken with a charming flower (girl), but I said to myself, No, it won't do. Besides, I have an equally pretty wife at home. Then, too, what would the world say? On the whole it would be policy to behave myself.' But his wife takes umbrage all the same. The thorns of her jealousy, however, instead of wounding him give him pleasure, for they excuse his inclination for the flower. Moral: See what comes of being good!"

On the contrary, the moral is that such off-the-mark commentary is what comes of ignoring the context of Blake's songs (that is, whether the poem is a song of innocence or a song of experience) and the point of view from which a given poem is written. "My Pretty Rose Tree" is not about virtue perversely rewarded, nor does it have to do with "policy" or morality in the ordinary sense of those words. Virtue by itself meant noth-

"Point of View and Context in Blake's Songs" by Robert F. Gleckner. From *Bulletin of the New York Public Library*, LXI, 11 (November 1957), 531-38.

Reprinted by permission of the editor of *Bulletin of the New York Public Library* and the author.

ing to Blake unless clarified and qualified by context: in the state of innocence it is *The Divine Image;* in experience it is perverted to *A Divine
Image* and *The Human Abstract.* Real virtue Blake defined in *The Marriage of Heaven and Hell*: "No virtue can exist without breaking these
ten commandments. Jesus was all virtue, and acted from impulse, not
from rules." In "My Pretty Rose Tree" the speaker acts from rules when
he refuses the offer of the sweet flower. For, as Blake wrote elsewhere,

> He who binds to himself a joy
> Does the winged life destroy;
> But he who kisses the joy as it flies
> Lives in eternity's sun rise.

The speaker in "My Pretty Rose Tree" not only has let the moment go,
but also has bound to himself a joy. Furthermore, since this is a song of
experience about the state of experience, the flower offered the speaker
is the opportunity for a joy, a love, an ascent to a higher innocence. We
recall that it was not just *any* flower, but a superb one, "such a flower as
May never bore." Still, the offer is refused—because the speaker already
has a rose-tree. Now, conventionally, this is admirable fidelity; for Blake,
however, it is enslavement by what he called the marriage ring. The
speaker thus passes up the chance of a spiritual joy (sweet flower) to return to the limited joy of an earthly relationship (pretty rose-tree). He is
sorely tempted—but his desire has fallen subject to an extrasensual force
symbolized by the existence of, and his relationship to, the rose-tree.

The result, of course, is the speaker's retreat from desire to the only
substitute for desire in Urizen's world of experience, duty:

> Then I went to my Pretty Rose-tree:
> To tend her by day and by night.

The last two lines of the poem are the crushing commentary on the whole
affair. Virtuous in terms of conventional morality, the speaker is rewarded
with disdain and jealousy, ironically the same reaction which would have
been forthcoming had the speaker taken the offered flower. It is Blake's
trenchant way of showing the "rules" to be inane.

How easily, then, in reading Blake's *Songs of Innocence and of Experience* we can ignore Blake's own individual method. Basically that method
is simple, its roots lying in his concept of states and their symbols. Like
many other artists Blake employed a central group of related symbols to
form a dominant symbolic pattern; his are the child, the father, and
Christ, representing the states of innocence, experience, and a higher innocence. These *major* symbols provide the context for all the "minor,"

contributory symbols in the songs; and my purpose here is to suggest a method of approach that is applicable to all of them—and thus to all the songs.

Each of Blake's two song series (or states or major symbols) comprises a number of smaller units (or states or symbols), so that the relationship of each unit to the series as a whole might be stated as a kind of progression: from the states of innocence and experience to the *Songs of Innocence* and *Songs of Experience,* to each individual song within the series, to the symbols within each song, to the words that give the symbols their existence. Conceivably, ignorance of or indifference to one word prohibits the imaginative perception and understanding of the whole structure. As Blake wrote in the preface to *Jerusalem,* "Every word and every letter is studied and put into its fit place; the terrific numbers are reserved for the terrific parts, the mild and gentle for the mild and gentle parts, and the prosaic for inferior parts; all are necessary to each other."

For the serious reader of Blake's songs, then, a constant awareness of the context or state in which a poem appears is indispensable; and since each state is made up of many poems, the other poems in that state must be consulted to grasp the full significance of any one poem. Each song out of its context means a great deal less than Blake expected of his total invention, and occasionally it may be taken to mean something quite different from what he intended. Blake created a system of which innocence and experience are vital parts; to deny to the *Songs of Innocence,* then, the very background and basic symbology which it helps to make up is as wrong as reading *The Rape of the Lock* without reference to the epic tradition. Without the system, Blake is the simplest of lyric poets and every child may joy to hear the songs. Yet with very little study the child of innocence can be seen to be radically different from the child of experience, and the mother of innocence scarcely recognizable in experience. The states are separate, the two contrary states of the human soul, and the songs were written not merely for our enjoyment, or even for our edification, but for our salvation.

Closely related to the necessity of reading each song in terms of its state is the vital importance of point of view. Often it is unobtrusive, but many times [a faithful interpretation of the poem depends] upon a correct determination of speaker and perspective. Blake himself suggests this by his organization of the songs into series, *Innocence* introduced and sung by the piper, *Experience* by the Bard. Superficially there seems to be little to distinguish one from the other since the piper clearly exhibits imaginative vision and the Bard "Present, Past, & Future sees." Yet for each, the past, present, and future are different: for the piper the past can only be the primal unity, for the present is innocence and the immediate future is experience; for the Bard the past is innocence, the present experience, the future a higher innocence. It is natural, then, that the piper's point of view is prevailingly happy; he is conscious of the child's essential divinity and assured of his present protection. But into that joyous context the elements of experience constantly insinuate themselves so that the note of sorrow is never completely absent from the piper's pipe. In experience, on the other hand, the Bard's voice is solemn and more deeply resonant, for the high-pitched joy of innocence is now only a memory. Within this gloom, though, lies the ember which can leap into flame at any moment to light the way to the higher innocence. Yet despite this difference in direction of their vision, both singers are imaginative, are what Blake called the poetic or prophetic character. And though one singer uses "mild and gentle numbers" and the other more "terrific" tones, both see the imaginative (and symbolic) significance of all the activity in the songs. The inexplicit, Blake said, "rouzes the faculties to act." The reader of Blake, then, must rouse his faculties to consider this imaginative point of view always, no matter who is speaking or seeing or acting in a poem.

Both singers are of course William Blake. And since he, or they, sing all the songs, [an understanding of] whether they are identifiable or not with a character in a poem contributes most importantly to the total meaning of the poem. To take an extreme example, in "The Little Vagabond" of *Songs of Experience* there are four points of view: that of the mother, who is now out of her element and can no longer protect her child as she did in *Songs of Innocence;* that of the parson, who is a part of the major symbol of experience, father-priest-king; that of the vagabond himself, a child of experience, not the carefree, irresponsible, thoughtless child of innocence; and that of the Bard, through whose vision each of the other points of view can be studied and evaluated. Without an awareness of this complexity in "The Little Vagabond" the poem dissipates into sentimental drivel. Another good example is "Holy Thursday" of *Songs of Innocence.*

From a conventional point of view it is thoughtful and kind of the "wise guardians of the poor" to run charity schools and to take the children occasionally to St. Paul's to give thanks for all their so-called blessings. But from the piper's point of view (and Blake's of course) the children clearly are disciplined, regimented, marched in formation to church in the uniforms of their respective schools—mainly to advertise the charitable souls of their supposed guardians. The point here (seen only through the piper's vision) is that in the state of innocence there is, or ought to be, no discipline, no regimentation, no marching, no uniforms, and no guardians—merely free, uninhibited, irresponsible, thoughtless play on the echoing green. Accordingly the children in *Holy Thursday* assert and preserve their essential innocence, not by going to church, but by freely and spontaneously, "like a mighty wind," raising to "heaven the voice of song." This simple act raises them to a level far above their supposed benefactors, who are without vision, without innocence, without love: "Beneath them sit the aged men, wise guardians of the poor." The irony is severe, but lost upon us unless we are aware of context and point of view.

As a final example consider the "Introduction" to *Songs of Experience.* The main difficulty here seems to be Blake's chaotic punctuation and the ambiguity it causes. Stanzas 1, 3, and 4 seem to be an invitation to Earth to arise from the evil darkness and reassume the light of its prelapsarian state. Such an orthodox Christian reading, however, is possible only if we forget (1) that this is a *Song of Experience,* and (2) that the singer of these songs is the Bard, not God or a priest. In similar fashion, while ignoring the context or the point of view, one might quickly point out the obvious reference in stanza 1 to Genesis iii, and forget that the speaker in that chapter is the Old Testament God, Jehovah, the cruel lawgiver and vengeful tyrant who became in Blake's cosmos the father-priest-king image. And finally, the Holy Word in Genesis walked in the garden not in the "evening dew" but in the "cool of day," not to weep and forgive but to cast out and curse his children, to bind them to the soil, and to place woman in a position of virtual servitude to man. In view of this, if the second stanza is read as a clause modifying "Holy Word," it is either hopelessly contradictory or devastatingly ironic.

Blake himself hints at the correct reading immediately by means of the ambiguity of the first stanza. There are actually two voices in the poem, the Bard's ("Hear the voice of the Bard"), and the Holy Word's ("Calling the lapsed Soul"); and the second stanza, because of its apparently chaotic punctuation, must be read as modifying both voices. The last two stanzas are the words of both voices, perfectly in context when the dual purpose of the poem is recognized. Only in this way can the poem be seen for what it is, an introduction to the state and the songs of experience, in which the Holy Word of Jehovah is hypocritical, selfish, and jealous, thinking and acting in terms of the physical phenomena of day and night and the earthly morality of rewards and punishments. The Bard, mortal but prophetically imaginative, thinks and acts by eternal time and according to eternal values.

But how does one discover the all-important point of view in Blake's songs? One way is to observe the reactions of various characters to the same symbolic act, object, or character, for both the characters and the symbols ultimately resolve themselves into aspects of the major symbol governing that particular poem. Thus the mother of *Songs of Innocence* is symbolic in that her protection of the child contributes to the overall picture of the child as major symbol of the state of innocence. In addition, many of Blake's symbols are recurrent, so that once a symbol's basic significance is revealed in a kind of archetypal context, each successive context adds association to association within the song series. When the beadle's wand appears in the first stanza of "Holy Thursday" of *Innocence,* for example, its immediate connotation is authority. But since a *beadle* wields the symbol, it is also religious authority, the organized church, institutionalized religion. It also represents an act of restraint which forces the children to act according to rule rather than impulse. The wand is "white as snow" to suggest the frigidity of man-made moral purity as opposed to the warmth of young, energetic, exuberant innocence. And finally, it suggests the worldly, non-innocent concept of duty (and its corollary, harm), the duty of worship which clashes with all of Blake's ideas of freedom and spontaneity. But all of this, it will be said, strongly suggests the world of experience, and "Holy Thursday" is a *Song of Innocence*; the overall point of view is the piper's. The point to be made here is simply this. If we do not read the poem as a *Song of Innocence,* about the *state* of innocence and its major symbol, the joyous child, we can read it as a rather pleasant picture of nicely dressed charity children being led to church by a gentle beadle to sing hymns, or as a terrible view of unfortunate, exploited charity children under the thumbs of their elders. And we would not see that despite outward appearance the children *are* innocent, essentially free and happy, as they spontaneously sing their songs. Without an awareness of context the symbols do not work as Blake intended them to, and the song becomes a fairly inconsequential bit of sentimental social comment.

Considering, then, the care Blake took with point of view, recurring symbols, and symbolic action, we can see that gradually many of Blake's characters merge. The final products of these mergers are what I have called the major symbols. Kindred points of view tend to unite the holders of those points of view; characters who are associated continually with the same or similar symbols tend to melt into one another; and a similar pattern of action reveals a fundamental affinity among the actors. In these ways the significance and value of any one character in any one song are intensified and expanded beyond the immediate context. The physical identity may shift, but the symbolic value remains constant—or better, is constantly enriched. When the beadle's wand in "Holy Thursday" is recognized as part of the basic scepter motif, the beadle's identity, while being retained as representative of church law, merges with that of Tiriel, say, and the father—and ultimately with the "selfish father of men" in "Earth's Answer," the pebble in "The Clod and the Pebble," the "cold and usurous hand" of "Holy Thursday," God in "The Chimney Sweeper," the mother, parson, and "Dame Lurch" in "The Little Vagabond," "Cruelty," "Humility," and the "Human Brain" in "The Human Abstract," and Tirzah in "To Tirzah." Within the identity are inherent all the other identities which combine to make up the major symbol of the context. The priests of "The Garden of Love" may bind with briars love and desire, but they do so because they are selfish, fatherly, cold and usurous, worldly, cruel, humble, hypocritical, and so forth.

One serious question remains: how does one distinguish among all these characters, or are they all precisely alike and hence redundant? Professor Mark Schorer answers the question this way—I know of no better [answer]: "The point is," he says, "that the individuality of these creations lies not in their rich diversity but in the outline that separates them from their backgrounds." That is, each individual identity in its specific context is . . . [an identity as] a part of the whole context and [identical with] the whole of which it is a part. Both the priest of "The Garden of Love" and the flower in "My Pretty Rose Tree" are self-sufficient for some understanding of these two poems. Blake simply asked his reader to do more than merely understand: that, he said, is a "corporeal" function. He wanted them to imagine as he imagined, to see as he saw, even to recreate as he created. Only then does his method make sense, only then can one see the minor symbols as parts of a major symbol, only then can the individual song take its rightful place as a song of innocence or [a] song of experience.

Fact and Symbol in "The Chimney Sweeper" of Blake's *Songs of Innocence*

by Martin K. Nurmi

A reader of William Blake's two chimney sweeper songs needs little more information concerning eighteenth century London "climbing boys" than the songs provide, in order to grasp their general humanitarian and symbolic significance. Yet familiarity with some additional details does, I think, help us see more clearly Blake's indictment of a society that allows children to be subjected to almost unbelievably wretched conditions, and it also gives more force and point to the symbolism. For in the songs Blake does not really describe the living and working conditions of the sweeps; he presupposes a knowledge of them. Writing at the time of the passage of the "Chimney Sweepers' Act" of 1788, when newspapers and reformers like Jonas Hanway were publicizing the treatment of the sweeps, Blake could depend on his readers' being aware of the facts in a way that modern readers are not. And he can therefore express his deep outrage obliquely and ironically, through the understated discourse of boys who, in the symbolic context of *Songs of Innocence & of Experience,* have somehow learned to preserve their humanity in circumstances that are all but completely dehumanizing. The details of chimney sweeping, which these notes will briefly review, do not, to be sure, reveal the poems in a new light. But a more sharply delineated picture of the lives of the sweeps than Blake's speakers in the poems can give strengthens our awareness of the ironic disparity between the tone of the boys' discourse and the conditions they allude to; it helps us to see some of the imagery of the poems a little more vividly; and it sets some badly needed limits on symbolic interpretations of the poems.

"Fact and Symbol in 'The Chimney Sweeper' of Blake's *Songs of Innocence*" by Martin K. Nurmi. Reprinted from *Bulletin of the New York Public Library,* LXVIII, 4 (April 1964), 249-56.
Reprinted by permission of the editor of *Bulletin of the New York Public Library* and the author.

As any reader of *Oliver Twist* is aware, the boys were indeed boys, the smaller the better. When Blake's sweep of *Innocence* says,

> When my mother died I was very young,
> And my father sold me while yet my tongue
> Could scarcely cry " 'weep! 'weep! 'weep! 'weep!" [1]

he is not exaggerating. Although the usual age at which children became sweeps, or apprentices, was six or seven, some did so at five or even four.[2] And the world "sold" is to be taken quite literally. Unlike the usual apprenticeship, in which the fee is paid to the master, binding children— both boys and girls[3]—to a master sweep usually brought a payment ranging from twenty shillings to five guineas from the master to the parent, if there was one, or to whoever had the child at the time.[4] Ostensibly the child was apprenticed for seven years, after which he was usually too large to go up small chimneys; but after his apprenticeship he was by no means assured of a living as a journeyman, since there was not enough work to go around. Often he was left to the parish to support, not only because work was scarce but because he was physically unable to work. Chimney sweeping left children with kneecaps twisted and spines and ankles deformed,[5] from crawling up chimneys as small as nine or even seven inches in diameter,[6] with "chimney sweep's cancer" of the scrotum resulting from the constant irritation of the soot,[7] with respiratory ailments,[8] and eye inflammations.[9]

Their living and working conditions were almost incredibly wretched. Although some masters took reasonably good care of their sweeps, most, to judge from evidence given before parliamentary committees and other contemporary sources,[10] kept them worse than animals. Sweeps arose lit-

---

[1] Blake, *Complete Writings,* ed. Sir Geoffrey Keynes (London and New York 1957), p. 117. All quotations from Blake [in this essay] are from this text.

[2] Jonas Hanway, *A Sentimental History of Chimney Sweepers in London and Westminster . . .* (London 1785), p. 25; "Extracts from Minutes of Evidence" taken before a Committee of the House of Commons, in June 1817, reprinted in *The Chimney-Sweeper's Friend, and Climbing Boy's Album,* arranged by James Montgomery (London 1824), pp. 169-84. References to the minutes reprinted in this volume will hereafter be given as CSF with a page number.

[3] Hanway, pp. 53-54; CSF 102, 170, 211, 228.

[4] Hanway, p. 25; CSF 169, 182. Small boys fetched a higher fee. Children were sometimes stolen and sold; see CSF 219.

[5] CSF 188, 200.

[6] CSF 170, 233.

[7] CSF 170, 199, 228.

[8] CSF 202.

[9] CSF 201.

[10] See, for instance, the reports issued annually by the Society for Superseding the Necessity of Climbing Boys which extracted reports of newsworthy abuses from the

erally "in the dark" and worked until about noon, when they "cried the streets" for more business until it was time to return, carrying heavy bags of soot, to the cellars and attics where they slept, often not on mattresses or even straw but on the bags of soot they had swept.[11] When Blake's sweep says "in soot I sleep," he is not talking metaphorically. Soot is his element day and night. Nor was there much relief from it, even temporarily, for sweeps often went without washing for six months.

Little Tom Dacre cried when they shaved his head, but not the ordinary child's tears that come from fear of the unknown. As the older sweep's remark makes clear, Tom's haircut is a ritual one, like those given [in] prison or the army, and he is aware of it. Tears will be common in his new life for awhile. The children did cry when forced, by fire,[12] slaps, proddings with poles, or by the pricking of the bottoms of their feet with pins,[13] to go up small chimneys. Because the chimneys were very narrow where small boys were used, climbing had to be accomplished by inching one's way up using knees and elbows, which at first became raw and bled but in about six months, after "the sores," developed a thick sole.[14] The most frightening aspect of climbing was going into a confined dark space, uncertain what would happen in the curves, where boys sometimes got stuck and suffocated.[15] To Tom Dacre, the new sweep, unaccustomed as yet to being shut up in a narrow black space but aware of the real possibility of death, a dream of being locked up in a coffin of black is more natural than symbolic. And a boy spending his days squeezed in sooty chimneys, being cleansed only when he was taken outside to be swept off, spending his nights sleeping on soot, would quite naturally dream wishfully of leaping, laughing, running, and being able to "wash in a river, and shine in the sun."

Tom's dreaming of sweeps sporting "naked & white," while it serves Blake's symbolic purpose in the *Songs,* also has a more specific significance. Nakedness is not here merely a symbol of Innocence. In dreaming of it Tom is making a connection between his dream imagery and his ordinary life. For sweeps often went up chimneys naked,[16] since clothes

---

papers. A good bibliography of contemporary accounts of climbing boys and chimney sweeping in general may be found in George L. Phillips, *England's Climbing Boys: A History of the Long Struggle to Abolish Child Labor in Chimney-Sweeping.* Publication No. 5 of the Kress Library of Business and Economics (Cambridge 1949).

[11] CSF 172; Society for the Superseding of the Necessity of Climbing Boys, etc, *Report,* 1826, p. 5.

[12] CSF 210; see also *Oliver Twist,* chapter III.

[13] CSF 187, 208-9, 227.

[14] CSF 186.

[15] Several accounts are given in the Society for Superseding, etc. *Report* of 1826.

[16] Hanway, pp. 53-54; CSF 194.

took up needed room, and bare skin, though it would bruise and scratch, did not catch on the rough plaster inside the chimney, and of course did not cost anything to replace. Protective clothing of leather had been used earlier in the century but was abandoned because the heat from the fires that were sometimes kept going while boys were in chimneys would parch and spoil the leather.[17] Naked immersion in soot, therefore, is Tom's normal state now, and naked white cleanliness is its natural opposite.

The sweeps were not simply children who were forced to clean chimneys. Tom's ritual haircut changes him into a different, somehow subhuman creature.[18] Even Charles Lamb, who was sympathetic with the sweeps, could not help regarding them as beings not quite the same as other people.[19] And Thomas Hood, despite his sympathies for the laboring poor, remarked with a callous detachment, in defending the practice of using children for sweeps, that it was just as natural for these creatures to make their call as it was for sparrows to chirp.[20] When Blake's sweep of *Experience* says that his parents have gone off to church, it is significant that he does not go: the sweeps were not welcome, if an anecdote told by Jonas Hanway is indicative of a common attitude:

> As an instance in what manner these poor children are treated, I remember an anecdote of a little band of them, who had the fortune to be supplied with Sundays clothing: their faces, however, proclaimed them *chimney-sweepers*. Curiosity, or information that the churches were houses of God, carried them within the gates of a church; but alas! they were driven out by the beadle, with this taunt, "What have chimney sweepers to do in a Church?" [21]

Blake's songs are not merely humanitarian poems, like those which Lamb characterized as being "colour'd by fiction," published in James Montgomery's *The Chimney Sweeper's Friend and Climbing Boy's Album*, where "The Chimney Sweeper" of *Innocence* was first reprinted.[22] To Lamb, who unsuccessfully "batter'd [his] brains . . . for a few verses" for the album, Blake's poem was "the flower of the set." [23] "The Chimney Sweeper" belongs only superficially in the genre of sad stories of little

[17] Hanway, pp. 101, 102. Children did not sweep in Germany, and the men sweeps wore leather suits like those used now by scuba divers.
[18] Becoming a chimney sweep "cuts them off from all society," says W. Tooke; see CSF 175.
[19] "The Praise of Chimney-Sweepers."
[20] "The Sweep's Complaint."
[21] Hanway, p. 35.
[22] The poem was sent to James Montgomery, the "arranger," by Lamb. See *The Letters of Charles Lamb & Mary Lamb*, ed. E. V. Lucas (New Haven 1935), II, 424-27.
[23] *Ibid.*

sweeps, for Blake deals with particular social evils symbolically in the comprehensive "prophetic" context of Innocence and Experience. But if this prophetic context of "the Two Contrary States of the Human Soul" reveals a larger meaning in the plight of the sweeps than can be seen naturalistically, we must nevertheless see the sweeps with as much harsh particularity as possible, not only to restore a factual context for Blake's allusive imagery to work in, but also to grasp them clearly enough as symbols. A symbolic interpretation of these songs that does not keep the cruel facts firmly in view is in danger of going badly astray.

The black skin of the sweep of *Innocence* is indeed, as Northrop Frye suggests, a symbolic "modulation" of the black skin of the African,[24] but it is a mistake to take the sweep as being too closely analogous in all respects to the Little Black Boy, as for instance, Robert F. Gleckner does:

> He sleeps in soot instead of the earthly mother's bosom or lap. But just as the mother shields the child from the intense beams of God's love until he is able to bear them alone, so the sweeper's soot is ironically his shield.[25]

A reading such as this is possible only if one takes a rather generalized view of the sweep's condition, for it is hard to imagine what the sweep's soot shields him from, ironically or otherwise. The dark pigment of the African's skin enables him to bear the beams of God's love, symbolized as sunbeams, and, in showing his closeness to God, Blake ironically reveals the clouded vision of the dominant white society which has enslaved him.[26] But the sweeps do not need protection from the beams of love, symbolically or naturally. Naturally, they do not see the sun, and symbolically they are far worse off than the Black Boy, since their humanity has been all but completely obscured. They live in a world of unrelieved blackness, rising in the dark, spending their days enclosed in black chimneys, and sleeping on bags of soot.

The difference between the blackness of the African and that of the sweeps is literally the difference between day and night, between eventual light and unrelieved darkness. The Negro boy is able to look forward to the day when he will be like the English boy—not "white," to be sure, but freed of his "black cloud"; the sweeps, who were white, are now black and, unless an angel releases them, will presumably stay that way. Blake uses blackness ironically in "The Little Black Boy" and "The Chimney Sweeper," but the irony twists in a different direction in each. In the for-

[24] *Fearful Symmetry* (Princeton 1947), p. 212.
[25] Robert F. Gleckner, *The Piper and the Bard* (Detroit 1959), pp. 108-9.
[26] Gleckner's analysis of "The Little Black Boy" is excellent; see also Jacob H. Adler, "Symbol and Meaning in the Little Black Boy," *Modern Language Notes*, LXXII (1957), 412-15.

mer, white society feels that it can enslave and hence dehumanize the Negro because of the blackness of his skin, which then becomes symbolic of his inferiority in the eyes of the whites, and also of his oppression. But a naturalistic fact about dark skin, its ability to withstand the sun's heat, allows Blake to manipulate the symbol to show the Negro boy, from the perspective of humanity, as superior to his oppressors. Naturalistic fact allows no positive reversal of blackness in "The Chimney Sweeper." The irony here is that the white victims of oppression are turned black and become, in the eyes of their oppressors, what they seem to be: creatures so different as to have no claims on humanity.

Although the sweep is like the Negro boy a slave and like him black, the Negro boy can envision a release from his slavery and blackness because his mother's wise teaching has enabled him to see life so comprehensively that he can feel tender now toward the English boy while he waits for the cloud of white supremacy to vanish. The hope held out to the sweep is much fainter. All the older sweep can tell Tom Dacre is that if his hair is shaved off the soot won't spoil it. This consolation could, perhaps, be taken as offering a hope of Tom's actually regaining his Innocence, his imaginative vision, but if so it is not very much to go on. It is more a counsel of endurance than of hope: if your outward appearance of Innocence is completely gone, you will be better able to survive in the world of Experience. In being shorn of his lamb-like hair and being plunged into a world of death and blackness, Tom has been stripped of all the Innocence that Experience can strip him of.[27]

Both poems are of course *Songs of Innocence,* belonging to that complex stratum of songs showing Innocence or imaginative perception of reality dwelling with bitter knowledge gained in the world of Experience. And part of the wonder of "The Chimney Sweeper" is that Blake can make us feel this Innocence as being alive even in the midst of such bitter oppression. But the imagery in which Innocence is represented, derived largely from the modest wishes of a little boy who would like to be liberated from black chimneys to wash in a river and run about in the warm sunshine, does not allow us to forget the realistic context, which even a symbolic view of the sweep's dream should not ignore.

The only hope actually held out to the boy in his dream is vague and distant, expressed by the angel in the language of a kind but stuffy adult:

> And the angel told Tom, if he'd be a good boy,
> He'd have God for his father, & never want joy.

---

[27] According to Gleckner, "the white hair cannot be spoiled because it is not there substantially; yet to the imagination the hair is there, unspoiled and in a sense protected" (p. 109).

Tom's wish to have God for his father is natural enough, since his real father sold him into his present condition.[28] But when is this to be? Being "a good boy" in Tom's situation can mean little more than being a good sweep and staying out of trouble, but he must find what consolation he can even in an admonition like this, which makes him feel that someone, if only in a dream, cares about him. Since no one will really come with a bright key to release him into the sunshine, he must, in order to endure, find in the angel's words a private meaning of more immediate hope than they actually hold out.

The moral appended by the older sweep, "So if all do their duty they need not fear harm," puts another conventional construction on the matter. Doing one's duty here means primarily going up chimneys without having to be forced, and the "harm" is the very real punishment given boys who would not climb. Joseph Wicksteed has suggested that doing one's duty means the dreaming of dreams.[29] I think this interpretation passes too easily over the facts. But the line could be taken to mean that if one adapts as well as possible to the present inhuman condition, sustained by such glimpses of Innocence as are possible, in dreams, then one may be able to keep from losing one's humanity altogether. In any case, there is nothing else that can be done.

If the facts of Tom Dacre's condition make the poem affecting in a way that limits critical ingenuity, I do not think the poem loses very much by that. It does not become sentimental; the speakers' understatements prevent it. Nor does it become simple; the tension between Innocence and Experience, on the contrary, becomes, when fleshed out, more compelingly complex than ever.[30]

Postscript on Legislation

The conditions of climbing boys began to be publicized in 1780. In June and December of that year a committee organized by Jonas Hanway and others sent out appears . . . for better treatment of sweeps [to all masters who could be located].[31] Another committee was formed in 1783 and yet another in 1788, which was instrumental in securing the passage

---

[28] The poem does not say that Tom's father sold him, but parents were usually the ones who sold children. The speaker of the poem was sold by his father. Cp. "The Song of the Poor Little Sweep," which closely parallels this passage: An orphan sweep says, "The gentleman said I'd a father in heaven,/Whose care never slumber'd, whose eye cannot sleep . . . ," CSF 254. This sweep too is filled with gladness, but in a much more conventional way.

[29] *Blake's Innocence and Experience* (London and New York 1928), pp. 109-10.

[30] I am grateful to Professor John E. Grant for valuable critical suggestions.

[31] Hanway, pp. 59-67.

of "An Act for the better regulation of chimney sweepers, and their Apprentices" (28 George III, c. 48). The act stipulated that a churchwarden or overseer of the poor, with the approval of two justices, could bind a boy of eight or older; that masters could have no more than six apprentices; that boys would not be let out for hire to other masters. [It] included in the indenture forms further stipulations that masters must provide "competent and sufficient meat, drink, washing, lodging, apparel"; provide working clothes and at least once a year, clothes to be worn when not working; "at least once a week . . . cause the . . . apprentice to be thoroughly washed and cleansed from soot and dirt"; require the apprentice to attend church and "permit and allow him to receive the benefit of any other religious instruction," when the apprentice would not wear his working dress; limit the hours at which apprentices would call the streets; and, finally, the forms stipulated that the master or other persons delegated by him could not "require or force him the said apprentice to climb or go up any chimney which shall be actually on fire, nor make use of any violent or improper means to force him to climb or go up any such chimney."

The act of 1788 helped a little, but it was weak and difficult to enforce.[32] Abuses continued. What was needed was an act prohibiting the use of climbing boys (and girls) altogether. Machines of various kinds were demonstrated during the next eighty-seven years, as efforts to gain the needed legislation continued.[33] Bills were passed in the Commons in 1804, 1818, 1819, the latter two as the result of a good deal of distressing testimony in committee hearings; but the Lords, for a variety of reasons, among them that of ostensibly not wanting to infringe upon property rights by dictating the kinds of chimneys that would be needed for effective mechanical sweeping, regularly defeated them. Bills regulating the trade were finally passed by both houses in 1834 (4 and 5 Guilielmi, c. 35), in 1840 (3 and 4 Victoria, c. 85), in 1864 (28 Victoria, c. 377). But it was not until 1875, when a bill introduced by Lord Shaftesbury was passed (38 and 39 Victoria, c. 70), that the practice of sending children up chimneys was at last made illegal.

[32] See the Society for Superseding, etc., *Report* of 1826, p. 9. See also David Porter, *Considerations of the Present State of Chimney Sweepers* (London 1792).

[33] See B. M. F[orster], "An Account of Some Attempts which have been made at different Periods to Benefit the Condition of Chimney-Sweepers," *The Philanthropist*, V (1815) 341-42. A very full account of later efforts is to be found in Phillips, *op. cit.*

Blake's Introduction to Experience

by Northrop Frye

Students of literature often think of Blake as the author of a number of lyrical poems of the most transparent simplicity, and of a number of "prophecies" of the most impenetrable complexity. The prophecies are the subject of some bulky commentaries, including one by the present writer, which seem to suggest that they are a special interest, and may not even be primarily a literary one. The ordinary reader is thus apt to make a sharp distinction between the lyrical poems and the prophecies, often with a hazy and quite erroneous notion in his mind that the prophecies are later than the lyrics, and represent some kind of mental breakdown.

Actually Blake, however versatile, is rigorously consistent in both his theory and practice as an artist. The *Poetical Sketches,* written mostly in his teens, contain early lyrics and early prophecies in about equal proportions. While he was working on the *Songs of Innocence and of Experience,* he was also working on their prophetic counterparts. While he was working at Felpham on his three most elaborate prophecies, he was also writing the poems in the Pickering MS, which include such pellucid lyrics as "Mary," "William Bond," and "The Smile." The extent to which the prophecies themselves are permeated by a warm and simple lyrical feeling may be appreciated by any reader who does not shy at the proper names. Hence the method, adopted in some critical studies, including my own *Fearful Symmetry,* of concentrating on the prophecies and neglecting the lyrics on the ground that they can be understood without commentary, may have the long-run disadvantage of compromising with a thoroughly mistaken view of Blake.

What I propose to do here is to examine one of Blake's shortest and best known poems in such a way as to make it an introduction to some of the main principles of Blake's thought. The poem selected is the

"Blake's Introduction to Experience" by Northrop Frye. From *Huntington Library Quarterly,* XXI (1957), 57-67.
Reprinted by permission of the editor of *Huntington Library Quarterly.*

"Introduction" to the *Songs of Experience,* which for many reasons is as logical a place as any to begin the study of Blake. I do not claim that the way of reading it set forth here is necessary for all readers, but only that for those interested in further study of Blake it is a valid reading.

> Hear the voice of the Bard!
> Who Present, Past & Future, sees;
> Whose ears have heard
> The Holy Word
> That walk'd among the ancient trees . . .

This stanza tells us a great deal about Blake's view of the place and function of the poet. The second line, repeated many years later in *Jerusalem* ("I see the Past, Present & Future existing all at once Before me"), establishes at once the principle that the imagination unifies time by making the present moment real. In our ordinary experience of time we are aware only of three unrealities: a vanished past, an unborn future, and a present that never quite comes into existence. The center of time is now, yet there never seems to be such a time as now. In the ordinary world we can bind experience together only through the memory, which Blake declares has nothing to do with imagination. There is no contact with any other points of time except those that have apparently disappeared in the past. As Proust says, in such a world our only paradises can be the paradises that we have lost. For Blake, as for Eliot in the "Quartets," there must also be another dimension of experience, a vertical timeless axis crossing the horizontal flow of time at every moment, providing in that moment a still point of a turning world, a moment neither in nor out of time, a moment that Blake in the prophecies calls the moment in each day that Satan cannot find.

The worst theological error we can make, for Blake, is the "Deist" one of putting God at the beginning of the temporal sequence, as a First Cause. Such a view leads logically to an absolute fatalism, though its devotees are seldom so logical. The only God worth worshipping is a God who, though in his essence timeless, continually enters and redeems time, in other words an incarnate God, a God who is also Man. There is a Trinity in Blake of Father, Son, and Spirit, but Blake takes very seriously the Christian doctrines that the Spirit proceeds from the Son and that no man can know the Father except through the Son, the humanity of God. Attempts to approach the Father directly produce what Blake calls "Nobodaddy," whom we shall meet again in the next poem "Earth's Answer," and who is the ill-tempered old man in the sky that results from our efforts to visualize a First Cause. Attempts to approach the Spirit directly produce the vague millennialism of the revolutionaries of Blake's time, where human nature as it exists is assumed to be perfectible at some time in the future. What Blake thinks of this he has expressed in the prose introduction to the third part of *Jerusalem.* For Blake there is no God but Jesus, who is also Man, and who exists neither in the past like the historical Jesus, nor in the future like the Jewish Messiah, but now in a real present, in which the real past and the real future are contained. The word "eternity" in Blake means the reality of the present moment, not the indefinite extension of the temporal sequence.

The modern poet or "Bard" thus finds himself in the tradition of the Hebrew prophets, who derive their inspiration from Christ as Word of God, and whose life is a listening for and speaking with that Word. In the Christian view, as recorded in *Paradise Lost,* it was not the Father but Jesus who created the unfallen world, placed man in Eden, and discovered man's fall while "walking in the garden in the cool of the day" (Gen. iii.8), the passage alluded to in the last line of the stanza.

> Calling the lapsèd Soul,
> And weeping in the evening dew;
> That might controll
> The starry pole,
> And fallen, fallen light renew!

"Calling" refers primarily to Christ, the Holy Word calling Adam in the garden, and the "lapsèd Soul" is presumably Adam, though the epithet seems curious, as Blake did not believe in a soul, but only in a spiritual body, as far as individual man is concerned. The word "weeping" also refers primarily to Christ. Neither in the Biblical story nor in *Paradise Lost,* where we might expect it, do we get much sense of Christ as deeply moved by man's fate, except in theory. Blake is making a much more definite identification than Milton does of Adam's "gracious Judge, without revile" with the Jesus of the Gospels who wept over the death of man as typified in Lazarus. Both the calling and the weeping, of course, are repeated by the Bard; the denunciations of the prophet and the elegiac vision of the poet of experience derive from God's concern over fallen man.

In the last three lines the grammatical antecedent of "That" is "Soul"; hence we seem to be told that man, if he had not fallen, would have had the powers as well as the destiny of a god. He would not now be subject to an involuntary subordination to a "nature" that alternately freezes and roasts him. On a second look, however, we see that Blake is not saying "might have controlled," but "might controll": the conquest of nature is now within man's powers, and is a conquest to which the poets and prophets are summoning him with the voice of the Word of God. We are very close here to Blake's central doctrine of art, and the reason for his insistence that "Jesus & his Apostles & Disciples were all Artists."

The ordinary world that we see is a mindless chaos held together by automatic order: an impressive ruin, but a "slumberous mass," and not the world man wants to live in. What kind of world man wants to live in is indicated by the kind of world he keeps trying to create: a city and a garden. But his cities and gardens, unlike the New Jerusalem and Eden of the Biblical revelation, are not eternal or infinite, nor are they identical with the body of God. By "Artist" Blake means something more like charitable man or man of visible love. He is the man who lives now in the true world which is man's home, and tries to make that world visible to others. "Let every Christian," urges Blake, "engage himself openly & publicly before all the World in some Mental pursuit for the Building up of Jerusalem."

The second stanza particularly illustrates the fact that what is true of time must be equally true of space. Just as the real form of time is "A vision of the Eternal Now," so the real form of space is "here." Again, in ordinary experience of space, the center of space, which is "here," cannot be located, except vaguely as within a certain area: all experienced space is "there," which is why, when we invent such gods as Nobodaddy, we place them "up there," in the sky and out of sight. But as "eternal" means really present, so "infinite" means really here. Christ is a real presence in space as well as a real present in time, and the poet's imagination has the function of bringing into ordinary experience what is really here and now, the bodily presence of God. Just as there is no God except a God who is also Man, so there is no real man except Jesus, man who is also God. Thus the imagination of the poet, by making concrete and visible a hidden creative power, repeats the Incarnation.

If all times are now in the imagination, all spaces are here. Adam before his fall lived in a Paradisal garden, a garden which is to be one day restored to him, but which since his fall has existed, as Jesus taught, within us, no longer a place but a state of mind. Thus Blake begins *Milton* by speaking of his own brain as a part of the Garden of Eden, which his art attempts to realize in the world. In the Bible the Garden of Eden is the imaginative form of what existed in history as the tyrannies of Egypt and Babylon. Similarly the Promised Land, flowing with milk and honey, is the imaginative form of what existed historically as the theocracy of Israel. England, along with America, is also the historical form of what in the imagination is the kingdom of Atlantis, which included both, but now lies under the "Sea of Time and Space" flooding the fallen mind. We begin at this point to see the connection between our present poem and the famous lyric, written much later as a preface to *Milton*, "And did those feet in ancient time." As all imaginative places are the same place, Atlantis, Eden, and the Promised Land are the same place; hence when Christ walked in the Garden of Eden in the cool of the day he was also walking on the spiritual form of England's mountains green, among the "Druid" oaks. We note that Blake speaks in the first line of his poem not of a poet or a prophet but of a "Bard," in his day an almost technical term for a tradition of *British* poets going back to the dawn of history. "All had originally one language, and one religion: this was the religion of Jesus, the Everlasting Gospel."

> O Earth, O Earth, return!
> Arise from out the dewy grass;
> Night is worn,
> And the morn
> Rises from the slumberous mass.

The first words spoken by Jesus through the mouth of his "Bard" are, appropriately enough, quoted from the Hebrew prophets. The first line refers partly to the desperate cry of Jeremiah faced with the invincible stupidity of his king: "O earth, earth, earth, hear the word of the Lord!" (Jer. xxii.29). A century earlier Milton, after twenty years spent in defending the liberty of the English people, helplessly watching them choose "a Captain back for Egypt," could express himself only in the same terms, in a passage at the end of *The Ready and Easy Way* that may have focused Blake's attention on his source:

> Thus much I should perhaps have said, though I were sure I should have spoken only to Trees and Stones; and had none to cry to, but with the Prophet, *O Earth, Earth, Earth!* to tell the very Soil itself, what her perverse inhabitants are deaf to.

There is also an echo in the same line from Isaiah (xxi.11-12):

> He calleth to me out of Seir, Watchman, what of the night? Watchman, what of the night? The watchman said, The morning cometh, and also the night: if ye will inquire, inquire ye: return, come.

Both in the Hebrew language and in Blake's, "cometh" could also be rendered by "has come": the light and the darkness are simultaneously with us, one being "here" and the other "there," one trying to shine from within, the other surrounding us. Hence a third Biblical allusion appears dimly but firmly attached to the other two (John i.5): "And the light shineth in darkness; and the darkness comprehended it not." The "fallen light," therefore, is the alternating light and darkness of the world we know; the unfallen light would be the eternal light of the City of God, where there is no longer need for sun or moon, and where we can finally see, as Blake explains in the prophecies, that no creative act of man has, in fact, really disappeared in time.

We notice in this stanza that the "Soul" is now identified, not as Adam, but as "Earth," a being who, as we can see by a glance at the next poem, is female. Thus the "Soul" is a kind of *anima mundi;* she includes not only the individual man and the "Church" but the totality of life, the whole creation that, as Paul says, groaneth and travaileth in pain together until now. She is also Nature red in tooth and claw, the struggle for existence in the animal world, of which man, in his fallen aspect, forms part. The prophet sees in every dawn the image of a resurrection that will lift the world into another state of being altogether. He is always prepared to say "the time is at hand." But every dawn in the world "out there" declines into sunset, as the spinning earth turns away into darkness.

> Turn away no more;
> Why wilt thou turn away?
> The starry floor,
> The wat'ry shore,
> Is giv'n thee till the break of day.

There are two ways of looking at the "fallen" world: as fallen, and as a protection against worse things. Man might conceivably have fallen into total chaos, or nonexistence, or, like Tithonus or Swift's Struldbrugs, he might have been forced to live without the hope of death. This world is pervaded by a force that we call natural law, and natural law, however mindless and automatic, at any rate affords a solid bottom to life: it provides a sense of the predictable and trustworthy on which the imagination may build. The role of natural law (called Bowlahoola in the prophecies) as the basis of imaginative effort is what Blake has in mind when he calls creation "an act of Mercy"; the providential aspect of time, in sweeping everything away into an apparent nonexistence, is brought out in his observation that "Time is the Mercy of Eternity." In the Bible a similar sense of the created world as a protection against chaos, usually symbolized in the Bible by the sea, as a firmament in the midst of the waters, comes out in the verse in Job (xxxviii.11): "Hitherto shalt thou come but no further, and here shall thy proud waves be stayed." It is this verse that Blake has in mind when he speaks of the "wat'ry shore" as given to Earth until the Last Judgment; it is the same guarantee that God gave to Noah in the figure of the rainbow. Similarly the automatic accuracy of the heavenly bodies, of which Earth of course is one, affords a minimum basis for imaginative effort. Newtonian science is quite acceptable to Blake as long as it deals with the automatism of nature as the "floor" and not the ceiling of experience.

In Blake's prophecies there are two perspectives, so to speak, on human life. One is a tragic and ironic vision; the other sees life as part of a redemptive divine comedy. The usual form taken by the tragic vision is that of a cyclical narrative, seen at its fullest and clearest in *The Mental Traveller* and *The Gates of Paradise*. Here there are two main characters, a male figure, the narrator in *The Gates of Paradise* and the "Boy" of *The Mental Traveller,* and a female figure who, in the latter poem, grows younger as the male grows older and vice versa, and who in *The Gates of Paradise* is described as "Wife, Sister, Daughter, to the Tomb."

The "Boy" of *The Mental Traveller* is struggling humanity, called Orc in the prophecies. The female figure is nature, which human culture partially but never completely subdues in a series of historical cycles. The relations between them are roughly those of mother and son, wife and husband, daughter and father. Very roughly, for none of these relations is quite accurate: the mother is an old nurse, the wife merely a temporary possession, and the daughter a changeling. The "Female will," as Blake calls it, has no necessary connection with human women, who are part of humanity, except when a woman wants to make a career of being a "harlot coy," or acting as nature does. The female will is rather the elusive, retreating, mysterious remoteness of the external world.

The "Introduction" to the *Songs of Experience,* despite its deeply serious tone, takes on the whole the redemptive or providential view. Hence the relation of the two figures is reversed, or rather, as they are not the same figures, the relation of a male and a female figure is used to symbolize the redemption of man instead of his bondage. The two characters correspond to the Bridegroom and Bride of Biblical symbolism. The male character is primarily Christ or the Word of God, which extends to take in the prophets and poets, and is ultimately Christ as the creative power in the whole of humanity. The "Bard" is called Los in the prophecies, the Holy Spirit who proceeds from the Son. The female character Earth embraces everything that Christ is trying to redeem, the forgiven harlot of the Old Testament prophets who keeps turning away from forgiveness. She has no name, as such, in the prophecies, though her different aspects have different names, the most important being

Ahania and Enion. She is in general what Blake calls the "emanation," the total form of what man, or rather God in man, is trying to create. This total form, a city, a garden, a home, and a bed of love, or as Blake says "a City, yet a Woman," is Jerusalem. But just as the female will is not necessarily human women, so Earth, the Bride of Christ, includes men, as in the more conventional symbol of the Church.

In her "Answer" Earth rejects with bitterness and some contempt the optimistic tone of the Bard's final words. She does not feel protected; she feels imprisoned, in the situation dramatized in Blake's poem *Visions of the Daughters of Albion*. She recalls Io, guarded by the myriad-eyed Argus, or Andromeda, chained on the seashore and constantly devoured by a possessive jealousy. Earth is not saying, as some critics accuse her of saying, that all would be well if lovers would only learn to copulate in the daytime. She is saying that nearly all of man's creative life remains embryonic, shrouded in darkness, on the level of wish, hope, dream, and private fantasy. Man is summoned by the Bard to love the world and let his love shine before men, but his natural tendency, as a child of fallen nature, is the miser's tendency to associate love with some private and secret possession of his own. This "dark secret love," or rather perversion of love, is what Blake means by jealousy.

The "Selfish father of men" who keeps Earth imprisoned is not God the Father, of course, but the false father that man visualizes as soon as he takes his mind off the Incarnation. To make God a Father is to make ourselves children: if we do this in the light of the Gospels, we see the world in the light of the state of innocence. But if we take the point of view of the child of ordinary experience, our God becomes a protection of ordinary childishness, a vision of undeveloped humanity. If we think of God as sulky, capricious, irritable, and mindlessly cruel, like Dante's primal love who made hell, or tied in knots of legal quibbles, like Milton's father-god, we may have a very awful divinity, but we have not got a very presentable human being. There is no excuse for keeping such a creature around when we have a clear revelation of God's human nature in the Gospels.

The source of this scarecrow is fallen nature: man makes a gigantic idol out of the dark world, and is so impressed by its stupidity, cruelty, empty spaces, and automatism that he tries to live in accordance with the dreary ideals it suggests. He naturally assumes that his god is jealous of everything he clings to with secret longing and wants it surrendered to him; hence he develops a religion of sacrifice. There are two other reasons for Earth's calling her tormentor the "father of the ancient men." In the first place, he is the ghost of what in the New Testament would be called the first Adam. In the second place, he is the god to whom the "Druids" sacrificed human beings in droves, as an eloquent symbol of their belief, quite true in itself, that their god hated human life. This false father still exists as the shadow thrown by Newtonian science into the stars, or what Blake calls the "Spectre." He is the genius of discouragement, trying to impress us with the reality of the world of experience and the utter unreality of anything better. His chief weapons are moral conformity, sexual shame, and the kind of rationality that always turns out to be anti-intellectual. If we could only get rid of him, "every thing would appear to man as it is, infinite."

In the three characters of these two poems we have the three generating forces, so to speak, of all Blake's symbolism. First is the Bard, representative of the whole class that Blake in *Milton* calls "Reprobate," personified by Los, and including all genuine prophets and artists. They are given this name because their normal social role is that of a persecuted and ridiculed minority. Earth includes the total class of the "Redeemed," or those capable of responding to the Reprobate. In the later prophecies Blake tends to use the masculine and purely human symbol of "Albion" as representing what the prophet tries to redeem. We can see part of the reason for this change in the poems we are studying: the Bard appeals to Earth, but Earth reminds him that man is responsible for his own evils, and that he should talk only to man if he is to do anything to help her.

The father of the ancient men is what in *Milton* is called the "Elect," because the idolatry of fallen nature incarnates itself in all natural societies; that is, the tyrannies of warriors and priests. In *Milton* too the Reprobate and Redeemed are called "Contraries," because the conflict between them is the "Mental fight" in which every man is obligated to engage. The Elect constitutes a "Negation": he is the aspect of the law that the Gospel annihilates, as distinct from the "starry floor," or basis of imaginative order which it fulfills.

Interpreting Blake's "The Fly"

by John E. Grant

Though "The Fly" is one of Blake's most popular lyrics, many readers have felt that they do not quite understand this elusive little poem. No accurate and thorough critical interpretation of "The Fly" has yet been published. The commentaries of S. Foster Damon and Joseph H. Wicksteed contain valuable insights, but they do not pretend to be systematic, while the article by the late Leo Kirschbaum, published two years ago in *Essays in Criticism* together with an "Editorial Postscript" by F. W. Bateson, contains serious errors and omissions, a number of which I discussed in a counterstatement.[1] One weakness of these interpretations is that they do not consider all the evidence provided by Blake for the reader, particularly the illustration of the poem. Blake himself demanded that no less attention be paid to his painting than to his poems: "As Poetry admits not a Letter that is Insignificant, so Painting admits not a Grain of Sand or a Blade of Grass Insignificant—much less an Insignificant Blur or Mark."[2] He might well have added that, in his extraordinary illuminated books, no correspondence or contradiction between the poetry and the painting should be considered insignificant either. But a comprehensive interpretation of the "design" of "The Fly" must be based on prior separate and detailed analyses of the poem and of the illustration. Since truth can best be distinguished from error

"Interpreting Blake's 'The Fly'" by John E. Grant. From *Bulletin of the New York Public Library*, LXVII, 9 (November 1963), 593-612.

Reprinted by permission of the editor of *Bulletin of the New York Public Library* and the author.

[1] S. Foster Damon, *William Blake: His Philosophy and Symbols* (Boston 1924) pp. 275-76, 285. Joseph H. Wicksteed, *Blake's Innocence and Experience: A Study of the Songs and Manuscripts* (London and New York 1928), pp. 181-82, 280-81. Leo Kirschbaum, "Blake's 'The Fly,'" *Essays in Criticism*, XI (April 1961), 154-62. F. W. Bateson, "An Editorial Postscript," *Essays in Criticism*, XI (April 1961), 162-63. John E. Grant, "Misreadings of 'The Fly,'" *Essays in Criticism*, XI (October 1961), 481-87. See also Harold Bloom, *Blake's Apocalypse: A Study in Poetic Argument* (Garden City 1963), pp. 136-37.

[2] Geoffrey Keynes, ed., *The Complete Writings of William Blake With All Variant Readings* (London and New York 1957), p. 611—hereafter cited as Keynes.

in criticism by specific quotation, comparison, and refutation, I shall also be quite explicit about what seems to me wrong in previous interpretations.

There are more things to be kept in mind when one is interpreting Blake than when one is interpreting most other writers. It should be helpful, therefore, to begin with a summary of the various perspectives and contexts in which the poem exists and from which it must be considered if a thorough understanding of it is to be achieved. The basic perspectives are three: the form of the poem, the literal meaning of the words and the literal action described, and the interpreted meaning of the poem as dramatic utterance. The third perspective is the most problematic, but the first two perspectives are not unmistakably obvious. There is also a fourth perspective, or total meaning of Blake's design [in] "The Fly," to be reckoned with; at this level several contexts are relevant. The first is the illustration; the second is *Songs of Innocence and of Experience* as a whole; the third is Blake's work as a whole; the fourth consists of affinities to works of other authors. There is also a fifth or genetic context provided by Blake's notebook drafts of the poem, but I believe this to be less illuminating for this work than the public contexts.

Such a survey should help the reader to place various kinds of critical comment in their proper relation to the poem. Obviously any attempt to provide an interpreted meaning must be evaluated in relation to the third context of Blake's work as a whole, though the critic should not assume that the poet simply repeats himself because he uses the same symbols elsewhere. Blake's ideas are more flexible than they are often given credit for being. For example, a frequent mistake in recent Blake criticism, to which Kirschbaum was particularly subject in his interpretation of "The Fly," is the intellectualistic error which assumes that when Blake uses words such as "mental" or "thought" he wishes to discredit all other modes of imaginative activity. But Blake had an aversion to such "Urizenic" reasoning because he believed that it ruled out three quarters of life. As Damon points out, there are crucial parallel passages in *Milton,* ones where Blake speaks in his own person about the significance of flies. I shall quote the first passage at somewhat greater length than Damon does:

> Now Albion's sleeping Humanity began to turn upon his Couch,
> Feeling the electric flame of Milton's awful precipitate descent.
> Seest thou the little winged fly, smaller than a grain of sand?
> It has a heart like thee, a brain open to heaven & hell
> Withinside wondrous & expansive: its gates are not clos'd:

I hope thine are not: hence it clothes itself in rich array:
Hence thou art cloth'd with human beauty, O thou mortal man.
Seek not thy heavenly father then beyond the skies,
There Chaos dwells & ancient Night & Og & Anak old.
For every human heart has gates of brass & bars of adamant
Which few dare unbar, because dread Og & Anak guard the gates
Terrific: and each mortal brain is wall'd and moated round
Within, and Og & Anak watch here: here is the Seat
Of Satan in its Webs: for in brain and heart and loins
Gates open behind Satan's Seat to the City of Golgonooza,
Which is the spiritual fourfold London in the loins of Albion.

(20: 25-40)

Damon comments that "Blake's love of every living thing expressed itself in the doctrine that they are all the works of God, and have God within them. . . . Blake interpreted everything in terms of man—as indeed we all are forced to do—but his recognition of this Anthropomorphism of Nature is sometimes puzzling at first. The human forms that he accords all things were what he called 'spiritual forms." But personification needs no excuse:

Thou seest the gorgeous clothed Flies that dance & sport in summer
Upon the sunny brooks & meadows: every one the dance
Knows in its intricate mazes of delight artful to weave:
Each one to sound his instruments of music in the dance,
To touch each other & recede, to cross & change & return:
These are the Children of Los [Poetry]."

(26: 2-7)[3]

Notice how different Damon's interpretation is from Kirschbaum's summary of the meaning of "The Fly":

Without vision [which Kirschbaum too simply equates with "thought"], it makes no difference whether one is a fly or a human being, a live man or a dead one. For without vision, a man is dead: he is an animal—which is what the scientists want to make him anyhow. He is dead because his essential humanity is not within him; he has been robbed of it by misleading and itself misguided experience. But line 18 is extremely sophisticated. It at last divides what a child is from what an animal is. (The deliberate confusion of the two started in Stanza I's "summer play.") A fly is "happy" in an *idiotic* way. It has its own "thoughtlessness." This is the opposite of what the child has, a human innocence that is perfectly happy—but not experienced innocence, not tested innocence, not the *thought* which is the opposite of *thoughtlessness* and which is true vision.[4]

[3] Damon, *op. cit.,* p. 275.
[4] Kirschbaum, *op. cit.,* pp. 159-60.

There is little doubt that Blake himself was opposed to any such Words-worthian glorification of "the philosophical mind" as is contained in Kirschbaum's summary, but the poem does literally say something very like what Kirschbaum interprets it to mean. However we need a little more information before we can evaluate the difference between what the poem literally says and what, as a dramatic utterance, it should mean to the reader.

There are certainly connections between the moods of "The Fly" and the . . . passages from *Milton*. For example, Bateson nicely refers to the "conviviality" contained in Stanza 3, thus using a word that partic-ularly well summarizes the feeling of the second passage from *Milton* cited by Damon. But we should be careful to distinguish the tones and significance of the passages from *Milton*, which are prophetic in the "Beulah" mode of threefold vision, from the tones and significance of "The Fly," a song of experience where twofold vision naturally pre-dominates. Who is actually talking in "The Fly"? "Blake," say Damon, Kirschbaum, and Bateson, without being sufficiently conscious that such an answer is indeterminate rather than specific. Damon means "Blake the Prophet"; Kirschbaum means "the speaker of the poem, who must be a poet because Blake was and because the poem echoes *Lycidas* in a passage about bad poets"; Bateson means "William Blake the man, who was writing poetry about 1792." I believe that all of these answers are either inaccurate or critically misleading.

From a literary point of view the ultimate narrator in all of the *Songs of Experience* is "the Bard," "who Present, Past, & Future sees," as an-nounced in the "Introduction," [5] but he is obviously not the speaker in "Earth's Answer," "The School Boy," "The Little Vagabond," or even, when the poem is carefully studied, the speaker in "The Tyger." [6] Least of all is he the speaker in "A Poison Tree." Similarly just because the personal pronoun "I" is used in "The Fly," the reader should not assume that the speaker is "Blake" in any of his several personae. On the con-trary, the speaker should be identified as a man *in* Experience, whose voice must be sharply distinguished from that of "the Bard," the pro-phetic observer of the fallen world described in this integrated anthology. Since he does not recognize this distinction, Kirschbaum often approaches

---

[5] Concerning the character of the Bard see Northrop Frye, "Blake's Introduction to Experience," [reprinted above]. A different view of the problem is presented by Bloom, *Blake's Apocalypse,* pp. 130-133.

[6] See my "The Art and Argument of 'The Tyger'," *Discussions of William Blake,* ed. John E. Grant (Boston 1961), pp. 64-82. I have not convinced all readers, however; see Hazard Adams, "Reading Blake's Lyrics: 'The Tyger'," *Discussions,* pp. 50-63 and Bloom, *op. cit.,* pp. 137-39.

what the poem is saying without understanding the visionary significance of what is said. An adequate interpretation must include an awareness of what this brief poem in iambic dimeter leaves unsaid. Neither the real ambiguities of the poem nor Blake's notebook provides a sufficient basis for reconstruction of the unstated context of the poem. Only by reference to other parts of Blake's work that he wished to make public can the interpreter ascertain how the poem as dramatic utterance should be understood.

The poem has a distinctive form, which is not quite the same thing as its meaning, and it is here that systematic criticism should start. "The Fly" begins with an anecdote in Stanza I in which the speaker's encounter with (and probable killing of) the Fly is narrated. This stanza is followed by two groups of two stanzas with the ideas arranged in quasi-logical relationships. The first of these groups, Stanzas II and III, asks hypothetical questions in similes about the relationship between the speaker and the Fly and then supports the hypotheses with the evidence that the speaker similarly revels and is similarly mortal as the eventual victim of "some blind hand." The second of these groups, Stanzas IV and V, sets forth the hypothetical proposition in metaphors that the presence of thought is equivalent to life and the absence of thought is equivalent to death. The conclusion is that the speaker is "a happy fly" whether he lives or dies.[7]

Even before he tries to work out exactly what the speaker is saying, the reader should feel that the poem is paradoxical, especially at the end. But it is part of the rhetoric of the poem that the speaker should show no awareness of having spoken paradoxically or, indeed, of having done anything more than tell an anecdote and then meditate about the relatedness of all life and the specific relationship between happiness and mortality. In other words, an essential aspect of the art of the poem is to set up a contrast between the artlessness of the speaker and the awareness of the reader. Let us see what is made of this contrast in the first stanza:

> Little Fly
> Thy summers play,

[7] This summary and all subsequent interpretation of the poem are based on the postulate of a single speaker, though it is conceivable that the last two stanzas, set off in a second column, are spoken by the Bard or Blake in a choric function. The fact that the fifth stanza of the poem was written before the fourth tends to weaken the possibility of two speakers, however, and I cannot see how the difficulties of the poem would be in any way clarified by such a distinction. It may be useful to discover two speakers in other *Songs*, even when Blake did not make the presence of more than one very explicit, but not here.

My thoughtless hand
Has brush'd away.

Kirschbaum discovered a number of implications in this stanza, not all
of which seem equally convincing to me. I have already criticized his
excessive ingenuity in having found a theatrical pun in the word "play."[8]
His other points may be summarized as follows: first, the suggestion that
the speaker is like an Olympian in that he was unconcerned about the
fate of the Fly; second, the possibility that "thoughtless" means "cruel";
third, the idea that there is a shift from childlike Innocence in the first
two lines to cruel Experience in the last two. Reflection, Kirschbaum
indicates (p. 155), "apparently is concomitant with cruelty." It is not
splitting hairs to find something wrong with each of these formulations.
For example, to gloss "thoughtless" as "cruel" brings in the idea of an
intention of causing pain, whereas what the poem says is that the speaker
was *inconsiderate* of the Fly and accidentally brought about its demise.
"Thoughtless" does not mean "ruthless." The third point, on the other
hand, is accurate for the poem but premature for the action of this
stanza because reflection is not at issue except as a *result* of the event.

The Olympian analogy has some justification in the poem as a whole
because it is strengthened by "blind hand" in Stanza III and because the
reader might recognize, in the initial action of "The Fly," an echo of a
direct Shakespearian reference to the Olympians. This is most clearly
appreciated when the reader recalls a couplet in Blake's *Auguries of
Innocence:*

The wanton boy that kills the Fly
Shall feel the Spider's enmity.

(lines 33-34)

This couplet contains an unmistakable allusion to Gloucester's famous
lines in *King Lear:*

As flys to wanton boys, are we to the gods;
They kill us for their sport.

(IV, i, 36-37).

There are important differences between these gnomes, which help to
bring out exactly what is being said in "The Fly." Gloucester has experi-

---

[8] "Misreadings," pp. 484-85. But in this context the word "play" is something of a
metaphor which humanizes the insect even before the speaker begins his formal analogies in the subsequent stanzas. From a merely descriptive point of view the Fly was not
playing (like a child), but simply acting like an (annoying) fly. The reader is left to
reflect that the speaker must have had an innate awareness of the place of the Fly in
the dance of life, signalized by his unconscious metaphor, but his deadly indifference
overcame his tendency toward fellow-feeling.

enced enough of providence to think that it is malicious, that the gods behave to men like boys who pull wings off flies for the fun of it. But in the couplet from *Auguries of Innocence* Blake does not wish to emphasize a comparable malevolence in the boy. He does not say that "the wanton boy that kills the Fly is like an irresponsible god who kills a man." For Blake such a god does not exist, except as a spectral projection of human malice. Instead he wishes to emphasize the unintentional cruelty resulting from the sportive play of the boy. It is significant that Gloucester's gods are not mentioned at all in Blake's couplet, though they continue to loom in the background as a result of the allusion and also because more manifest hints of providence are contained in other couplets in the poem. Consequently, the episode should be understood primarily on a naturalistic level: the Spider feels "enmity" and will sting the boy because, in the struggle for existence, he was deprived of his food when the boy squashed the fly. But the speaker in the Song of Experience is an adult "who ought to know better" than the boy that carelessness can be culpable, and it is clear enough why Blake the poet was tempted in the draft to permit the speaker to call himself "guilty." Nevertheless, the speaker in the printed version makes no such judgment of himself anywhere in the poem.

How the reader responds to the speaker's callousness depends on the reader's presuppositions. Kirschbaum (p. 160) implies that Blake wished to avoid a sentimental response and he assumes that Blake must have had an "adverse reaction" to Uncle Toby's famous dismissal of a fly in *Tristram Shandy*. But Blake had not been instructed by neo-Stoic New Critics that sentimentalism is always illegitimate in poetry. Blake was the author of a number of couplets in *Auguries of Innocence* such as: "He who shall hurt the little Wren / Shall never be belov'd by Men," which provoked Babbitt to sneer.[9] Even more relevant is the fact that the "little winged fly," in the first passage from *Milton* quoted above, "has a heart like thee." I shall return to some larger implications of this problem below, but it is evident that Blake considered sentiment to be part of the decorum of threefold Beulah vision.

In the second stanza the speaker begins to reflect on the relationship between himself and the Fly:

> Am not I
> A fly like thee?
> Or art not thou
> A man like me?

[9] Irving Babbitt, *Rousseau and Romanticism* (New York 1919), p. 196.

The mood of this stanza is difficult to capture if the hypothetical questions are translated either into assertions or into rhetorical questions. Kirschbaum (p. 155) understands Blake to argue as follows: "It is not that the fly is important; it is that the man is like a fly and hence unimportant." To be sure Kirschbaum recognizes that the thoughts are "set down" as questions, but he treats them as "conclusions [that] follow from the implications of Stanza I." I have already ("Misreadings," p. 486) criticized his idea that William Blake could have believed either a fly or a man to be unimportant, but even the speaker of the poem does not commit himself to such a covert assertion.

In the first place, as Stanza III makes clear, the speaker does not primarily compare himself and the Fly with respect to their *importance*, but with respect to their *mortality*. Moreover, the hypothetical questions of Stanza II do not necessarily follow from Stanza I because other kinds of men might either feel sorry (like the speaker in the first draft) or feel positively happy about having exterminated a fly. It is precisely the tentative quality of the speaker's reflections, which begin in Stanza II, that characterizes him. In the second and third stanzas it becomes clear that prophetic sympathy is not part of the makeup of the speaker in the finished poem. Elsewhere it is Blake's reiterated assertion that "Every thing that lives is Holy," [10] but the speaker knows nothing of that. This voice of experience becomes mildly concerned about what he has done and quietly meditative about what it implies for his own life and death. To glance ahead to the end of the poem, the speaker does not resolve to change and become thoughtful. Instead he seems to decide to make the best of life's transientness, come what may, like a character in the *Rubáiyát*. Certainly thought has little place in his ordinary way of life (though the death of a fly makes him pensive): "For I dance / And drink & sing." The reader should probably not condemn this thoughtless way of life, as Kirschbaum (p. 156) seems to do when he alludes to "Nepenthe." Such a life is at worst pathetic, and the suggestion of conviviality would have pleased Blake, who evidently enjoyed a pint now and then. Though it has been called "sentimental drivel," the reader should bear in mind the naïve irreverence of the Little Vagabond, who wishes that there were ale for all in church so that the Parson could "drink," as well as sing and preach.

Let us look more closely at the third stanza:

> For I dance
> And drink & sing:
> Till some blind hand
> Shall brush my wing.

[10] Keynes, pp. 160, 199, 289.

Kirschbaum makes some good observations about "blind hand" as opposed to "wing" in this stanza, but several of his remarks must be adjusted to fit the context of "The Fly." [11] "Blind hand" does imply, to the reader of Blake, philosophic generalizations about authority, science, and "a corrupted church of Christian God," [12] but the reader must also recognize that the speaker is not thinking clearly about any of these things. For him it is "some blind hand" or other, to which he cannot give a name, that will do away with him. Yet the speaker is imaginative enough to know, not only that he is fragile like a fly, but also that he too has "wings" that can be "brushed." If one were wholly unsympathetic to the speaker, he might feel that with this periphrasis the speaker is trivializing and thus minimizing the tragic certainty of his own mortality. From a prophetic perspective, on the other hand, it appears that the speaker has enough imagination to see that he is not only mortal like a fly, but that he has super-mortal potentialities, signified by his use of the word "wing." No doubt the speaker himself would say that this is a mere analogy, but it is the ability to see analogically that redeems a man from the Ulro of "Single vision & Newton's sleep." Moreover, the oxymoronic force of "blind hand" combines with the gentle horror of the line "Shall *brush* my wing" in a way that is admirable as a comprehensive account of both the finality and mildness of such a death.[13] One has only to substitute the word "crush" for "brush" to see how easily the balance could be disturbed. But this speaker could not bear to entertain such a brutal vision of his own death. Such a vision is only tolerable for a prophetically strengthened imagination which has steadily considered every one of the doors of death. Blake elsewhere gives the reader this kind of awareness as well: in plate 11 of *The Gates of Paradise,* a blind old man is depicted clipping the wings of a youth with a huge pair of shears (Keynes, p. 767).

The last two stanzas present the speaker's philosophic conclusions:

> If thought is life
> And strength & breath:

[11] I see no reason, however, to believe with Kirschbaum (p. 158) that in this poem the "hand" is "holy" from any relevant point of view. His references to the sanctified hands of Christ, John the Baptist, and in *King Lear* merely point to archetypal potentialities for symbolic hands. Nowhere in *Songs of Experience* are "hands" unequivocally good. In "Holy Thursday" and "Infant Sorrow" they are clearly sinister, in "The Tyger" they are ambiguous (see my article mentioned in footnote 6) and only in "The Little Girl Found" (line 27) is there any suggestion that they are sanctified. This poem is clearly a transitional poem between Innocence and Experience, which Blake relocated in Experience after first including it in Innocence. The reader should also recall the sinister giant Son of Albion, who is named "Hand" in *Jerusalem.*

[12] Kirschbaum, *op. cit.,* p. 157.

[13] Compare "the unimaginable touch of time" in Wordsworth's great "Mutability" sonnet.

> And the want
> Of thought is death;
>
> Then am I
> A happy fly,
> If I live,
> Or if I die.

The reader of Blake will recall that in *An Island in the Moon* much fun
is made of philosophers, especially Aradobo (Keynes, p. 49), who are be-
mused by Cartesian formulae about thinking and being. But in "The
Fly" such derisiveness is absent as the thought of this speaker in Experience reaches its climax, the maximum certainty possible for such a man.
This is rhetorically signaled by the fact that in Stanza IV the speaker
uses metaphors to express his hypothesis, rather than the more tentative
similes and questions employed in Stanza II. Kirschbaum excellently describes the force of the key word "if" in Stanza IV as an ostensible condi-
tional that means, in effect, "since"; the speaker at this point does feel
considerable assurance about his hypothesis. Nevertheless, the premise-
conclusion form of the speaker's logic should strike the reader as lacking
in visionary conviction as compared, for example, with the prophetic
downrightness of the thirty-sixth "Proverb of Hell": "One thought fills
immensity" (Keynes, p. 151), or, for that matter, with the declarative form
of the proposition. Blake had first written simply: "Thought is life"
(Keynes, p. 183). It should also be observed that the second line of the
stanza is ambiguous. If the speaker is simply saying that "strength and
breath" are attributes of "life," he is making an assertion that seems self-
evident and even redundant, though the Fly had no obvious strength.
But the word "And" at the beginning of the second line can only very
loosely mean "that is." What I believe occurs at this point in the poem is
that an awareness of a more energetic mode of being almost dawns on the
speaker, only to die away again with the reiterated "And" of line three.
The movement of the speaker's mind might be paraphrased as follows:
"I am not a particularly thoughtful fellow, but what I've done has made
me think. What if being thoughtful is *really* living—and not being
thoughtful is death (but so what? all men are mortal)?" For the reader
these lines may imply that an unthoughtful man, even when he is thinking, does not really care enough for life to live.

Kirschbaum's account of the meaning of the final stanza contains a
number of good observations, but if the reader has followed the develop-
ing form of the speaker's thought, there are several other essential points
to be made. Notice that there is a crucial ambiguity of emphasis in the
expression "happy fly." Because of the line of thought that leads out of

Stanza II, the speaker would probably give "fly" the stronger emphasis, because he is naturally thoughtless, as flies themselves are proverbially assumed to be, and he is aware that his mortality is comparable to that of the Fly, when he stops to think about it. The rhyme "fly-die" tends to reinforce this reading. The speaker also believes, however, that even if he is mortal he can be as happy as a mortal fly by living it up while there is yet time, like the grasshopper in the fable. At this point the reader may be tempted to feel self-righteous and to say that this sort of life in the Orc cycle is as good as being dead, that stupid happiness is a fool's paradise, that it is better to be miserable, etc. But such censoriousness is at least premature; the speaker does want to have it the other way too. He believes that he can also be a *happy* fly if he thinks and therefore (since "thought is life") "lives." Nevertheless, the reader can hardly discover what such a speaker imagines the philosophic implications of such an immortality may be. Perhaps the speaker supposes that as long as he has his wits about him, like Camus' Stranger, he is not dead. Possibly the speaker is a nominal Christian who has the notion that he has a place reserved if only he will entertain some serious thoughts. It is highly unlikely, at any rate, that the speaker would have such Blakean thoughts as Wicksteed propounds in his interesting commentary.[14] On the basis of what the speaker has said in the poem, "if I live" is a puzzle that he himself could not finally explain.

In short, there are loose ends in the last stanza such as I find in this line and such as Bateson has identified in the last line.[15] If Blake is the speaker, he must assume responsibility for these oversights and the poem is demonstrably imperfect. But if the speaker is a voice of Experience, the reader should expect that the speaker's reasonings will not quite add up because his first principles are erroneous.[16] As I have indicated, the

[14] Wicksteed, *op. cit.*, pp. 181-82. See the final paragraph of this article.

[15] Bateson, *op. cit.*, p. 162, acutely points out that the idea is a rationalization that seems to justify the speaker's unintentional cruelty to the Fly "by suggesting that the fly is happy in death."

[16] A defense of communicatory incoherence must consider whether there is any limit to the amount of unintelligibility than can be excused in a literary work if the speaker is presented as mad or idiotic. Critics who subscribe to the "imitative fallacy" theory constantly ask where the line is to be drawn that separates artistic success from artistic failure. Like all theories of literary value, however, the imitative fallacy should be used as a rule of thumb. Some poetry fails by being incoherent, whereas some poetry is gloriously successful in dramatizing incoherence. Much outstanding twentieth century literature, notably that of Joyce, Faulkner, and Beckett, can be seen as an experiment in stretching the bounds of the imitative fallacy. But even the greatest poets may fall foul of this fallacy. I have argued elsewhere that Shakespeare himself sometimes nodded. See Jack M. Davis and J. E. Grant, "A Critical Dialogue on Shakespeare's Sonnet 71," *Texas Studies in Literature and Language*, I (1959), esp. pp. 219-20. In "The Fly," however, the speaker is immersed in Experience and if he is to be presented as reason-

speaker does not have the visionary perspective on the Fly available to the poet in *Milton,* and thus he draws the wrong conclusions about both the nature of the fly and his own human nature. For the Fly of Innocence has "a brain open to heaven & hell" and it "knows the dance . . . in its intricate mazes of delight," which is all it needs to know in order to fulfill its essential nature. But the speaker and Kirschbaum (p. 155) presuppose a great chain of being in which each higher level is more excellent than the one beneath it, whereas Blake, as Damon has clearly shown, in contrasting "The Fly" with Gray's "Ode I: On the Spring," made no such assumption of a stratified creation. On the contrary, Blake's fourfold vision is apocalyptic and inclusive so that every living thing is recognized as equal to every other living thing, every object of perception is potentially infinite, and every creature, whether a fly, a little Black Boy, or a white English Protestant is as good as every other creature. "Everything that lives is Holy."

What Kirschbaum has given us, then, is a Urizenic reading of the poem that attempts to justify the twofold vision of the speaker, whereas Damon has given us a mistakenly prophetic reading of the poem that assumes the speaker of this Song of Experience is a visionary. I believe that the speaker is in error, but that Blake does not despise him for it. The Bard is "indignant" when the guardians of Experience are maliciously self-righteous (as in "A Little Girl Lost"), but the speaker in "The Fly" was only insensitive, and the Bard is saddened by his confusion.[17] But the Bard must deplore both the thoughtless indifference that leads to the extermination of flies (as well as of men) and rationalizations that justify the inhumanity of all creatures to one another. Notice how the final rationalizations of the speaker in "The Fly" are inspired by his dim vision of "some blind hand" of Nobodaddy, and compare the prophetic warning in the first quoted passage from *Milton* against a belief in a "heavenly father beyond the skies."[18] Dostoevsky's attitude toward the Underground Man's rational-

---

ing, he must betray some confusion. What he says might pass for serious thinking in the world of Experience, but it is certainly not wisdom and Blake expects his reader to be able to see through such a pseudo-Koan. On the other hand, I am inclined to agree with Robert F. Gleckner that Blake failed to construct a poetically intelligible dramatic situation in "The Human Abstract" and that this poem is not an unqualified artistic success. See his "William Blake and The Human Abstract" *PMLA,* LXXVI (September 1961), 373-79.

[17] It is possible to discover prophetic irony in the title of the poem, which is presumably supplied by the Bard. According to almost any reading, the poem must tell not about the Fly but about the speaker. Since the narrator becomes increasingly certain that he is a fly, the Bard must finally concede the point: "Yes, you are 'The Fly.'" But the mood of this awareness is more piteous than sardonic.

[18] I have several times referred to this passage in order to provide a corrective perspective on the speaker of "The Fly." There are other details that might usefully be

ization of his cruelty to the prostitute Lisa is comparable. Both Blake and Dostoevsky condemn the sin but forgive the sinner.

"Live and let live," like other proverbs of Experience, is not the summit of wisdom, but only a church porch virtue. Nevertheless, if man cannot achieve even this virtue, the world must be in a parlous state—and prophetic writers are unanimous that it is. No amount of double talk can justify a more "realistic" attitude than is contained in this proverb of Experience, but the poets have always been attracted to a more Innocent view, though wise critics have called them naïve or sentimental for succumbing to it. A glance at some other works that are imaginatively related to "The Fly" will show the Innocent vision in action.

Blake loved Spenser not only because he wrote a great mythological poem, *The Faerie Queene,* but also because he saw fit to write "Muiopotmos" about the pathetic fate of a butterfly ambushed by a spider and because he thought it important to translate "Virgil's Gnat" about an insect whose life was brushed away by a sleeping shepherd, whose own life was threatened by a lurking serpent. Blake would certainly have remembered that the gnat was not happy with his fate, though the shepherd had to be reminded. And when Blake's own age, which Northrop Frye has called "The Age of Sensibility," [19] rediscovered the greatness of Spenser and the community of all living things, work after work was written exploring this innocent relationship. This vision was strongly entrenched in the archetypal imagery of English poetry, of course, as such poems as Googe's "The Fly," Herrick's "Upon a Flie" and "The Amber Bead," and Oldys's "On a Fly drinking out of his Cup" indicate. But in Blake's age there are many works that have close affinities with the feelings involved in "The Fly." We have seen the relevance of the Uncle Toby episode mentioned by Kirschbaum and Gray's "Ode I" discussed by Damon. I think that Blake had also read Burns's "To a Mouse," as the rejected stanza beginning "the cut worm forgives the plow" suggests.[20] And the pathetic vision specifically employing insect imagery has been recreated in many con-

---

cited, such as the image of the "Webs" of Satan, which implies that he is a giant spider lurking to catch the fly of Innocence. In this prophetic counterstatement, the Bard not only shows what is wrong with the vision in the Song of Experience, but he also explains how this error depends on a false metaphysics. Here, as so often in his later work, Blake seems to be at pains to correct possible misunderstandings of his earlier work.

[19] Northrop Frye, "Towards Defining an Age of Sensibility," *Eighteenth-Century English Literature: Modern Essays in Criticism,* ed. James L. Clifford (New York 1959), pp. 311-18, esp. p. 316.

[20] I recall hearing Margaret Mead assert that, according to the ethos of modern England, the greatest sin that children can commit is cruelty to animals. Such an idea could hardly have obtained before the age of sensibility. Is it possible, after all, that poets are unacknowledged legislators?

temporary poems. Though the modern poet must eschew sentimentality, Robert Frost implicitly engages all the familiar images and feelings for an insect victim in his great small poem "Design." And Karl Shapiro's fine poem "The Fly" seems to be an exercise in expressing every possible attitude that one might have toward a housefly, though the central idea of his poem is human cruelty whereas the central idea in Blake's poem is human mortality. The eschatological implications latent within the quotidian event of killing an insect are most fully explored by Dylan Thomas in "Today, this insect, and the world I breathe." In this poem the fragility of the small creature, together with its metamorphic capacities, are developed into a universal parable of human fall and regeneration toward which half a dozen famous myths are declared to be less centrally relevant. Blake chose to build his poem on a sub-apocalyptic scale, but the reader should feel that the reflections of the speaker in "The Fly" are not too grandiose, but too limited. A wise man does not have to be warned, in the words of *Auguries of Innocence* (Keynes, p. 432):

> Kill not the Moth or Butterfly,
> For the Last Judgment draweth nigh.

The Illustration

If one attempts to grasp the imaginative relationship between Blake's poem and design, he will receive little help from the commentators. Damon (p. 285) described the illustration as follows: "A mother teaches her baby to walk. Behind her a little girl is playing battledore. The shuttlecock was no doubt intended to suggest the Fly. On the mother's left is a barren trunk of a tree." Wicksteed (p. 182) is even briefer: "The design shows Life's frailty and joy," though elsewhere (p. 61) he says, in a valuable passage generally neglected, that in Experience girl poems are about love and boy poems are about thought, especially thoughts about God, and he notes: "In 'The Fly' the little boy is in the illustration only." I can find no other interpretive comment on this design except for Ellis's assertion that the depicted children are "happy flies." [21]

Songs of Experience gives every evidence of being a carefully organized anthology of poetry and painting. For this reason I shall reject, as an initial postulate, Bateson's implication (pp. 162-63) that Blake used the design in spite of the fact that he had engraved it earlier for a poem he never got around to writing. Instead I shall begin with the contrary assumption that there must be some sort of oblique relationship between

---

[21] Edward J. Ellis, "Introduction" to the Quaritch facsimile of *Songs of Innocence and of Experience* (London 1893), p. xxi.

the poem and the illustration, and that Blake hoped that the apparent lack of relationship between them might tease his reader into thought. As Blake later explained, he believed that "what is not too Explicit [is] the fittest for Instruction, because it rouzes the faculties to act" (Keynes, p. 793). But the small connections between the poem and the illustration noted by Damon and Wicksteed would hardly have satisfied Blake. If no more comprehensive relationship exists, the total design is a failure whatever the merits of its parts. My hypothesis is that since the Bard is not the speaker of the poem, it is probable that the prophetic illustrator depicts things as they appear from a true visionary perspective. Any literal illustration of the poem would be redundant and consequently unilluminating because it could show no more than the man of experience musing over the corpse of the Fly—which in any case is too tiny to be visually interesting in such a small design.[22] This hypothetical illustration reminds us again, however, that the poem is really not about the killing of a fly by a man but about the mortality they both share. The slaughter of a fly is simply one of the innumerable cases of inhumanity that characterize the fallen world of Experience. Though it inspired an average man in Experience to thought, that event can hardly have the same significance for a visionary whose constant activity is mental, but must neccessarily be assigned to a subordinate place. Therefore, lest man become inured to Experience and come to terms with inhumanity, it is essential that the prophet show a visionary alternative, a light shining in the midst of darkness, as a corrective to despair. Blake certainly does so in the redemptive major illustrations to "London." We should expect him to be doing something comparable here.

The first task for systematic interpretation is to provide an accurate

[22] I have pointed out in my "Misreadings" article that Blake depicted a comparable incident in his fifth illustration for Gray's "Ode I: On the Spring" (reproduced in *William Blake's Designs for Gray's Poems*, ed. H. J. C. Grierson, Oxford 1922). There a two-winged human housefly has been slain on a dead tree and another is lying dead on the ground. They have been "brush'd by the hand of rough Mischance," who is visualized as a brutish human giant holding a third human fly in his right hand. But in this illustration Blake was free to intensify the images of Gray's poem to a degree that would be inappropriate and misleading for his own poem. The single fly is multiplied so that there is a carnage of crushed flies; moreover, these flies are visibly humanized, a symbolization which would make the speaker's hypothetical comparisons in Blake's poem seem ridiculously tentative. Even more important, Blake's poem is grotesquely misread if the speaker is imagined to be a monstrous exterminator, rather than an average man. On an elephant page of the designs for Gray's poems, Blake was able to reveal a sublime image of "Mischance," the executioner (together with his sinister companion "Age"), but on a small page of *Songs of Experience* he wisely did not attempt the grandiose. Blake's world of Experience corresponds to his state of "Generation," not to his state of Ulro, and his painting in *Songs of Experience* ordinarily observes the artistic limits imposed both by the size of his paper and the symbolic decorum of this state.

description of the picture. The three human figures, who dominate the lower part of the design, appear to be engaging in innocent activities. Facing the reader, a woman is teaching a small boy to walk, while an older girl with unbound hair is playing the harmless game of shuttlecock, with her back turned toward the reader. But there are several sinister symbols as well, notably the barren tree with a serpentine root (clear in copy Z)[23] on the reader's right. The lowest limb of this tree follows the curve of the woman's back, thus tending to cut off these two figures from the girl, who plays a game requiring *two* players by herself. There is also a barren sapling in the other margin that arches above the whole left side of the design and then falls unnaturally between the two columns of the poem until it crosses a higher branch of the lowest limb of the barren tree on the right. A cloud in the sky covers the top of the picture from the lower limb of the tree on the right to the sapling on the left. It forms a background for the girl from the waist up, including her right arm, and for the woman from the hips up, except for her left arm and right forearm. Beneath it is an unclouded area of sky, painted a vivid blue in copy AA. The cloud is more prominent in copy Z, but the area of blue is less intense.[24] Copy O, on the other hand, does not emphasize either sky effect. The ground is distinctly divided into two slopes, which in copy Z places the woman and child and both trees in a yellow-barren foreground, while the girl is off by herself in the background. Finally there is a dis-

---

[23] The standard lettering code for the copies of the Songs is that of Geoffrey Keynes and Edwin Wolf II, *William Blake's Illuminated Books: A Census* (New York 1953). Because Blake's plates were differently inked for the various impressions and because he painted the pages by hand, many small variations occur among the various copies. Though I have examined other versions, my description of "The Fly" is based on four copies that can be seen in reasonably accessible reproductions. These are: copy A, 1794, British Museum, in Wicksteed, *op. cit.*, p. 182c; copy O, 1800, Harvard College Library; copy Z, 1826, Lessing J. Rosenwald Collection, Library of Congress, Blake Trust Facsimile (color, 1955), p. 40; copy AA, 1826, Fitzwilliam Museum, Micro-Reproduction, Micro-Methods, Ltd. (Wakefield, Yorkshire, 1960) (color). (The dates of the earlier copies are largely conjectural.)

[24] Since no black and white reproduction can bring out the tonal qualities in the washes of copy Z, a brief description of other variants in the facsimile of this version will indicate what the interpreter must consider. The only area of cloud that has not been painted with enough blue or pink wash to qualify its sinister suggestions is that which surrounds the woman. But the edge of the boy's head has been tinted with gold and his chest has also been touched with gold. Thus the sky background for the girl is mostly light blue (the line of the cloud having been almost obliterated) and her racket and the base of the shuttlecock are gilded. Even the sapling on the left has a gilded area. The text of the poem is also in a light blue area, though parts of Stanzas III, IV, and V have an odd pinkish-white streak running through them. All of these details are compatible with the general interpretation I shall present, but it is significant that the woman is exempted from the general increase in redemptive symbolism that distinguishes the page in copy Z from earlier versions.

tant bird [25] flying above the complex lower limb of the tree on the right near the ends of the last two lines of text.

The trees in the design are barren, though their limbs arch in fairly graceful and realistic curves as compared with the squat and bushy tree depicted in "A Poison Tree." But in this, the only double-columned poem in the *Songs*, the dividing ornament is made distinctly serpentine. This device seems to imply a pictorial criticism of the action and reasoning of the unknowing speaker of the poem. It is also possible to interpret the device as a grotesquely unnatural branch of the left sapling, the main twig of which continues down to make contact with the large tree of death on the right. The shorter left twig ends in what appears to be a leaf. Ink blots are notoriously the inspiration for free association. But Blake, who counseled his audience not to neglect any "Blur or Mark," would not have been offended if a problematic detail were used as the basis for amplification of thoughts already implicit elsewhere in the design. Thus a residual leaf suggests that the sapling of death may regain its leaves in a spring of renewal. If the Fly were indeed recognized as being human, an identification that the speaker of the poem never really makes, the winter of Experience would come to an end. But the chief implications of the design are not optimistic. For the predominant right branch of the sapling joins with the major tree of death so as to constitute a pictorial parody of the innocent union of trees like that depicted in the design of "The Lamb." Indeed, the tree symbolism is one indication that "The Fly" is as much a "contrary" of "The Lamb" as "The Tyger" is.[26]

The fact that the text of "The Fly" is printed in a cloud tends to support the implications of the speaker's confusion that are latent in the poem and strengthened by the serpentine branch that writhes through the text. Though Blake's decorative use of washes on the cloud in copy Z obliterates this aspect of pictorial symbolism, it does not invalidate the implications of error in these copies of the design that Blake did not paint so elaborately. The most Blakean hypothesis is that every variant must be regarded as a potentially significant change in the pictorial context that may qualify the meaning of the design. Thus the meaning of "The Fly" is the meaning of every particular version, not an abstraction based on what the particular versions have in common after all the variants have been subtracted.

Criticism may never undertake a thorough exposition of this ideal

---

[25] It may, indeed, not be a bird but rather a butterfly, a moth, or even a bat. See the Appendix: Blake's Birds and other Winged Creatures, reprinted below.

[26] Blake's most explicit literary text dealing with the innocent phase of tree symbolism is contained in the beautiful Song, "Love and harmony combine" in *Poetical Sketches*, Keynes, p. 7.

meaning, but actual criticism should note that those versions of "The Fly" in which the text is unmistakenly printed in a cloud are pictorially linked with the "Introduction" to *Songs of Experience* where the text is always (as far as I know) printed in a cloud. Since I have asserted that the speaker in "The Fly" is entirely different from the Bard who speaks in the "Introduction," this linkage seems inexplicable at first. But this apparent contradiction can be explained if we assume that the words of the Bard shine down on the cloud or floor of Eternity, whereas in "The Fly" the words of the voice in Experience appear beneath the cloud seen as an upper limit, like "the vault/ of paved heaven" in the great "Mad Song" of *Poetical Sketches* (Keynes, p. 9). Clouds unmistakably divide the eternal World and the temporal World in Blake's illustrations for the Book of Job.

Relatively little critical attention has been devoted to Blake's artistic "minute particulars," so that any attempt to explain them must be quite speculative.[27] But when we turn from the blurs or marks to the major symbolic details in the illustration of "The Fly," it is possible to proceed with somewhat greater certainty. The woman may be identified as the boy's mother, as Damon states, because she wears a characteristic cap and collar such as those worn by the mother in "Infant Sorrow," whereas the sinister frustrated nurse depicted in the related "Nurses Song" of *Experience* has no cap and wears a décolleté dress. Furthermore, her activity is a good thing in itself, as is that of the mother in such a picture as "Teach those Souls to Fly," [28] though the reader may reflect that the mother in "The Fly" does hover over her boy in a solicitous manner which seems stifling, and that, after all, walking is not flying. The girl, on the other hand, is engaged in play, which is also good in itself, but the fact that she is playing a game for two by herself suggests that something is wrong. Moreover, though her aim is more deliberate, her stroke with the battledore resembles that of the wanton boy who has slain a girl and who is trying to catch a flying boy with his hat on page 7 of *The Gates of Paradise*.[29] Damon too implies that there may be something dubious about her play when he asserts that the shuttlecock suggests the Fly of the poem. Notice also that the girl advances her left foot (though her right one is

---

[27] The most recent attempt to deal extensively with Blake's pictorial details is Claudette Kemper's "The Interlinear Drawings in Blake's *Jerusalem*," *Bulletin of The New York Public Library*, LXIV (November 1960), 588-94.

[28] See Martin Butlin, ed., *William Blake (1757-1827): A Catalogue of Works in The Tate Gallery* (London 1957), pp. 37-38 and plate 3. The same design, without a title, appears on plate 2 of *The Book of Urizen*.

[29] Keynes, p. 765. John Sampson, ed., *The Poetical Works of William Blake* (London 1905), p. 109, seems to have been the first critic to relate this emblem to "The Fly." See also the illustration on plate 13 of *Jerusalem*.

revealed), whereas the mother and boy advance their right feet (though the mother's left thigh is strikingly highlighted in copy A). The significance the reader attributes to these positions depends on what one makes of Wicksteed's theory of Blake's pictorial symbolism according to which right = spiritual good, left = material evil, that he sometimes uses to great interpretational advantage.[30] Finally, the boy and the girl are both looking up, while the mother is looking down out of the cloud—with a troubled look in copy Z.

Such discordant notes in the human activities tend to undercut the reader's first impression that the human activities and relationships depicted are basically innocent. The presence of the mother begins to seem as oppressive as that of the trees of death when the reader realizes that her head is in the cloud, that the line of her back is repeated in the curve of the limb of the tree of death, and that her right foot (in some versions) seems to proceed from her left leg in a way comparable to the transposed foot of the befuddled Nobodaddy depicted on the title page of *The Book of Urizen*. These details suggest that the mother is really Tirzah or the terrible crucifying woman in the first phase of action described in "The Mental Traveller." Her bearing and presence are very different from those of the exemplary and truly helpful Virgin Mary shown in Blake's painting of "The Infant Jesus Riding on a Lamb." [31] So far as the children are concerned, both practice in walking and practice at games are entirely legitimate, but a three-year-old boy has no need to be taught to walk and a twelve-year-old girl, according to Blake's schedule of maturation, is wasting her life playing games. The reader should recall the adventures of Lyca, who is "seven summers old" in "The Little Girl Lost" (Keynes, p. 112), or those of Ololon, who is "a Virgin of twelve years" in *Milton* (Keynes, p. 527). Even before the advent of psychoanalysis it must have been evident to people that slashing at a shuttlecock, or swatting flies, can be substitute activity for interdicted love.

The human relationship depicted in "The Fly" is a modulation of that shown in the "Nurses Song" of *Experience* in which the woman is older and the boy is younger and is more emphatically separated from the girl by the looming body of the mother. The essence of Experience is isolation whereas the essence of Innocence is communion, but neither isolation nor communion is an absolute condition. The distinction is really between uncreative and creative relationships. In "The Fly" the girl may well be

---

[30] See Wicksteed, *op. cit.*, p. 37, and especially his *Blake's Vision of the Book of Job* (London and New York, revised ed. 1924), *passim.*

[31] Reproduced in Darrell Figgis, *The Paintings of William Blake* (London 1925), plate 41.

too old for the game, but in any case she cannot properly play it by herself, whereas the boy is certainly too old to be taught to walk and probably too young to play with the girl. Thus the reader is presented with a scene of frustration in which the boy and girl are evidently incapable of relating to one another and they are still more isolated by the presence of the unnecessary mother. All these sinister overtones unmistakably indicate that the illustration could never have been designed for a Song of Innocence.

But Experience has not overwhelmed the possibility of Innocence, for the young people are at least looking up. And what of the bird seen through the tree of death? Though it appears in a clouded area of sky and though it is not as graceful, it is surely related to the solitary bird in the illustration of "The Tyger," which I have elsewhere described as the most redemptive feature in that mixed design, the portion of the Tyger's imagination that is most likely to escape from the two trees of death depicted there.[32] Compare:

> How do you know but ev'ry Bird that cuts the airy way
> Is an immense world of delight, clos'd by your senses five?

and "Proverbs of Hell" 15, 39, and 54.[33]

Exactly how do the shuttlecock and the bird relate to the Fly? At this point plate 7 of *The Gates of Paradise* is again illuminating. The girl is slain by the wanton boy, but the flying boy escapes, as the "Keys of the Gates" makes clear.[34] In the design for "The Fly" the shuttlecock (made with bird feathers) corresponds to the corporeal part of the slain fly, whereas the bird corresponds to the spirit of the Fly, "a portion of genius," as a bird is called in "Proverb of Hell" 54, that has never been imagined by the speaker of the poem. Wicksteed's discussion (p. 181) of Blake's complex ideas about immortality is relevant here, but his summary in a maxim of Epicurus will suffice: "Where I am death is not: where death is I am not." And since the bird hovers above the head of the little boy, this child is revealed to have the potentiality of being more human than the girl with the unreflecting hand depicted at play, or than the man with the thoughtless hand in the poem. If the boy realizes his potentiality and if the girl should reject her segregation, they will "rise from Generation free," [35] as their Maker had done, or as the youth and the virgin do in "Ah! Sun-Flower."

[32] "The Art and Argument of 'The Tyger'," *Discussions of William Blake*, p. 80.
[33] Keynes, pp. 150-52.
[34] One Dies! Alas! the living & Dead,
   One is slain & One is fled. (Keynes, p. 771)
[35] "To Tirzah," line 3. Presumably the children must then say, as Jesus did, "Thou

Appendix:
Blake's Birds and other Winged Creatures

Very little systematic work has so far been done on Blake's iconography, especially on the relationship of the various pictorial symbols to one another. The following is an attempt to clarify some of the problems involved in interpreting the rather indistinct but undoubtedly significant winged creature depicted in "The Fly." It is important to identify the creature as precisely as possible, but the essential problem is to decide how much difference the various possibilities would make in the total meaning of the design.

Of the several kinds of winged creatures, the bat seems to be ruled out because Blake was careful precisely to delineate the characteristic webbed trailing edge of bat wings. But the possibility that the creature is a butterfly or moth cannot be neglected, especially for this design, because the word "fly" was a generic term meaning "winged insect" in the eighteenth century. I indicated in my article on "Misreadings" (pp. 483-84) why the finished poem cannot be made to declare whether the fly is a housefly or a butterfly, but I also showed that Blake's illustration of Gray's "Ode I: On the Spring" suggests the Fly in the poem should be imagined as a housefly. On the other hand, the delta-winged creature depicted in "The Fly" is certainly not a housefly, but it does bear a general resemblance to the moth-winged human forms depicted (together with indubitable birds and butterflies) on the title page of *Jerusalem*. Moreover, there is a delta-winged creature, closely resembling the one depicted in "The Fly," associated with two flying insects on page 13 of *The Book of Urizen* (clearer in the Dent Photographic facsimile of copy A [1929] than in the Blake Trust stencil facsimile of copy G, p. 15 [1958]). There is also a large pointed-winged dragonfly at the top of page 13 in *Jerusalem* that bears a fairly close resemblance to the creature in "The Fly" except that its abdomen is obviously much longer. Another connection between the plates, the fact that a man is trying to catch another insect in his cap, relates this

Mother of my Mortal part [who] with cruelty didst mould my Heart . . . what have I to do with thee?" (lines 9, 10, and 16). In my "Misreadings" article (p. 486) I carelessly stated that the notebook drawing, "Begone and trouble me no more," depicting the rejection of a woman by a man, which appears on the same page (reversed) as the drafting of "The Fly," has nothing to do with *The Gates of Paradise*. Mr. Bateson in a letter has pointed out to me that the drawing was indeed a draft for *The Gates of Paradise*, though Blake never used it in that book. I am glad to acknowledge my error, but I am still not convinced that the drawing gives reliable evidence for the dating of the poem. However, the drawing does (probably coincidentally) depict the apocalyptic rejection required to overcome a dominant mother such as the one shown in the illustration of "The Fly."

plate both to plate 7 of *The Gates of Paradise* and to the poem and picture in "The Fly." Thus it would be convenient for the interpreter if the two insects in *Jerusalem* were identical, but unfortunately they are not.

Scenes in which a human attempts to catch a winged creature occur frequently enough in Blake's work to constitute a distinct motif. In Blake's first poem, "How sweet I roam'd . . ." (Keynes, p. 6), the girl who was caught in a cage speaks of herself in bird imagery as she tells her story. Pictorially this motif is employed in Blake's first illuminated book, *There is no Natural Religion,* series a, plate 5, which accompanies the text "II. Man by his reasoning power can only compare & judge by what he has already perceiv'd." [36] There a woman holds back a child who stretches out his arms after a flying bird while behind them is a barren tree. This scene also appears later in one of a pair of designs in Blake's water-color illustrations for Young's *Night Thoughts.* The other design in this pair has as its prototype the only drawing in Blake's notebook that is closely related to the action described in the text of "The Fly." On page 42 Blake depicts a bearded old man with a stick who gropes with his left hand toward a small indistinct flying figure. But this old man resembles the "blind hand [who] shall brush my wing" more closely than he does the speaker whose "thoughtless hand" ended the "summer's play" of the fly. This connection seems the more probable because the man in the notebook drawing is very similar to the figure in the drawing dated c. 1788 of "God Creating the Universe." [37] The solitary man-flying creature relationship is again depicted in plate 26 of the illustrations to *Night Thoughts* ("Night the First," p. 21, lines 296-313) where a travel-worn pilgrim reaches up with his left hand in an attempt to catch a butterfly, whereas in the following plate (the seventh, p. 1é, in the engraved series of 1797) a boy eagerly reaches out for a bird that is flying from him. As in the plate of *There is no Natural Religion,* the boy is being restrained by his mother, but behind them the father has been killed by a serpent. This scene purports to illustrate Young's lines, "Misfortune . . . makes a scourge of past Prosperity,/ To sting thee more . . . ," but the moral, stated in Blakean terms, is: "The wanton boy who would seize the bird shall eventually feel the serpent's enmity." The hand and flying creature motif, as it appears in these counterpart designs of age and youth, is employed to symbolize the vanity of aspiration, but Blake always wishes to subordinate this notion to more energetic wisdom and certainly these pictures do

---

[36] Reproduced in Geoffrey Keynes, ed., *William Blake's Engravings* (London 1950), plate 80.

[37] Reproduced in Geoffrey Keynes, ed., *The Pencil Drawings of William Blake: Second Series* (London 1956), plate 34.

nothing to justify the thoughtless speaker in "The Fly." Perhaps the most judicious conclusion, insofar as these examples aid in identifying the creature depicted in the design for the Song, is that it is somewhat more likely to be a bird than an insect. Since an insect is the usual target for an aged man, and a bird for a boy being restrained by his mother, the fact that a boy held by his mother is the main figure indicates that the creature in question should be a bird.

The evidence for the problematic creature in "The Fly" being an insect does not appear very convincing and the preponderance of the evidence suggests that it is a bird. There are no other birds depicted in *Songs of Innocence and of Experience* that are exactly like it, though at least two of the thirteen ostensible birds in "My Pretty Rose Tree" are similar, as is one of the approximately twenty-four in "A Little Girl Lost." Creatures resembling the problematic one are also to be found on plates 22, 54, and 61 of *Jerusalem* and plates 3 and 5 of *The Book of Urizen* (both very similar) in the Blake Trust facsimiles. To be sure, it would be difficult to prove that all of these creatures are birds though most viewers assume that they are.

It does not seem possible to find a decisive analogy to the creature depicted in "The Fly" in Blake's published illustrations to the work of other writers. In Blake's illustrations to Milton's poems, for example, the evidence is splendidly inconclusive. If one disregards the slight suggestion of secondary wings on the problematic creature, he will notice the close resemblance to the pointed wings (and angle of ascent) of the angelic figure of the Lark of Dawn in the fine picture, "Night Startled by the Lark," in the "L'Allegro" series. But wings (similarly without a secondary set) of almost the same shape belong to a humanized creature described by Blake as an "Insect raised by the Sun's heat" in the upper right of the illustration "Milton led by Melancholy" in the "Il Penseroso" series. The same wing shape may be observed on allegorical figures, notably the personified Dream in "Milton Sleeping on a Bank" [38] and on Peace in "The Descent of Peace and Nature's Adoration" in the Nativity Ode Series.[39] And if the investigation is broadened to cover Blake's iconography of round-winged insects, such as bees, hornets, and houseflies—which abound in *Europe*—the conclusion seems similar, namely, that Blake probably did not observe careful biological distinctions among the various species of winged creatures he depicted or invented.

When a symbol-complex is so ambiguous, the chief task for interpreta-

---

[38] Reproduced in Adrian Van Sinderen, *Blake: The Mystic Genius* (Syracuse 1949), pp. 63, 103.

[39] Reproduced in Figgis, *op. cit.*, plate 35.

tion is to describe the extent of possible error. Both because of their gay appearances and metamorphic characteristics moths and butterflies are generally treated as benign symbols by Blake, though he did not forget the Biblical observations about the tendency of the nocturnal insect to corrupt. Thus a monstrous amalgam of moth and bat symbolizes the departing night in the great picture "Albion rose," traditionally called "Glad Day." [40] But though a barren season is depicted in "The Fly," there is no doubt that it is a daylight episode, and the creature is probably a butterfly or a bird. These two symbols are not sharply distinguished, but some differentiation may be observed. Though winged creatures are always associated with love by Blake, a connection at least as old as Plato's *Phaedrus,* something more specific is involved in both cases. In the drawing of "The Virgin Mary Hushing the Young Baptist," [41] John brings a butterfly to Jesus, who is sleeping in Beulah, while outside the door another butterfly is visible. Since the butterfly is a traditional image of the soul, this picture indicates that Blake used the butterfly as a threshold symbol, either of the descent of the soul into Experience or of the return of the soul through the "Western Gate" from Generation to Eternity. Though Wicksteed brilliantly interpreted the annunciation of the messenger with butterfly wings, depicted in "Infant Joy," by identifying the butterfly as a symbol of "resurrection," [42] such an equation is too specific to fit every context. The bird symbol is also employed in both *Innocence* and *Experience,* but because a bird is more energetic and less fragile than a butterfly it tends to imply more extreme states of freedom or bondage: as "an immense world of delight" or "a portion of genius" it represents Eden, but when a "Robin Red breast" is in a cage the bondage is characteristic of Ulro. Even the humblest flies may also achieve Eternity, as the quoted passages from *Milton* indicate, but Blake usually presents them as victims of Experience, undoubtedly because of their traditional associations with mortality. A complete explanation of Blake's symbolism of winged creatures will doubtless be provided by a critic skilled in ornithology, entomology, and angelology. But the fundamental question at issue here is whether the creature depicted in "The Fly" has optimistic implications (butterfly) or very optimistic ones (bird). Since the total meaning of the design remains almost the same in any case, there need be no confusion if the creature is somewhat arbitrarily called a bird.

[40] Geoffrey Keynes, ed., *William Blake's Engravings* (London 1951), plate 1.
[41] Geoffrey Keynes, ed., *The Pencil Drawings of William Blake: Second Series* (London 1956), plate 9; cf. Keynes, ed., *William Blake's Illustrations to the Bible* (London 1957), plate 99.
[42] Wicksteed, *op. cit.,* p. 123.

The Complexities of Blake's "Sunflower": An Archetypal Speculation

by William J. Keith

> Ah, Sun-flower, weary of time,
> Who countest the steps of the Sun,
> Seeking after that sweet golden clime
> Where the traveller's journey is done:
>
> Where the Youth pined away with desire,
> And the pale Virgin shrouded in snow
> Arise from their graves, and aspire
> Where my Sun-flower wishes to go.

The current critical fashion attempts to prove that Blake's Prophetic Books are simpler than they appear; my aim here is to reverse the procedure and argue that the apparently simple lyrics can be far more complex than they seem. Blake's own reference to

> My happy songs
> Every child may joy to hear

in the introductory poem to the *Songs of Innocence* is certainly misleading in its implication of simplicity. While the literal surface-meaning of the *Songs of Innocence and Experience* is easily appreciable, the images and themes employed, as might be expected from a poet like Blake, contain far deeper significances and possibilities than appear at a first reading. "Ah Sun-flower" offers itself as a particularly interesting example.

Commentators have generally been content to point out a moral, allegorical meaning, and it is often considered sufficient to state that the poem is about sexual repression. Yeats and Ellis, who might have been expected to make some comment on the symbolic undertones, merely observe that "the 'Sunflower' shows love, as the guide to imagination, or eternity." [1]

"The Complexities of Blake's 'Sunflower': An Archetypal Speculation" by William J. Keith was written especially for this collection.

[1] E. J. Ellis and W. B. Yeats, eds., *Works of William Blake* (London: Quaritch, 1893), II, 14.

Apart from the fact that these two explanations seem difficult to reconcile, the main point to notice is that they offer no explanation to the curious reader who may ask: "Why sunflower? why the youth? why the pale virgin shrouded in snow?" They seem to assume that the poem's sole *raison d'être* is to be the medium for some detachable moral comment. A sensitive response to the poem suggests that much more remains to be said.

A considerably more helpful commentary is to be found in C. M. Bowra's *The Romantic Imagination,* where attention is paid to the poetic symbolism:

> The central spring of the poem is the image of the sunflower. The flower which turns its head to follow the sun's course and is yet rooted in the earth is Blake's symbol for all men and women whose lives are dominated and spoiled by a longing which they can never hope to satisfy, and who are held down to the earth despite their desire for release into some brighter, freer sphere.[2]

More recently, G. M. Harper has suggested that the sunflower image may have been derived from Thomas Taylor's translations and commentaries of Platonic and Neoplatonic texts. He quotes Proclus discussing "those plants called heliotropes, that is attendants on the sun, moving in correspondence with the revolutions of its orb," and asserting that "the sunflower, as far as it is able, moves in a circular dance towards the sun." [3] This is a helpful and convincing suggestion, though we should not neglect another, perhaps more conventional origin in Ovid's *Metamorphoses,* which Northrop Frye has described as one of Blake's essential sources.[4] Ovid gives a detailed account of the story of Clytie who pined away with desire for the sun-god and was transformed into the heliotrope which perpetuates her action of counting the steps of the sun. It will be as well to note at this point that the sunflower and the heliotrope are identified popularly but not, of course, botanically; the sunflower derives its name from its appearance, not from any habit of turning its face toward the sun. In earlier centuries, however, a number of sun-like flowers were called heliotropes, including the marigold which, as Harper notes, appears in Blake in the opening lines of the *Visions of the Daughters of Albion.*

[2] C. M. Bowra, *The Romantic Imagination* (London: Oxford University Press, 1950), p. 45.
[3] Thomas Taylor, *The Mystical Initiations; Or, Hymns of Orpheus.* Quoted in G. M. Harper, *The Neoplatonism of William Blake* (Chapel Hill: University of North Carolina Press, 1961), pp. 121, 122.
[4] See Northrop Frye, *Fearful Symmetry* (Princeton: Princeton University Press, 1947), p. 11.

This background material provides a useful introduction to a more detailed consideration of the lyric. The phrase "weary of time" in the first line is interesting, for it carries two different, but equally appropriate, meanings. Primarily it implies that the flower is trying to ascend out of the natural world, which is subject to Time, into the higher world of Eternity. Nonetheless, the careful reader cannot fail to recognize the phrase as an adaptation from *Macbeth*. But Macbeth's speech runs:

> I gin to be aweary of the sun,
> And wish th' estate o' th' world were now undone.
>
> (V, v, 49-50)

Macbeth, then, is weary of the very thing which the sunflower is aspiring toward; on the other hand, Macbeth's second line implies a desire to escape from the present world, which is ironically paralleled by the aspiration of the sunflower.

The "steps of the Sun" are the sections of the sun's course through which he has to pass each day, and the "sweet golden clime" is an obvious variant of the legendary Golden Age which is supposed to be restored to earth when the constellations have returned to their original places—i.e., when the sun's course has been truly completed. The first verse, then, establishes the central archetypes of the poem. We have the sunflower, a member of the vegetable world, continually striving upward, and the sun continually moving across the sky. Both movements, we note, are continuous, for the vegetable cycle recurs from year to year, and the sun cycle from day to day. This draws attention, however, to the possibility of another latent irony in the poem: the sunflower, continually aspiring toward the sun of which it is itself a symbol, is engaged on a quest which is doomed to failure, for it is the very heat of the sun which will eventually cause the plant to wither, its quest unattained.

The second verse introduces us to the figures of the youth and the virgin, and here the complexities proliferate for, although most commentators seem to assume that no particular references are intended, I can never silence an obstinate inclination to associate "the Youth pined away with desire" with Narcissus, whose story Blake would also have found in Ovid's *Metamorphoses*. Narcissus, we remember, was punished by Nemesis for spurning the amorous advances of Echo, who similarly pined away with desire for Narcissus. When the youth saw his own reflection in a fountain, he became so enamoured of it that he wasted away for love of what was unattainable. Ovid continues: "The pyre, the tossing torches, and the bier, were now being prepared, but his body was nowhere to be found. Instead of his corpse, they discovered a flower with a circle of white petals around a yellow centre." [5] Other versions suggest that Narcissus stabbed himself in sorrow at his fate, and that the white flower with its *red* center grew from the place where his blood soaked the earth.[6] What is of interest to us is the classical reference which brings us round once again to flower symbolism. The youth who pines away with desire and is later seen rising from his grave is not only the classical Narcissus attaining to some kind of celestial paradise, but the narcissus-flower arising from the grave of "mother Earth."

My suggestion, then, is that an Ovidian metamorphosis-theory lies at the very core of the poem. Just as the sunflower image has human application (and this is strengthened by the Clytie story), so the youth and, as we shall see in a moment, the pale virgin have flower connections which are also explicable through an underlying myth. It is unnecessary to insist that Blake had specific prototypes in mind, but we have every right to explore the suggestions and possibilities arising out of the images which he presents. Blake may not be working directly from Ovid, but he may well be working freely in the Ovidian manner. He was certainly profoundly conscious of the connections between the vegetable and human worlds. As he writes in *Vala*:

> Wherever a grass grows
> Or a leaf buds, The Eternal Man is seen, is heard, is felt,
> And all his sorrows, till he reassumes his ancient bliss.
> (Night the Eighth, ll. 581-83)

It is less easy to find a traditional correspondence in myth for the "pale Virgin shrouded in snow." I suggest, however, that she is another treatment of the Persephone figure which Blake uses and adapts for his own purposes in the *Book of Thel* and the *Visions of the Daughters of Albion*. According to the classical version, Persephone, while gathering flowers in Enna, was seen by Pluto who fell in love with her and carried her off to the infernal regions to be his queen. Her mother Ceres sought her frantically throughout the world, and, finally learning of her whereabouts, descended into Hell to claim her. Eventually it is arranged that Persephone shall come back to earth for part of the year, but must dwell with her husband in Hell for the other part. There are other versions of the story, with various complications, but I give the general outline of the myth, which obviously refers to some kind of vegetation cycle. Persephone is the seed planted in the earth (i.e., Hell) in which it stays during the winter

---

[5]Ovid, *Metamorphoses*, trans. Mary M. Innes (Harmondsworth: Penguin Books, 1955), p. 94.

[6] See, for instance, Robert Graves, *The Greek Myths* (Harmondsworth: Penguin Books, 1955), I, 288.

months; in the spring it returns to the surface and remains on the earth until autumn when it dies down and the same process is repeated once again.

But what were the flowers that Persephone was gathering when she was abducted? The question seems relevant here, and it proves, as Sir Thomas Browne would say, "not beyond all conjecture." There are, in fact, various answers. Ovid says "violets and shining lilies." [7] Shakespeare gives basically the same answer in *The Winter's Tale,* though he reverses the order, substitutes the English daffodil for the Mediterranean lily, and adds a few more for good measure:

> O Proserpina,
> For the flowers now that, frighted, thou let'st fall
> From Dis's waggon!—daffodils,
> That come before the swallow dares, and take
> The winds of March with beauty; violets, dim
> But sweeter than the lids of Juno's eyes
> Or Cytherea's breath . . .
>
> (IV, iv, 116-22)

Indeed, daffodil or its equivalent seems to be the favorite answer. The qualification is necessary because there is a confusion throughout English literature between daffodil and asphodel. I quote from Geoffrey Grigson's *The Englishman's Flora:*

Narcissus pseudonarcissus [the Wild Daffodil] owes a debt also to its English name, which goes back, through the Mediaeval Latin *affodilus* and Latin *asphodilus* to the Greek *asphodelus,* name of that plant which grew across the meadows of the underworld and which belonged to Persephone, the Queen of Hell.[8]

The asphodel is, of course, traditionally associated with Hell, from Homer onward. We can find our next clue most conveniently in *Brewer's Dictionary of Phrase and Fable* under the entry for daffodil, and it possibly throws some light on Blake's phrase "shrouded in snow":

Legend says that the daffodil, or "Lent Lily," was once white; but Persephone, who had wreathed her head with them and fallen asleep, was captured by Pluto, at whose touch the white flowers turned to a golden yellow. Ever since the flower has been planted on graves. Theophilus and Pliny tell us that they grow on the banks of the Acheron, and that the spirits of the dead

[7] Ovid, *Metamorphoses,* p. 137.

[8] Geoffrey Grigson, *The Englishman's Flora* (London: Phoenix House, 1955), p. 416.

delight in the flower, called by them the Asphodel. In England it used to be called the Affodil.[9]

The botanical complications here are considerable. The real asphodel, as it grows in the Mediterranean, is white, but the daffodil, of course, is yellow. Poets have traditionally called the asphodel yellow—examples include Pope's

> By those happy souls who dwell
> In yellow meads of Asphodel

from the "Ode for Music on St. Cecilia's Day." Indeed, Pope seems to have consistently confused the two, telling Joseph Spence that the asphodel was "nothing else but that poor yellow flower that grows about our orchards," and flippantly retranslating Homer to the effect that

> the stern Achilles
> Stalked through a mead of daffodillies.[10]

Moreover, to complicate the matter still further, the English flower commonly called Bog Asphodel is also yellow, but has no connection whatever with the true asphodel family.[11] But for a last answer to the question about Persephone's flower gathering we may turn to Thomas Taylor once more, and he is quite explicit. The flower in question was the Narcissus "who fell a victim to the love of his own corporeal form." To Taylor, who sees Persephone's rape as an allegorical representation of the soul's descent into the material world of generation, there is a moral significance in her being found plucking "this fatal flower." [12] And the Narcissus, as I have already noted, is basically white.

But, to return to the pale virgin, why should she be described as "shrouded in snow"? I suggest that the phrase is meaningful on three levels. If we take the pale virgin as a general type, the snow in which she is shrouded represents the coldness and frigidity of the situation in which she is trapped; snow has obvious connections with barrenness and sterility. If we take her as Persephone, the snow is metaphorical and describes the white flowers which covered her as she was dragged off to Hell, her grave;

[9] *Brewer's Dictionary of Phrase and Fable,* revised and enlarged edition (London: Cassell, 1952), p. 266.

[10] Quoted in Geoffrey Tillotson, *Pope and Human Nature* (Oxford: Clarendon Press, 1958), p. 63.

[11] For an interesting discussion of the asphodel in literature, see the name essay in Robert Graves, *The Common Asphodel* (London: Hamish Hamilton, 1949).

[12] Thomas Taylor, *A Dissertation on the Eleusinian and Bacchic Mysteries.* Quoted in Harper, *op. cit.,* p. 258.

in this sense "shrouded" is extremely precise in meaning. Thirdly, if we take her to be representative of the daffodil, then the snow is literally snow which covers the earth and the seed during the winter. We may add that the association with the myth of the daffodils changing from white to gold is strengthened by the antithesis presented clearly in the poem of the virgin shrouded in snow and the "sweet *golden* clime" to which she is aspiring. The same antithesis is found in the *Visions of the Daughters of Albion* where Oothoon, another pale virgin, plucks the sun-like marigold which is immediately described as a "Golden nymph." [13]

It may be objected that, while I have argued some kind of association between Narcissus and Persephone as flowers, I have failed to demonstrate any connection between them as mythological characters. I am not convinced that such a demonstration is necessary. It must be emphasized that I am only exploring possibilities, and Blake would have considered himself, here as elsewhere, perfectly free to remold and adapt the traditional myths at will. The mythological stories I have been discussing are analogues, in some cases perhaps even subliminal sources, but they are not the fixed and unalterable contents of the poem. Yet if I am right in seeing traces of a Persephone myth in the poem, it is not irrelevant to point out that Blake elsewhere uses the myth, like Taylor, to represent the descent of the soul into matter from which it afterward yearns to escape. The primary aim, then, is not sexual satisfaction but escape from the world of generation. This is true of Thel, another pale virgin in "a white veil" (Plate 5, l. 7), who views the fallen world but is privileged to return to the "vales of Har" unmolested. On the other hand, in the *Visions of the Daughters of Albion* where satisfaction and escape seem identical, Oothoon plucks the golden marigold and so descends into the material world where, after her fall, she sings a lament which includes a remarkable parallel to the second verse of the sunflower poem:

> The moment of desire! the moment of desire! The virgin
> That pines for man shall awaken to enormous joys
> In the secret shadows of her chamber: the youth shut up from
> The lustful joy shall forget to generate & create an amorous image
> In the shadows of his curtains and in the folds of his silent pillow.
>
> (Plate 7, ll. 3-7)

In the "sweet golden clime" all things are possible, and the sexual repressions suffered in this life are resolved or transcended. But from our viewpoint in the world of experience—and this is one of the *Songs of Experi-*

---

[13] It is interesting to note that this scene at the opening of the *Visions of the Daughters of Albion* reminds G. M. Harper of the Narcissus myth. See Harper, *op. cit.*, p. 259.

ence—youth and virgin remain isolated, and we are not invited to inquire into their relationship beyond the material world.[14]

It may be agreed that the pattern of the poem is more complex than appears at first sight, and it is time to examine the two verses in conjunction. In the first verse, the image of the sunflower leads us on to the world of men—we naturally react to the symbol and see its application to human life. In the second verse this process is inverted; we begin with the world of men, the world of the youth and the virgin, and the underlying significance of the symbols leads us back to the vegetation cycle. It is a poem about a cyclical process, and its form fits perfectly with its content in being itself circular.

It is important, however, that we do not miss the essential ambivalence of the poem, an ambivalence that affects our whole outlook to its poetic meaning. It is possible to read the poem as confident and optimistic or, on the contrary, as pessimistic and even hopeless. In the optimistic reading the poem consists of a straightforward image of aspiration. Here the dignity and persistence of the quest is emphasized. The sunflower, symbolic of mankind, is striving toward a form of existence where the bonds and restraints which suppress the individual in this world are swept aside, and humanity attains to a world of satisfaction and perfection. It is a poem which looks forward to a time when paradise is regained, and suggests that it can be regained.

The other reading, a more "ironic" view, stresses the fact that the sunflower can never attain its goal—and that man cannot either. It emphasizes the cyclical process and points out that the sunflower must inevitably wither in autumn. Moreover, it concentrates on the last two lines of the poem which we have so far ignored. The image of the youth and the virgin arising from their graves is impressive, but the rest is, to say the least, equivocal. What exactly does "aspire / Where my Sun-flower wishes to go" imply? The difficulty is with the word "aspire." Though there is some

---

[14] Before leaving the youth and the virgin, I should perhaps consider the possibility that Hamlet and Ophelia may be relevant in this context. There are certainly some interesting analogues. Hamlet tells Ophelia: "Be thou as chaste as ice, as pure as snow, thou shalt not escape calumny" (III, i, 135-36), and warns her father: "Let her not walk i' th' sun" (II, ii, 183). In her madness, Ophelia sings:

> White his shroud as the mountain snow
> Larded with sweet flowers;
> Which bewept to the grave did not go
> With true love showers;

(IV, v, 34-8)

and she knows more about flower symbolism than any Shakespearean heroine, Perdita included.

dictionary authority for the meaning "reach" or "attain," the more usual meaning is simply "aim at" or "long for," and the final line suggests that the youth and the virgin are in no better position than the sunflower itself. In other words, they are as helpless and entrapped on the other side of the grave as they were on this. The very use of the word "sunflower" in the first and last lines of the poem helps to draw attention to the fact that no progression is made in the course of the poem at all. The goal is just as far away, and the implication is even that it is completely unattainable. Both readings appear defensible, though perhaps, as so often in such cases, a full response to the poem will be able to hold both possibilities in suspension.

Finally, a word must be said in defense of the present exegesis, and this will include an important qualification. It may be objected that at certain points in the preceding discussion I have ventured far beyond the boundaries of the poem. Indeed, the more conservative critic might even argue that such an examination is of value only as a kind of awful warning. I would reply that my approach is justified so long as I do not insist that Blake intended it all, or that it is vital to an intelligent appreciation of the poem. The latter argument would be absurd; as far as I know, my approach is original, and to suggest that it was the key to the poem would imply that none of the previous commentators had really understood it. The discussion began as a speculation, and remains one. What can be said is that, if my commentary is at all legitimate, it realizes a potential which was in the poem as it came forth from the mind of the poet. I may be accused of rewriting Blake's lyric and so producing something which is really my own; I can only reply that I am aware of what I am doing and of the dangers that surround it. The fact remains, however, that the process has deepened my own appreciation of Blake's lyric, and if it does the same for anyone else, I shall consider it justified.

Little Girls Lost:
Problems of a Romantic Archetype

by Irene H. Chayes

The poetry of the English Romantics has been closely associated with the development of the archetypal approach in literary studies; it is not necessary to recall the importance of Coleridge to Maud Bodkin or of Blake to Northrop Frye. Despite the precedents set by these two critics, however, especially by Frye in his suggestive essays and lectures of recent years, there has been no true extension of the work of either. (In his study of the "correspondent breeze," which might legitimately be called an archetype, M. H. Abrams refuses to use the term.[1]) For the student of a particular literary period, as distinguished from the aesthetician or the general critical theorist, there are certain practical difficulties in this approach which perhaps have prevented its wider adoption. How, for example, are the various levels of archetypes related to each other? Do the psychological archetypes in which the Jungians are interested, and the cultural archetypes of ritual and myth, take precedence over the archetypes of literature? Or should literature be considered as autonomous, supporting certain archetypal relations inside its own boundaries but remaining free of entangling foreign alliances? Is identifiable recurrence the sole criterion of an archetype? What, especially, can the study of archetypes tell the practical scholar or critic about a literary period as complex as the Romantic?

Within the limits of this paper, I shall try to illustrate some of these problems, and others more specific to the topic, by considering three examples of a recurring figure, an archetype, which is both universal and peculiarly Romantic. The first, which will be the model for the others,

"Little Girls Lost: Problems of a Romantic Archetype" by Irene H. Chayes. From *Bulletin of the New York Public Library*, LXVII, 9 (November 1963), 579-92.

Reprinted by permission of the editor of *Bulletin of the New York Public Library* and the author.

[1] "The Correspondent Breeze: A Romantic Metaphor," *English Romantic Poets: Modern Essays in Criticism*, ed. M. H. Abrams (Galaxy Books 1960), p. 49.

is Lyca, the heroine of the two companion poems in Blake's *Songs of Innocence and of Experience*, "The Little Girl Lost" and "The Little Girl Found." In many ways, these poems are pivotal to the whole double sequence, having first been in *Innocence* and then been transferred to *Experience*, and the complexity of their interrelations with other "songs" in both groups tends to obscure their more universal aspects for the specialist. But if an ideal, unspoiled but sensitive reader were to come to the Lyca poems for the first time, one who was not acquainted with Blake scholarship but did have some knowledge of the archetypes outside literature, he probably would have little trouble in placing their protagonist. She would belong to the archetype described by Jung and Kerényi as Kore, the primordial maiden of Greek myth, who has analogues in other traditions as well.[2] More specifically, Lyca would be Kore in the form of the particular mythological maiden in Persephone.

In the more familiar versions of her myth, Persephone, out gathering flowers on the plains of Enna, is seized by Hades and carried away to his Underworld kingdom. Lyca, also alone in the midst of nonhuman nature, is discovered by the beasts of prey and taken underground to their caves. Like Demeter, Lyca's parents search for her in grief and hardship and do not succeed in bringing her back; their meeting with the lion-king, who to enlighten them puts off his animal shape, implies that Lyca already is, or is to become, his consort in his "palace deep," as Persephone has become the consort of Hades when Demeter finds her. With the account by Ovid in particular, the very titles of Blake's poems have an arresting point of contact. In *Metamorphoses V* Ceres-Demeter comments sadly:

> I have sought her long, and found her
> At last, if you can call it finding
> To lose more surely, if you call it finding
> To know her dwelling-place.[3]

(Nata quaesita diu, reperta est tandem mihi; si vocas reperire amittere certius, aut si vocas reperire scire ubi sit.)

The rape of Persephone has been related to the Lyca poems by less direct means: through the double filter of a Neoplatonic allegorization of the myth, and the translations and adaptations of the Neoplatonic texts that were made by Blake's contemporary Thomas Taylor.[4] The detailed

[2] C. G. Jung and C. Kerényi, *Essays on a Science of Mythology: The Myth of the Divine Child and the Mysteries of Eleusis*, trans. R. F. C. Hull, Bollingen Series XXII (New York 1949), Chaps. III, IV.

[3] Trans. Rolfe Humphries (Bloomington, Ind. 1955), p. 123.

[4] Kathleen Raine, "The Little Girl Lost and Found and the Lapsed Soul," *The Divine Vision: Studies in the Poetry and Art of Willam Blake,* ed. Vivian de Sola Pinto

and dogmatic Neoplatonic interpretation of the poems that is the result—Lyca lost and found is the soul descending into corporeal existence and returning to eternity—shows the superiority of the more straightforward and at the same time more flexible archetypal approach, I feel, for it is this approach that permits recognition of the significant differences as well as the resemblances between Lyca's story and the myth.[5] Whereas Persephone is unsuspecting and is carried away by force, Lyca lies down to sleep in willing surrender and is gently received by the beasts; the lion, corresponding to Hades the abductor, makes obeisance to her and weeps in pity. When we first see her, Lyca is already "lost," having "wander'd long" in the desert, and she is "found" in effect when she is carried underground. When she is found by her parents, they learn that she is lost to them as Persephone is not lost to Demeter; there is no hint of a seasonal return. Yet when they are shown their "sleeping child," Lyca's parents are consoled and settle without fear in "a lonely dell," presumably in the same desert world in which she has been lost.

Evidently, then, Lyca is a figure of some complexity, and other images and allusions in the two poems lead to other "larger unifying categories"[6] and other contexts in which she also finds a place. There are motives from folklore and fairy tale; fleetingly identifiable are Sleeping Beauty, Beauty and the Beast, the Children in the Wood. (The Orphan Child, abandoned and alone in the wilderness, sometimes nursed by wild animals, is another psycho-mythological archetype which Lyca assimilates.[7]) There are also specifically literary echoes: Lyca and the compassionate lion recall Una and her lion protector in *The Faerie Queene* (I, iii, 5-9).[8] Una too is lost in a desert and is asleep when the lion discovers her: he too fawns and bows before her, "And mightie proud to humble weake does yield." Moreover, the events preceding Una's meeting with the lion suggest what those preceding the situation in the Lyca poems might

---

(London 1957), pp. 19-63. A similar interpretation via Taylor's writings has been made of Blake's *The Book of Thel* and *Visions of the Daughters of Albion*; see G. M. Harper, *The Neoplatonism of William Blake* (Chapel Hill 1961), Chap. XV.

[5] Miss Raine (p. 46) cites Jung and Kerényi on myth in general but does not distinguish between the primordial image and the Neoplatonic allegory. Taylor's Persephone (*A Dissertation on the Eleusinian and Bacchic Mysteries,* London 1790?) is actually at third or fourth remove from the Kore.

[6] "By an archetype I mean an element in a work of literature, whether a character, an image, a narrative formula, or an idea, which can be assimilated to a larger unifying category." Northrop Frye, "Blake's Treatment of the Archetype," *English Institute Essays 1950,* ed. A. S. Downer (New York 1951), p. 191.

[7] Jung and Kerényi, *op. cit.,* pp. 38-42.

[8] Una and the lion are included in "Characters from Spenser's *Faerie Queene*," one of Blake's watercolors (1809?). See *The Paintings of William Blake,* ed. Darrell Figgis (London 1925), plate 100.

be. Una is wandering alone because Archimago, or Hypocrisy, by the use
of magic made her appear guilty of unchastity, and the jealous and virtuous Red Cross Knight thereupon abandoned her (I, ii, 3-6). Another song
of Experience with a companion title, "A Little Girl Lost," is virtually a
Blakean parody of this episode. Ona—who just misses being named
Una—is condemned by her father for unchastity of her own, and it is as
much by the grieving condemnation as by the act itself that she is "lost,"
although in her case the act is real enough.[9]

By their common relation to Spenser's heroine, Blake's two "little
girls" thus are brought into clearer relation to each other. Tentatively,
at least, it appears that Ona undergoes a fall for which Lyca by her
wandering performs penance; Persephone in an earlier phase—or, in
Blake's own term, an earlier "state"—is Magdalen, or perhaps Eve. Associations with the Fall in the Book of Genesis seem, in fact, to have been
intended by Blake. The design on the title plate for *Songs of Innocence
and of Experience* shows Adam and Eve in their aprons of leaves being
driven outward, presumably from paradise; on the first of the three continuous plates of the Lyca poems the fatal fruit is being plucked by a
full-grown young woman (*not* a child!) who is in the embrace of a lover
and who might be Ona before her condemnation.

I

Other contexts that become relevant to the story of Lyca are the
tradition of vision literature, including the Bible, and the body of Blake's
other works. "The Little Girl Lost" opens with a prophecy of the awake-
ening of the sleeping earth which echoes affirmatively the "voice of the
bard" in the introduction to *Songs of Experience* ("O Earth, O Earth,
return!"):

> In futurity
> I prophetic see
> That the earth from sleep
> (Grave the sentence deep)
>
> Shall arise and seek
> For her maker meek;
> And the desart wild
> Become a garden mild.

---

[9] Cf. Frye's comparison (*Fearful Symmetry: A Study of William Blake* [Princeton
1949], p. 143) of Archimago to Urizen, Blake's "father of jealousy," of whom Ona's father is an early manifestation.

Persephone as a fertility goddess brings about such a rebirth in nature when she returns from the Underworld; since Lyca retires into sleep in the poem that follows, it becomes apparent that she is identifiable with the earth and, further, that she too will wake. Yet it is not her retirement into sleep and her descent underground that turn the earth into a desert; it is already a desert when she closes her eyes. In "Earth's Answer," the first song of Experience according to the arrangement now generally adopted, earth protests that she is helplessly captive to "starry Jealousy" (that is, to Urizen) and calls for release; the primal fall that blighted the garden, therefore, was the kind undergone by Ona, at an earlier time. When Lyca is the protagonist, the situation is changed. The reaffirmed prophecy, the strange actions of the animals, Lyca's serene and confident acceptance which her parents come to share, all suggests that she has advanced further than any of the other "children" in these songs toward a resolution of the problem of "the two contrary states of the human soul."

"Without contraries is no progression." *The Marriage of Heaven and Hell,* in which this famous key statement occurs, is usually dated about the time *Songs of Experience* was being added to *Songs of Innocence,* and there is especially no reason to exclude the principle of dialectical progression from the dual work that explicitly names contrariety in its descriptive subtitle.[10] In "A Little Girl Lost," Ona enters the state of Experience; at the beginning of "The Little Girl Lost," Lyca prepares to pass out of it. Her surrender in sleep in the midst of the fallen, desert world is not a second fall, nor an admission of defeat, but a necessary, ritual step toward the predicted awakening, by which earth will be able to break the "heavy chain" that holds her in bondage. That progression as well as contrariety is foreseen is evident in the designs. A tree, which has a withered counterpart in the design accompanying "A Little Girl Lost," is shown on the three plates of the Lyca poems in three successive stages of growth; on the last, a thick, twisted bole puts forth new leaves, while in the foreground the maiden lies asleep, now naked and disposed in much the same attitude as the figure that decorates the introductory song of the bard. Like the sleep of Vala in *The Four Zoas,* Night the Ninth (lines 455ff.), Lyca's sleep itself is a form of the sleep of Beulah, which is regenerative as well as nuptial and takes place in "lower paradise," where, temporarily, "Contrarieties are equally True." [11]

---

[10] A scruple against "progression" unnecessarily limits the recent readings of the Lyca poems by R. F. Gleckner, *The Piper and the Bard: A Study of William Blake* (Detroit 1959), Chap. XI.

[11] *Milton,* II, 30.

And what of the animal guardians, in whose company the rescued Lyca is left? Isaiah's prophecy (XIII, 21-22) of the desolation of Babylon shows them in the role they most often play for Blake: "But wild beasts of the desert shall lie there; . . . And the wild beasts of the islands shall cry in their desolate houses, and dragons in their pleasant palaces." "The wrath of the lion is the wisdom of God," Blake says in one of his Proverbs of Hell.[12] There and elsewhere he calls his beasts of prey "portions of eternity"[13] and "guards" of the "fold,"[14] which "cease" when "Empire is no more."[15] They seem to represent part of the violence of the Last Judgment, in Blake's full meaning of the term: a last manifestation of material power, including the human passions, that is also the first manifestation of divine power and is indispensable to a return to the state of Eden.

The lion and the wolf, which usually stand for the beasts collectively (the "tyger," famous as he is, belongs peculiarly to *Songs of Experience* and its limited point of view), had a long history before Blake adopted them. As mythographers of his own time noted, both were often associated symbolically with the sun and even gave their names to constellations. In the Norse Edda, the wolf Fenris was bound for safety, like Blake's Orc; at the end of the world, it was predicted, he would break out of his fetters and devour the sun.[16] In the tradition of moral allegory, a tapestry by Bronzino shows Innocence being rescued by Justice from the powers of evil, among which are Fury and Greed, represented respectively by a lion and a wolf.[17] And since Blake in his later career was to execute a distinguished series of designs for the *Divine Comedy*, it may be remembered especially that a lion and a wolf are two of the three symbolic beasts—the third, the leopard, is named incidentally in "The Little Girl Lost"—that block the path of the pilgrim at the beginning of the *Inferno*, so that he must go by "another road," descending even lower than the dark wood in which he is, like Lyca or like Spenser's Una, lost.

But the "wolvish howl" and the "lions' growl" are what Lyca's parents learn *not* to fear, and instead of blocking her way the beasts make it possible for Lyca to complete her journey, which requires that she, like

---

[12] *The Marriage of Heaven and Hell,* plate 8.

[13] *Ibid.*

[14] Letter to Thomas Butts, October 2, 1800, *The Complete Writings of William Blake,* ed. Geoffrey Keynes (London and New York 1957), p. 805.

[15] *America, A Prophecy,* plate 6.

[16] P. H. Mallet, *Northern Antiquities,* trans. Bp. Thomas Percy (London 1770), II, 90-94.

[17] Erwin Panofsky, *Studies in Iconology: Humanistic Themes in the Art of the Renaissance* (Harper Torchbooks 1962), p. 84.

Dante's pilgrim, descend beyond the point to which her own powers bring her. The beasts for their part are tamed when and, it appears, even because Lyca makes her trusting surrender; it is only after they have "view'd" her asleep that, led by the lion, they begin to gambol about her, "O'er the hallow'd ground." For the moment at least, the "wild beasts of the desert" are turned into kindly friends and protectors, like those in another vision of Isaiah (XI, 6) which has often been cited in relation to these poems: "The wolf . . . shall dwell with the lamb, and the leopard shall lie down with the kid; and the calf and the young lion and the fatling together; and a little child shall lead them." The last design shows beside the sleeping Lyca just such a "little child," leaning trustingly against the massive head of a lion, while two more children play about a reclining lioness: a dream of the state of "higher innocence" to come, perhaps, or a pictorial gloss on Lyca's surrender and rescue which indicates their significance by way of what seems to be an overt allusion to Isaiah.

There is another consideration, which cannot be overlooked and which is peculiarly relevant to the Persephone archetype. The lion and the wolf are evoked in the last two lines of "The Little Girl Found" with their familiar associations and in their familiar pairing, although in neither poem has a wolf previously been named among the animals. Yet in both the lion plays a role which is less prominent than only one other, and if the pairing is to be consistent, there remains only one personage to supply the missing term. Lyca 's name, one of the few specifically used in *Songs of Innocence and of Experience,* was not an improvisation, for it had appeared first in one of the pastoral songs found written in a copy of *Poetical Sketches.*[18] It has been plausibly derived from Greek *λύκη, "light";[19] at the same time, as a word it suggests another origin, if a more bizarre one, which is done other than the missing term itself, with an unexpectedly appropriate Dantesque turn: λύκαινα, or "she-wolf." Mythologically, at least, the two meanings of what is very nearly a pun are not necessarily incompatible; according to one of the Neoplatonists translated by Thomas Taylor, for example, in the Mithraic Mysteries animal names were applied to the gods, and among these was Diana (another Kore figure), who was called a she-wolf.[20] Persephone herself in becoming the bride of Hades acquired a new, sinister character which was another aspect of the triple goddess Hecate, the most fundamental

---

[18] Keynes, *op. cit.,* p. 63.
[19] Raine, *op. cit.,* p. 26n.
[20] "On Abstinence from Animal Food," *Select Works of Porphyry* (London 1823), p. 155.

among Greek feminine archetypes, who comprised in herself maiden
(the Kore), mother, and Mistress of the Spirits.[21] When Lyca becomes the
consort of the lion-king, dwelling in his caves, does she similarly become
part of the "wolvish" terror which like leonine wrath will continue until
the completion of the Last Judgment? Or is "wolvishness" the state she
is leaving immediately behind, appropriate only to her exile in the desert
after her fall as Ona? The poems in the Pickering Manuscript that might
well have been songs of Experience, "The Crystal Cabinet" and "The
Mental Traveller," show something of what might have happened between the fall and the surrender—an unremitting struggle between male
and female wills that brings victory to neither but which neither can give
over, continuing without end in a setting very much like that in "The
Little Girl Lost." [22]

Actually, the implied symmetry between Lyca and the lion, as well as
the ambiguity of her name and her relation to Persephone, justifies both
alternatives. As far as the weeping lion of "The Little Girl Lost" is from
the "couching lion" that attacks the parents in "The Little Girl Found,"
so far is "lovely Lyca" of the first poem from the howling wolf signified
by one aspect of her name and evoked at the conclusion of the second
poem. There is also a further step, which is taken by the lion and on
analogy remains in the future for Lyca. As he reveals himself to the
wondering parents, he is a "spirit arm'd in gold," with a crown and flowing golden hair, and it is primarily his metamorphosis that reassures
them. The regeneration of the lion is already under way when Lyca
makes her surrender, having begun in another poem, "Night," one of the
later songs of Innocence, which like the Lyca poems might be placed in
either series because it hints of a way out of the dilemma of contrariety.
There, as angels watch, the lion is moved to tears of pity by the sight
of the suffering sheep the other beasts of prey have wounded. His pity in
turn leads him to a state of "meakness" which will permit him to lie
down with the naturalistic lamb, as he might in Isaiah's Peaceable Kingdom, and even to become an agent of Christ the symbolic Lamb:

> For, wash'd in life's river,
> My bright mane for ever
> Shall shine like the gold
> As I guard o'er the fold.

To be "wash'd in life's river" is the equivalent of a passage into and
through Experience; in "The Little Girl Lost," therefore, Lyca at her

---

[21] Jung and Kerényi, *op. cit.*, pp. 152-58.
[22] See my "Plato's *Statesman* Myth in Shelley and Blake," *Comparative Literature,*
XIII (1961), 361ff.

surrender moves into equality with the lion. If the symmetry between them is to be preserved, she too must be destined to undergo a final transformation beyond the states of both she-wolf and "little child," one that will bring her ultimate state into accord with the second meaning of her name, making her a queen of light beside the sunlike lion-king.[23] In the meantime, until the Last Judgment is completed and empire is no more, the wolvish howl and the lions' growl continue in the world of Experience.

II

As an archetypal figure, Blake's Lyca thus is a delicately sustained synthesis of a number of images of different orders and from different contexts, with different associations, all subtly interconnected and interacting, all relevant. She is not only a new adumbration of Persephone, the lost daughter and queen of the Underworld. She is also the sleeping maiden of nursery folklore; an Orphan Child who voluntarily separates herself from her parents; Una, the Christian Kore; a Magdalen who recovers innocence; a second Eve who reverses the Fall; a Dantesque pilgrim who does not flee from the beasts of prey, and perhaps even becomes one of them; Isaiah's "little child" as a redeemer, leading the way for others to follow; a foreshadowing of Blake's own persecuted and exiled Jerusalem, who prepares to become the Bride of the Lamb by first becoming the bride of the lion. Yet the other images acquire their function in the whole mainly by their relation to the basic image of Persephone, and it is therefore all the more remarkable that the values implied by the full story of Lyca are at variance with the values reflected in the Greek myth. Demeter wins the limited consolation of the seasonal cycle, a compromise between death and life; Lyca and her parents accept total separation and a radical change of character in the implied certainty of an eventual awakening to totally new life. The difference is perhaps part of the general difference between classical values and Christian; but it extends beyond Blake, who for all his heterodoxy was probably the most Christian among the English Romantics. The ways in which "The Little Girl Lost" and "The Little Girl Found" resemble and differ from the Greek myth are precisely the ways by which the broad mythological archetype is modified into a Romantic literary archetype.

To turn from Blake's Lyca poems to Wordsworth's "Lucy Gray" is to

---

[23] In the Edda (Mallet, II, 166-67) the sun, before being devoured by Fenris, was to give birth to a daughter who would become the sun of the new earth. Persephone herself as Kore was identified with the sun by the mythographer Jacob Bryant; see *A New System, Or, An Analysis of Antient Mythology*, 3rd ed. (London 1807), II, 304.

find the Romantic Persephone already established. Lucy is consistently called a "child," although without the complex overtones of Lyca's "little girl." Her name too has a root meaning of light, and the moon appears at the beginning of her journey as the moon of Beulah rises at the beginning of Lyca's sleep. (As it happens, the moon, that pervasive Romantic image, was also the special emblem of the goddess Hecate.) For Lyca's desert there is Lucy's moor, and for the beasts of prey, the terrors of nature, there is the storm, which overwhelms her and at the same time delivers her from her former life. Lucy disappears in the storm, is sought by her parents, and is traced to the middle of the bridge, where her footprints end—that is, to the point at which she leaves behind the parents and their world. Thereafter, like Lyca, she is free to continue her way in a realm in which they have no place.

Even more striking than the narrative parallels between Blake and Wordsworth is their common divergence from the values of the myth each approaches independently. Both in the initial situation reverse the solicitude of mother for daughter which naturalistically and mythologically would be expected. Before she closes her eyes, Lyca has only one doubt: "How can Lyca sleep/If her mother weep?" (The disastrous effects of parental weeping, of course, are shown in "A Little Girl Lost.") Anticipating the search that later will be made for her, Lucy Gray in her turn sets out in the snow at first as a rescuer, carrying a lantern (which also serves as an emblem appropriate to her name) to light her mother home, like the questing Demeter with her torch. (Or, it might be observed, like the glow-worm that rescues the wandering emmet mother in Blake's "A Dream," still another song of Innocence on the lost-and-found theme.) In both instances, too, the parents' grief is to be understood as the result of their limited vision; Lyca's parents are enlightened and reassured, but Lucy's are left with only the hope that "In heaven we all shall meet." The perspective in all three poems widens out from the world that is being left behind toward the final state that awaits both Lyca and Lucy, although neither attains it in view of the reader—a state for both of release and fulfillment rather than of alienation, bondage, or loss. As Lyca presumably is headed toward what was later to be particularized as Blake's Eden, so the lost Lucy Gray, mingling with the sound and motion of the moor wind, gives promise that she will eventually join her namesake, the heroine of the Lucy poems, in absorption into the Wordsworthian world-soul, to be "Rolled round in earth's diurnal course,/With rocks, and stones, and trees."

Blake and Wordsworth are closely in agreement in presenting their Persephone figures as literal or symbolic children who are lost and found in nature. My third example confirms the Romantic archetype from another direction, for it combines the same reversal of values with an erotic encounter that recalls the sexual aspects of the myth. But instead of possession by force, there is a ritualized seduction that amounts to a quasi-mystical consummation, like the symbolic weddings in the Mystery religions to which the rape of Persephone itself may ultimately be related.

In Keats's "The Eve of St. Agnes," Madeline is a nubile maiden who, like Lyca, serenely lies down to sleep in the presence of what should be danger and over whose preparations the moon also presides; unlike Lyca, she does wake. Angela the nurse is a substitute mother-figure, of minor importance now and even used as an accessory to the seduction; Porphyro, the intruder, seducer, and abductor,[24] an analogue of Hades by his acts, is a hero and deliverer by their effect.[25] The climax of the poem is another departure from ordinary material human existence, which is represented by the society of the castle and, as Keats pictures it, resembles Blake's world of Experience, with the ascetic Beadsman praying in the chapel and "barbarian hordes" of guests revelling in the "level chambers." As an image, the castle itself is an archetype. Once more *The Faerie Queene* comes to mind, and with it the Castle of Alma (II, xi), the fortress body in which the senses are bulwarks for the defense of the virgin soul within.[26] Keats, however, reverses the characters of the besiegers and the defenders, so that the "wicked band of villeins" are actually those entrenched inside the castle.

Like Lucy Gray, Keats's lovers vanish into a storm, which is called "an elfin-storm from faery land," and like Wordsworth's storm is a means of deliverance—"Of haggard seeming, but a boon indeed." In one sense, like Lyca's underground sleep and Lucy Gray's disappearance, the flight of Porphyro and Madeline should probably be understood first of all as simple physical death—and death without the promise of the mythological Persephone's periodic return. But at the same time, it is principally death of another kind, with connotations of transcendence, release, and fulfillment, passage to a higher and happier state of being. Parallel allusions elsewhere suggest that the departure actually may have overtones of the Elizabethan and seventeenth century erotic "death," by way of the

---

[24] Cf. Jack Stillinger, "The Hoodwinking of Madeline: Scepticism in 'The Eve of St. Agnes,'" *Studies in Philology*, LVIII (1961), 539-46.

[25] Cf. Dorothy Van Ghent, "Keats's Myth of the Hero," *Keats-Shelley Journal*, III (1954), pp. 7-25, esp. 16-17.

[26] Spenser's Castle of Alma may be supplemented by an image of Keats's own, sometimes cited in relation to this poem—the "Mansion of Many Apartments." See his letter to J. H. Reynolds, May 3, 1818, *The Letters of John Keats, 1814-1821*, ed. H. E. Rollins (Cambridge, Mass. 1958), I, 280-81.

image of the storm. In both a sonnet ("A Dream") and the account of its genesis in one of his letters, Keats transforms the episode of Paolo and Francesca, driven in eternal punishment by winds symbolic of their earthly passion, into what might be an illustration of his own concept of mortal pleasure immortally "repeated in a finer tone." [27]

Like the parents of Lyca and of Lucy, the inhabitants of the castle are left behind; but, by an irony whose immediately unpleasant effects Keats insisted upon,[28] they are either dead or uneasily sleeping. Instead of being mourners for the lost Madeline, guests, hosts, and retainers all together play the role of a stricken corpse, abandoned as though by a soul rapt away in ectasy. Alma is set free through the senses rather than imprisoned by them, and her destination, which perhaps is indistinguishable from the journey, may be just such an Inferno-heaven of blissfully perpetual, storm-enveloped flight as Keats himself dreamed of.

III

Considerably more could be said about the Romantic Persephone and the poems in which she appears. Coleridge's Christabel and the Lucy of Wordsworth's Lucy poems, for example, are Kore figures, each with her moon-symbol, who for different reasons do not quite attain the full stature of a Lyca, Lucy Gray, or Madeline. In the Lucy poems there is an extra turn to the variation on the myth, for it is the analogue of Demeter— Nature personified, who sets out to "make/A Lady of my own"—who receives Lucy in death, while the earthly lover is the one left bereaved. In the unfinished "Christabel," where a lover is mentioned but does not make an appearance, Geraldine, the mother-spirit, and Christabel herself represent in their curious triangular relationship much the same aspects of the triple goddess that are dramatized in the myth, emerging in Coleridge's poem almost as though for the first time in human culture. And, on another level, the Romantic Persephone in her lyric "fortunate fall" takes her place beside a very different variant, within a continuity that both precedes and follows the Romantic period and is found in

[27] "The fifth canto of Dante pleases me more and more— . . . I dreamt of being in that region of Hell. The dream was one of the most delightful enjoyments I ever had in my life—I floated about the whirling atmosphere as it is described with a beautiful figure to whose lips mine were joined [as] it seem'd for an age—and in the midst of all this cold and darkness I was warm—even flowery tree tops sprung up and we rested on them sometimes with the lightness of a cloud till the wind blew us away again— . . . o that I could dream it every night." Letter to George and Georgiana Keats, April 16, 1819, Rollins, II, 91.

[28] Letter of Richard Woodhouse to John Taylor, September 19-20, 1819, Rollins, II, 162-63.

drama and the novel, embodying a third and very different set of values: the spring fertility goddess who is sacrificed to a barren code of society, and is destroyed.[29]

What has been said, however, is sufficient to indicate some of the problems the critic is likely to meet in approaching Romantic poetry from the standpoint of archetypal recurrence. In the case of Blake's Lyca poems, one problem is the preservation of the basic mythological image, the archetype that is recognizable as the governing one, among the multiplicity of secondary images and allusions. If Lyca is not continuously understood as a figure of Persephone, more than the broader perspective of myth may be lost: the sense of overall pattern in the two poems; their relation to other poems by Blake; and the relevance of the secondary images and allusions themselves. Yet without the interrelations and associations of such additional images as Spenser's Una, Dante's pilgrim, and Isaiah's "little child," to say nothing of the she-wolf, the full implications of what a "Persephone figure" actually means in Blake would be lost. Blake's own concept of "states," by which the personages of legend and myth remain to be met again while man passes through and beyond them,[30] is itself a sophisticated theory of archetypes that illuminates his practice and might be a useful modification of present-day theories. As for the subsidiary images in their own right, they occupy a region somewhere between universal archetypal recurrence and individual imaginative creation, where some degree of knowing selection and adaptation must be assumed on the part of the poet. An altered conception of the study of "sources" and "influences" might be suggested by the relations that have been seen of the Bible, Ovid, the eighteenth century mythographers, and especially Dante and Spenser—both of whom are relevant to both Blake and Keats[31]—to the Romantic rediscovery of Persephone.

There is also a problem for the critic in the radical change in value that accompanies the archetypal image in its Romantic phase, as well as some of the minor images assimilated to it. Is Persephone really Persephone if her disappearance is not a calamity? How far may image and value be separated—or, on the other hand, how closely may they be

---

[29] See Dorothy Van Ghent, "Clarissa and Emma as Phèdre," *Modern Literary Criticism, An Anthology,* ed. Irving Howe (Boston 1958), pp. 139-51.

[30] *A Vision of the Last Judgment,* ed. Keynes, pp. 606, 607.

[31] Coleridge, too, might be included. Christabel at prayer in the moonlight, like Lyca or Madeline, is seen kneeling in a Dantesque "midnight wood." And a non-archetypalist critic recently has compared the relation between Christabel and Geraldine to that between Una and Duessa. See R. H. Fogle, *The Idea of Coleridge's Criticism* (Berkeley and Los Angeles 1962), pp. 133-34.

united—without the destruction of the whole concept of the archetype? What is most strongly demonstrated by the poems that have been considered, I believe, is the interdependence of *both* image and value, and their effects on each other. The Lyca poems, "Lucy Gray," and "The Eve of St. Agnes" all express the Romantic version—better, *three* Romantic versions—of the familiar paradox that in order to gain life it is necessary to lose it; in order to be "found" one must first be irretrievably "lost." Attaching itself to the archetypal image of the lost and found maiden, the Romantic value is able to modify it, reduce or extend it, and even overturn its most firmly established traditional meanings. At the same time, the traditional meanings and accumulated associations of the image provide a test of the new value as it emerges, in an encounter from which both the value and the archetype gain. If the general theory of archetypes affirms a conservatism in literature as a whole as well as in culture and the human psyche—and its conservatism is one of its chief attractions at this point in the twentieth century—the study of a particular literary period like the Romantic can affirm equally a dynamism which, though it may not in absolute novelty create, can transform.

"The Crystal Cabinet" and "The Golden Net"

by Hazard Adams

Judging from the lack of commentary upon it, "The Crystal Cabinet" has been one of Blake's most enigmatic poems. A close reading of "The Mental Traveller" and "My Spectre around me . . ." provides a background . . . [against] which the poem's action can be more clearly understood. At least two important principles emerge from a study of those two poems, and they can be applied here successfully. First, there is the principle of the interchangeability of macrocosm and microcosm. In Blake's visionary world the substance of things may fade, but the form of things is constant. All speakers are in some way a form of Albion himself, the macrocosmic world. Second, there is the principle of perspective. The speaker may be Albion, it is true, but each poem presents the speaker in a slightly different position or state of mind, for in the fallen world, the single form tends to dissolve whereas the substance of things does not. At least that is the illusion through which Blake's actors travel. . . . In the fallen world, where forms change and substance remains, it is not at all surprising to see Albion take what appear to be different forms of himself. We know that one of his forms is Orc and another Urizen. We know, too, that the female, once separate from the male, moves through Tirzah to Rahab. In the fallen world, shape-changers are the rule:

The Crystal Cabinet

The Maiden caught me in the Wild
Where I was dancing merrily
She put me into her Cabinet
And lockd me up with a golden Key

This cabinet is formd of Gold
And Pearl & Crystal shining bright

" 'The Crystal Cabinet' and 'The Golden Net' " by Hazard Adams. From *William Blake: A Reading of the Shorter Poems* (Seattle: University of Washington Press, 1963). Copyright © 1963 by University of Washington Press.
Reprinted by permission of the publisher.

And within it opens into a World
And a little lovely Moony Night

Another England there I saw
Another London with its Tower
Another Thames & other Hills
And another pleasant Surrey Bower

Another Maiden like herself
Translucent lovely shining clear
Threefold each in the other closd
O what a pleasant trembling fear

O what a smile a threefold Smile
Filld me that like a flame I burnd
I bent to Kiss the lovely Maid
And found a Threefold Kiss returned

I strove to sieze the inmost Form
With ardor fierce & hands of flame
But burst the Crystal Cabinet
And like a Weeping Babe became

A weeping Babe upon the wild
And Weeping Woman pale reclined
And in the outward air again
I filld with woes the passing Wind
                    (The Crystal Cabinet, K 429-30) [1]

The speaker recalls a state of unrestrained innocence represented by his dance. He has discovered there a shape-changing female, who performs an act analogous to the crucifixion of Orc in "The Mental Traveller." The difference is that the maiden has seduced the speaker. Distinctions rigidly adhered to in "The Mental Traveller" are somewhat blurred or collapsed, for this speaker is not certain about the experience himself. Tirzah the mother and Rahab the seductress are not distinguished from one another, for the speaker is time-borne. Tirzah is forgotten, though her action is described as accomplished by Rahab. In considering the sexual aspect of the symbolism—cabinet, lock, key, etc.—we move at once to encompass a simple Freudian reading and see that the clearly sexual imagery is symbolic of a meaning larger than itself; for the female is the whole of the outer world as well as her sexual self. In the speaker's eyes, the two actions of "The Mental Traveller"—capture by the earth mother

[1] Citations marked "K" are to Geoffrey Keynes, ed., *The Complete Writings of William Blake* (London: The Nonesuch Press; New York: Random House, 1957). References are to page numbers. [ED.]

and rape of the virgin bright—are suddenly one and the same in remembrance. We can think of the capture of the speaker as following the last part of the cycle of "The Mental Traveller," if we assume that the speaker *remembers* the female not as a Tirzah but only as a Rahab.

What we discover is that the male has been contained by the female rather than encompassing her. The crystal cabinet is an area just short of vision, holding within itself all the possibilities of vision. It is clearly related to what Blake calls Beulah, the state of threefold vision, passive pleasure, and moony nights. But Beulah is part of the fallen world here, the uppermost area below Eden; it is a part of the triple form which is nature—Beulah, Generation, and Ulro. In some respects it is a gate, but a gate has two directions and no one is capable of staying in the gate itself for long, just as each moment in fallen time must disappear.

The action in Beulah is very nearly successful, but the danger of Beulah is its seductivity and the tendency of the passive dreamer of moony nights to abstract his vision from himself and assume its separate existence. The result is the familiar fall into multiplicity, seen here as an infinite regress in which the vision of the "other," really the self, becomes a series of mirrors or a crystal. The "other maiden" whom the speaker sees is really, then, the same maiden split into a triple form by the process of "reflecting" upon an outer world. The number three in Blake is associated with a vision of nature halfway between the chaotic area of Generation and the fourfold vision of Eden. In Beulah, if man externalizes the threefold maiden and thus fails to encompass within his own imaginative form the triple world of nature which she represents, he falls into Ulro.

We notice, then, that within Beulah a choice is presented to the speaker. He may expand his vision to encompass all of a beautiful spiritual England, all of London—a city like the woman that Albion finally marries in *Jerusalem*. The vision is that of London *within* England (Albion). To make this choice would be to expand inward in that paradoxical Blakean fashion that always puts Eden at the still point of the circle and Ulro at the circumference. Or to put it another way:

> What is Above is Within, for every-thing in Eternity is translucent:
> The Circumference is Within: Without, is formed the Selfish Center
> 　　　　　　　　　　　　　　*(Jerusalem*, Ch. 3, K 709)

Such an interpretation seems to contradict the preceding statement, but the terms are simply reversed. The real or upright world is really the world of mental forms without material substance. The true expansion to the infinite circumference of God, which is traditionally both everywhere and nowhere in measurable space, is therefore within, while to assume oneself the center of the material universe is to enclose oneself in the Urizenic cave of the ego. The speaker, in other words, can proceed from the sexual to the human vision, where nature is no longer a surrounding physical existence but a city within the spirit.

The second choice, or perhaps we should call it temptation, is to turn around, or inside out, and instead of looking within look without. Then the true England becomes a triple female named Rahab, an indefinite cyclical conception or crystal mirror suggesting something beyond herself (translucent) but actually reflecting a debased image of the self. Although this mirror woman can return a kiss, to grasp her is as impossible as to reach successfully through a mirror. The result is, of course, a shattering of the glass itself.

Now any bursting forth might, on first appearance, suggest an apocalyptic assertion of new life similar to breaking the shell of the traditional cosmic egg or ascension from the grave. But if we accept Blake's paradoxical spatial imagery we see that the true rebirth does not come from breaking out of the crystal cabinet into another merely larger cyclical world. Such action might go on indefinitely, the infinite space of modern physical science providing the wanderer with shell after shell to be broken through. Instead, proper vision lies in an inward expansion in which one's own spiritual body surrounds that "other England" within the grain of sand. Any violent reading out destroys the vision. From within the crystal cabinet the translucence, which is really reflection, suggests a tantalizing possibility of something beyond the perceivable or visionary fact. And yet with that translucence smashed, the reflection of the self is apparently translucent again, on a larger more remote concave surface. This should be the spiritual lesson of modern science.

We may note the paradoxical aspects of the crystal cabinet by observing that it is related, on the one hand, to the "crystal house" of *Europe,* where it is a symbol of the cyclical enclosure of fallen time and space ruled over by a nature-goddess, Enitharmon:

> Then Enitharmon saw her sons & daughters rise around.
> Like pearly clouds they meet together in the crystal house.
> *(Europe,* "A Prophecy")

On the other hand, it has aspects of "the grain of sand" image in Blake which appears frequently to illustrate the paradox of inward visionary expansion. The grain of sand appears most prominently in the following places: at the beginning of "Auguries of Innocence," where it is used to express the identity of macrocosm and microcosm (that which is above is that which is within); in the poem "Mock on Mock on . . . ," from the Rossetti MS, where it is used in an attack against the reality of the outer world, [as assumed in] all theories of a material substratum in nature; and finally in *Jerusalem,* where it is associated with Beulah.

In "Mock on Mock on . . . ," Voltaire and Rousseau, at the base of whose mockery there is a materialist assumption, turn out to be mocking only themselves in that cyclical pattern we have come to associate with delusion:

> Mock on Mock on Voltaire Rousseau
> Mock on Mock on tis all in vain
> You throw the sand against the wind
> And the wind blows it back again

If we assume that the sun is like a guinea instead of a choir of the heavenly host, we must live with the implications of that assumption. So too with the materialistic assumption above. One's own atomic particles, tossed on the wind, blind the self. Just as the "translucent" mirror shows only a self mistaken for an outer female, so does the assumption of matter, thrust back into the physical eye, blind the perceiver to an inner world:

> And every sand becomes a Gem
> Reflected in the beams divine
> Blown back they blind the mocking Eye
> But still in Israels path they shine

The pillar of sand is really a pillar of visionary fire, though this is not apparent to someone who tries to look *with* instead of *through* the eye:

> The Atoms of Democritus
> And Newtons Particles of light
> Are sands upon the Red sea shore
> Where Israels tents do shine so bright
>   (K 418)

Just as materialist mockery is self-blinding, in a kind of cyclical return, so are the atomic particles which form the physical basis of the material delusion. They are caught in the cycle of tides, tossed on the shore, and tossed again unless they are seen as spiritual universes which contain the shining tents of Israel.

Blake tells us that each grain of sand is a gem, reminding us of the crystal cabinet itself. And he makes the relationship even more explicit in *Jerusalem* . . . :

There is a Grain of Sand in Lambeth that Satan cannot find
Nor can his Watch Fiends find it; tis translucent & has many Angles
But he who finds it will find Oothoons palace, for within
Opening into Beulah every angle is a lovely heaven.

(Jerusalem, Ch. 2, K668)

Relation to "The Crystal Cabinet" is even more apparent here. Satan, who is associated with Urizen and is indeed his spectral form, cannot find this grain of sand because he operates on the same premises as Voltaire and Rousseau—that is, he assumes the material substratum in nature which is symbolized by the grain of sand. Therefore, he cannot conceive of looking inside it. If he did he would be introduced to Beulah and the window into Eden. Blake adds, incidentally, that even if the watch fiends did find it, they would call it sin, evoking "morality" against that which violates their materialistic premises as well as their sexual mores. This is exactly what happens to Oothoon in Blake's *Visions of the Daughters of Albion.* Oothoon's "union of innocence and experience in the free act of love," as Peter F. Fisher describes it, is frustrated by Enlightenment, common sense and tyrannical moral law. Her palace is the vision her act represents.

The word "translucent," which appears above and in Blake's description of Rahab in *Jerusalem* as well as in "The Crystal Cabinet," points up the delusions possible in Beulah. From within the cabinet the endless reflection of light leads the speaker to assume that it is shining through from without. This leads him to burst through the crystal. But the speaker's striving does not result in a return to the same kind of innocent "wild" in which he originally danced. Quite the contrary, the wild is now transfigured; time has passed, and with it innocence. The "weeping babe" is a creature of the realm of experience, the sulking infant Orc of "Infant Sorrow." The wild is now a wasteland of woes and wind. The imagery is that of flux—dissolving form. The speaker has grown young, the maiden has become a woman. They are now, as the poem ends, taking part in a scene we remember from "The Mental Traveller." Soon, as she grows older and he even younger, she will nail him down upon the rock in an act similar to his attempt to seize her inner form. The "outward air," in which all of this occurs, is similar to the terrain of "My spectre around me . . ."; and, in Blake's terms, certainly the man and woman have again taken on aspects of specter and emanation.

Erdman, relating the action of "The Crystal Cabinet" to Blake's own life, points out that it was written during a period when Blake, having returned from Felpham (the "wild") to London with high hopes, saw those hopes for a return to "the pleasant aspects of his Lambeth days" dwindle away in a series of personal difficulties, including perhaps the illness of his wife. If Erdman is correct, we are also correct in assuming that the wild into which the speaker is thrust at the end is not the same wild in which he was caught. It is the desolation of a London in which Blake's wife (the weeping woman) is ill and in which other things do not go well. But the symbolic details of the poem do not all fit, or at least are not all explained by, the biographical evidence available to us. I am not sure that the poem is necessarily biographical at all, for if it is we must assume that the speaker is Blake. And there seems to be too great a sense of detachment in the tone for this to be certain.

One of the lessons the speaker should have learned is that the female or outer nature cannot be "grasped." It is the specter that must be wrestled with and brought under control:

> Each Man is in his Spectres power
> Untill the arrival of that hour
> When his Humanity awake
> And cast his own Spectre into the Lake
>
> (K421)

To wrestle with the emanation is to assume that it is somewhere beyond, not back through the eye or window of the mind. When the speaker of "The Crystal Cabinet" saw in Beulah for a timeless moment the glory of the true city, he confused his spiritual direction. The city became the reflecting mirror Rahab, and he fell back into the triple world of the Orc cycle. He became a part of nature rather than encompassing the triple world into his own fourth being.

The ultimate enclosure is the idea of a material body, an unchanging nature out of which form struggles to escape. The crystal cabinet is a symbol for such a body—the inert sleeping Albion. Like the crystal cabinet, the material form of humanity is "translucent all within"—the spiritual world turned inside out. This we are told in the introductory poem to Chapter II of *Jerusalem:*

> He [Satan] witherd up the Human Form
> By laws of sacrifice for sin;
> Till it became a Mortal Worm;
> But O! translucent all within.
>
> (K651)

Another symbol for the fallen body appears in "The Golden Net," where, like the cabinet, the net is associated with a threefold female of delusory powers:

Three Virgins at the break of day
Whither young Man whither away
Alas for woe! alas for woe!
They cry & tears for ever flow
The one was Clothd in flames of fire
The other Clothd in iron wire
The other Clothd in tears & sighs
Dazling bright before my Eyes
They bore a Net of Golden twine
To hang upon the Branches fine
Pitying I wept to see the woe
That Love & Beauty undergo
To be consumd in burning Fires
And in ungratified desires
And in tears clothd Night & day
Melted all my Soul away
When they saw my Tears a Smile
That did Heaven itself beguile
Bore the Golden Net aloft
As on downy Pinions soft
Over the Morning of my day
Underneath the Net I stray
Now intreating Burning Fire
Now intreating Iron Wire
Now intreating Tears & Sighs
O when will the morning rise

(K424)

Central to the poem is the problem of misplaced pity or erroneous
action resulting from that emotion. We are reminded at once of Los and
the necessity of holding to the higher form of pity, which is creative
action. The speaker here has been deceived into pitying three females,
thinking them damsels in distress. And indeed they have cried out for
his aid. The three females are, like the crystal cabinet, "dazling bright"
and represent the familiar Rahab or external nature. They also, of course,
represent the false, hollow social forms that cause subservience in relations between the sexes. In calling for pity the females take advantage of
the subservient state in which pity often places the giver. Our speaker
should have been wary of those images we have learned to associate
with delusion and enclosure—the triple form, the tree, and the net—
but he is consumed with pity for the women, who are putting on quite
a show of grief. His interest, however, is undoubtedly sexual, for his own
distress is that he imagines what woes love and beauty undergo when

held in a state of repression, which well may be a reflection of his own condition.

His initial feelings are perfectly correct. In this world, . . . love and beauty *are* consumed in "ungratified desires," but the false female, or nature, is not really representative of love or beauty and actually revels in the fallen state, using it to trap and consume the male. This lesson is also the lesson of "My Spectre around me. . . ." It is only that our speaker has misunderstood his adversary. He thinks he is, and perhaps he may even at the outset be, acting upon the emotion of pity. But he is also acting out of his own repressed sexual desires; therefore his own pity cannot be pure. He wishes to save beauty, as the good knight wishes to save the damsel. But reaching out, he discovers the net and tree, the flames, the iron wire, the tears and sighs; and he discovers that they are his prison as well. He falls. And now it is he who is "intreating" the female for pity. In such a "natural" society, then, the direct human relationship seems perverted.

A main point is that the speaker attributes the best of motives to himself. Perhaps he is merely the pawn of nature, like Keats's pale knight; on the other hand, perhaps his own materialistic assumptions have enclosed him in his dazzling prison. To have seen the triple female is to have looked outward. Having looked outward, he discovers the dazzling brightness which we have found to be the paradoxical light of the concave walls of nature—Rahab and the crystal cabinet itself. The three virgins *are* the net which they hold; the tree on which they hang the net is the tree of knowledge of good and evil, the fallen world itself; and in a sense the females compose an Eve figure holding out a golden temptation. We have been shown that moment which is recognizable as the fall from Beulah. Nature is no longer a mother but a virginal outer being whom our Orc seeks to grasp and control. "The Golden Net" is therefore associated not only with the enclosure of "The Crystal Cabinet" but also with "The Mental Traveller." We note, for example, that the poem begins with morning, the state of innocence and growth. The speaker describes himself as in the transitional period between innocence and experience. He is still somewhat lamb-like ("Underneath the net I stray"), but at the end of the poem he is seeking another morning, the rebirth from his own day, which has become the dark night of experience. The dazzling brightness of Rahab is curiously associated with a kind of cloudiness ("downy Pinions soft"), and has shown itself to be as paradoxical as the dark fires of Dante's Hell.

Blake's Vision of Slavery

by David V. Erdman

The fire, the fire is falling!
Look up! look up! O citizen of London enlarge thy countenance:
O Jew, leave counting gold! return to thy oil and wine. O African!
black African! (go, winged thought widen his forehead.)

"A Song of Liberty"

I

When Blake came to believe, in the decade after Waterloo, that the revolutions in America and France had been merely bourgeois revolutions, destroying colonial and monarchic restraints only to establish the irresponsible "right" to buy and sell, he concluded that nearly everything of value in those revolutions had been lost—at least as far as his own countrymen were concerned. When he declared that most Englishmen "since the French Revolution" had become "intermeasurable by one another" like coins in a till and had reduced all values to the experiment of chance, he meant that such Englishmen had absorbed nothing of the real meaning of Republican culture, had not learned that everything that *lives* is holy and without price and that each "line or lineament" is *itself* and is "not intermeasurable by anything else." [1]

Most of his life Blake was more or less confident that the sons and daughters of Albion would learn; would enlarge their views rather than their investments, would "look up" and open their minds to the visions in the air. For "counting gold" is not abundant living; and grasping

---

"Blake's Vision of Slavery" by David V. Erdman. From *Blake: Prophet Against Empire* (Princeton: Princeton University Press, 1954). Copyright © 1954 by the Princeton University Press.

Reprinted by permission of the publisher.

[1] To Cumberland, Apr. 12, 1827 (Geoffrey Keynes, ed., *The Complete Writings of William Blake* [London: The Nonesuch Press; New York: Random House, 1957], p. 927; hereafter referred to as "K" with page number). Blake says "Englishmen are *all*" etc., but excepts himself and his friend. On the opposition of Money to Art see Laocoön (K581).

colonies and shedding blood whether in the name of royal dignity or in the name of commerce is not living at all, but killing. When Blake urges the London merchant to turn from banking to the exchange of useful commodities (Biblical "oil and wine") he is thinking on the one hand of the need to abolish hunger; on the other hand he is thinking of the gold amassed from colonial plunder, traffic in slaves, and open war. The winged thought which must inspire the African slave to revolt must also inspire the British citizen to let "the British Colonies beneath the woful Princes fade" and to desist from coveting the colonies of France. And it must also inspire the sexes to *love* and let *live* without possessive jealousy.

Blake sees all these matters as interrelated. War grows out of acquisitiveness and jealousy and mischanneled sexual energy, all of which grow out of the intrusion of possessiveness into human relations. "Number weight & measure" signify "a year of dearth." [2] The Rights of Man are not the rights of dealers in human flesh—warriors, slavers, and whoremongers. When Fayette was "bought & sold" in the service of the royal whore, his and other people's happy morrow was also "bought & sold." Purchase and sale only bring the old relationship of tyrant and slave out into the open market.

The economic side of Blake's myth is often expressed in images of fertility and sterility, fire and frost and seasonal growth. The soul of America who sings passionately of "lovely copulation" is a woman and also a continent longing for fruit in her fertile valleys. To say that she wants to be loved, not raped, is to say, economically, that she wants to be cultivated by free men, not slaves or slave-drivers; for joy, not for profit. The revolutionary energy which appears in history as Orcus pulling tyrants down to the pit appears in husbandry as the plower, sower, and reaper of abundant harvests, symbolized as ὄρχεις, the root of sexual growth in the womb of the earth. Orc as the spirit of living that transcends the spirit of trading is the divine seed-fire that exceeds the calculations of Urizen, god of commerce. The portrait of Urizen with golden compasses is made in the image of Newton, the mighty spirit of weighing and measuring who thought to reduce the prolific universe to an orrery of farthing balls. When Newton's trump marks the end of weight and measure, the great starry heavens prove to be as light as leaves.

In the symbolic Preludiums of *America* and subsequent poems, the rich sexual-agrarian implications of Blake's economics are condensed into a cryptically ritualized myth. But some of the reasoning behind this myth,

---

[2] "Proverbs of Hell," *The Marriage of Heaven and Hell*, 7 (K183); cf., the motion in The House of Commons, Feb. 5, 1790, for "a return from all cities and market towns of the different weights and measures now in use."

or more properly the questioning behind it, is available in *Visions of the Daughters of Albion,* 1793, a dramatized treatise on the related questions of moral, economic, and sexual freedom and an indictment of the "mistaken Demon" whose code separates bodies from souls and reduces women and children, nations and lands, to possessions.

Superficially the *Visions* appears to be a debate on free love with passing allusions to the rights of man, of woman, and of beasts and to the injustices of sexual inhibition and prohibition, of life ruled by "cold floods of abstraction," and of Negro and child slavery. Yet love and slavery prove to be the two poles of the poem's axis, and the momentum of its spinning —for it does not progress—is supplied by the oratory of Oothoon, a female slave, free in spirit but physically bound; Bromion, the slave-driver who owns her and has raped her to increase her market value; and Theotormon, her jealous but inhibited lover who fails to recognize her divine humanity. As a lament over the possessiveness of love and the hypocrisy of moral legislators, the poem has been widely explored in the light of Blake's notebook poems on this theme and in the light of Mary Wollstonecraft's *Vindication of the Rights of Woman.* The other pole, equally important in the dynamics of the work, has scarcely been discovered. Yet we can understand the three symbolic persons of the myth, their triangular relationship, and their unresolved debate if we recognize them as, in part, poetic counterparts of the parliamentary and editorial debates of 1789-1793 on a bill for abolition of the British slave trade—the frustrated lover, for example, being analogous to the wavering abolitionist who cannot bring himself openly to condemn slavery although he deplores the *trade.*

Blake, in relating his discussion of freedom to the "voice of slaves beneath the sun" (*V.D.A.* 31), was directing the light of the French Revolution upon the most vulnerable flaw in the British constitution, and in doing so he was contributing to the most widely agitated reform movement of the time. The Society for the Abolition of the Slave Trade, formed in 1787, had begun at once to gather evidence, organize town meetings, and enlist the help of artists and writers. Wedgwood produced a cameo of a suppliant Negro, widely used on snuffboxes, bracelets, hairpins. William Cowper wrote a number of street ballads such as *The Negro's Complaint* and *Sweet Meat Has Sour Sauce.* And Blake's *Little Black Boy* coincided with the early phase of this campaign. But the Parliamentary phase began in 1789 and coincided with the revolution in France and the ensuing revolution of slaves in 1791 in French Santo Domingo. It reached its height in 1792-1793, and Wordsworth, returning to

England early in 1793 after more than a year in France, was struck by the extent of the English movement: "little less in verity Than a whole Nation crying with one voice" against "the Traffickers in Negro blood." [3] The abolitionists nevertheless were "baffled." The bill was defeated in Parliament by the pressure of Antijacobin attacks from Burke and Lord Abingdon and various slave-agents, of whom Blake's thundering Bromion is a caricature.

This movement "had diffus'd some truths And more of virtuous feeling through the heart Of the English People," but its breadth was due partly to the fact that relatively few had any direct stake in the trade. Conservative as well as liberal humanitarians were not unwilling to dissociate British honor and British commerce from "this most rotten branch of human shame." Moreover, the slaves themselves made the trade a risky one, both for slave drivers and for ship owners. Scarcely a year went by without its quota of slave ship mutinies, battles on the African coast, and insurrections in the plantations. Military statesmen complained that merchant seamen died off twice as rapidly in the slave trade as in any other, effecting a loss of manpower for the British navy. And many active abolitionists were merchants who preferred to invest in well-behaved cargoes manufactured in Manchester and Birmingham. It is Blake's view that the movement failed because of an insufficient diffusion of "truths" and a considerable misapplication of "virtuous feeling," to use Wordsworth's terms.

In *Visions of the Daughters of Albion* the true feelings which the Heart must "know" before there can be human freedom are discussed by Oothoon, Bromion, and Theotormon for the edification of the "enslav'd" Daughters of Albion—an almost silent audience or chorus, who lament upon their mountains and in their valleys and sigh "toward America," and who may be considered the Blakean equivalent of traditional personifications of the trades and industries of Great Britain: in *The Four Zoas* some of them appear as the textile trades whose "needlework" is sold throughout the earth. They are of course, in the moral allegory, "oppressed womanhood," as Damon points out. They are shown that as long as possessive morality prevails, all daughters remain slaves; and that while the trafficker in Negro blood continues to stamp his signet on human flesh, none of the traffic on the golden Thames is untainted. In short, freedom is indivisible, and Oothoon's is a test case. [4]

[3] *The Prelude*, X, 202-27, here and below.
[4] For documentation and illustration of this section and the next, see *Journal of the Warburg and Courtauld Institutes*, XV (1952), 242-52.

II

Blake's knowledge of the cruelties of slavery came to him doubtless through many sources, but one was directly graphic. In 1791 or earlier the bookseller Joseph Johnson distributed to Blake and other engravers a sheaf of some eighty sketches of the flora and fauna and conditions of human servitude in the South American colony of Dutch Guiana during some early slave revolts. With more than his usual care Blake engraved at least sixteen plates, including nearly all those which illustrate slave conditions. We know he was working on them during the production of his *Visions of the Daughters of Albion* because he turned in most of the plates in batches dated December 1, 1792, and December 2, 1793. The two-volume work they illustrate was finally published in 1796 as *A Narrative, of a five Years' expedition, against the Revolted Negroes of Surinam, in Guiana, on the Wild Coast of South America; from the years 1772 to 1777,* by Captain J. G. Stedman. We may assume that Blake was familiar with the narrative, available in Johnson's shop—at least with the portions explanatory of the drawings.

Blake's engravings, with a force of expression absent from the others, emphasize the dignity of Negro men and women stoical under cruel torture: the wise, reproachful look of the *Negro hung alive by the Ribs to a Gallows* (pl. 11) who lived three days unmurmuring and upbraided a flogged comrade for crying; the bitter concern in the face of the Negro executioner compelled to break the bones of a crucified rebel; the warm, self-possessed look of his victim, who jested with the crowd and offered to his sentinel "my hand that was chopped off" to eat with his piece of dry bread: for how was it "that he, a *white man,* should have no meat to eat along with it?" Though Blake signed most of the plates, he shrank from signing his engraving of this bloody document, *The Execution of "Breaking on the Rack"* (pl. 71); but the image of the courageous rebel on the cruciform rack bit into his heart, and in the Preludium of *America* he drew Orc in the same posture to represent the spirit of human freedom defiant of tyranny.

For the *finis* page Blake engraved according to Stedman's specifications "an emblematical picture" of *Europe supported by Africa & America*— three comely nude women tenderly embracing each other, the Negro and the European clasping hands in sisterly equality. Roses bloom auspiciously on the barren ground at their feet. Yet there is a curious difference between this pictured relationship of Europe *supported* by her darker sisters, who wear slave bracelets while she wears a string of pearls, and the "ardent wish" expressed in Stedman's text, that all peoples "may henceforth and to all eternity be the props of each other" since "we only differ in colour, but are certainly all created by the same Hand." The bracelets and pearls may be said to represent the historical fact; the handclasp, the ardent wish. For one plate Blake had the ironic chore of engraving a "contented" slave—with Stedman's initials, J.G.S., stamped on his flesh with a silver signet.[5] "Stampt with my signet," says Bromion (*V.D.A.* 21).

In his *Narrative* Stedman demonstrates the dilemma, social and sexual, of the English man of sentiment entangled in the ethical code of property and propriety. A hired soldier in Guiana, Captain Stedman was apologetic about the "Fate" that caused him to be fighting bands of rebel slaves in a Dutch colony: " 'Twas *yours* to fall—but *Mine* to feel the wound," we learn from the frontispiece, engraved by Bartolozzi: *Stedman with a Rebel Negro prostrate at his feet.* The fortitude of the tortured Negroes and the "commiseration" of their Negro executioners impressed Stedman and led him to conclude that Europeans were "the greater barbarians." Yet he could repeat the myth that these same dignified people were "perfectly savage" in Africa and would only be harmed by "sudden emancipation." His "ears were stunned with the clang of the whip and the dismal yells"; yet he was reassured by the consideration that the tortures were legal punishment and were not occurring in a *British* colony.[6]

To the torture of female slaves Stedman was particularly sensitive, for he was in love with a beautiful fifteen-year-old slave, Joanna, and in a quandary similar to that of Blake's Theotormon, who loves Oothoon but cannot free her. Stedman managed "a decent wedding" with Joanna, for which he is shamefaced, and a honeymoon during which they were "free like the roes in the forest." But he was unable to purchase her freedom, and when he thought Joanna was to be sold at auction, he fancied he "saw her tortured, insulted, and bowing under the weight of her chains, calling aloud, but in vain, for my assistance." Even on their honeymoon, Stedman was harrowed by his inability to prevent the sadistic flagellation of a slave on a neighboring estate. We have Blake's engraving of this *Flagellation of a Female Samboe Slave* (pl. 37). Naked and tied "by both arms to a tree," the "beautiful Samboe girl of about eighteen" had just received two hundred lashes. Stedman's interference only prompted the overseer to order the punishment repeated. "Thus I had no other remedy but to run to my boat, and leave the detestable monster, like a beast of prey, to enjoy his bloody feast." The girl's crime had been "refusing to submit to the loathsome embraces of her detestable executioner." The

---

[5] Pl. 68; see Stedman's text I, 206.

[6] I, 109, 203, 90; II, 298.

captain's own Joanna, to prove the equality of her "soul" to "that of an European," insisted on enduring the condition of slavery until she could purchase freedom with her own labor.[7] Blake's Oothoon invites vultures to prey upon her naked flesh for the same reason. Her lover, Theotormon, is also unable to interfere or to rescue her:

> Why does my Theotormon sit weeping upon the threshold;
> And Oothoon hovers by his side, perswading him in vain
>
> *(V.D.A.* 44-45)

The persons and problems of Stedman's *Narrative* reappear, creatively modified, in the text and illustrations of Blake's *Visions*: the rape and torture of the virgin slave, her pride in the purity and equality of her soul, and the frustrated desire of her lover and husband. Oothoon advertised as pregnant by Bromion is the slave on the auction block whose pregnancy enhances her price; Oothoon chained by an ankle in plate 4 is the *Female Negro Slave, with a Weight chained to her Ancle*[8]—or the similarly chained victim of the infamous Captain Kimber, cited in Parliament in 1792. The cold green wave enveloping the chained Oothoon is symbolic of the drowning of slaves in passage from Africa; the flame-like shape of the wave is symbolic of the liberating fires of rebellion. Her friend beside her hears her call but covers his eyes from seeing what must be done. In another picture Oothoon is fastened back-to-back to Bromion; yet the most prominent chains are on *his* leg, and she has not ceased struggling to be free.[9] Impotent beside these two squats Theotormon, the theology-tormented man,[10] inhibited by a moral code that tells him his love is impure. A caricature of paralyzed will power, he simultaneously clutches himself, buries his face in his arms, and scratches the back of his head. Despite his furtive sympathy ("secret tears") he makes no effective response to

> The voice of slaves beneath the sun, and children bought with money,
> That shiver in religious caves beneath the burning fires
> Of lust, that belch incessant from the summits of the earth.

[7] I, 99-106, 208, 312, 319, 325-26; II, 83, 377.

[8] Pl. 4, engraved by Bartolozzi.

[9] *V.D.A.* Plate printed variously as frontispiece or tailpiece—an emblem of the *situation.*

[10] The names Oothoon, Theotormon, Bromion, and Leutha have been traced to Ossian's Oithona, Tonthormod, Brumo, and Lutha. But the oo-oo doubling may come from African words in Stedman: apootoo, too-too, ooroocoocoo (snake). A *toremon* is a shiny black bird whose name means "a tale-bearer, or a spy"; and the rebels "have an invincible hatred against it." I, 367-368. If *Theo* is God, an accuser of sin might be considered God's spy, *Theo-toreman.* Unquestionably Theotormon torments and is tormented.

[11] *V.D.A.* 31-33.

Stedman's anxieties shed light on the moral paralysis of Theotormon; yet we must also be aware of the analogous but more impersonal and political quandary of the Abolition Society, whose trimming announcement in February 1792 that they did not desire "the Emancipation of the Negroes in the British Colonies" but only sought to end *the Trade* for Slaves" conflicted with their own humanitarian professions and involved an acceptance of the basic premises of the slavers: that slaves were legitimate commodities and that the rebellion of slaves was legally indefensible.[12] William Wilberforce, the Society's zealous but conservative spokesman in Parliament, became increasingly preoccupied in 1792 with clearing his reputation of the taint of republicanism in an attempt to carry water on both shoulders: to be known as a great friend of the slaves yet as an abhorrer of "democratical principles." Also he had obtained a "Royal Proclamation against Vice and Immorality" and was promoting what became known as the Vice Society, based on the proposition that woman's love is Sin and democracy is Blasphemy. Blake's deliberate emphasis on the delights of "happy copulation" could be expected to shock such angelic moralists, as if to say: you cannot free any portion of humanity from chains unless you recognize the close connection between the cat-o'-nine-tails and the moral code.[13]

The situation or story of Blake's poem is briefly this. Oothoon, a candid virgin, loves Theotormon and is not afraid to enter the experience of love. She puts a marigold between her breasts and flies over the ocean to take it to her lover; she is willing, that is, to give him the flower of her virginity. But on the way she is seized by Bromion, who rapes her despite her woeful outcries, and advertises her as a pregnant slave (harlot).[14] Her lover responds not by coming to her rescue but by accusing her and Bromion of adultery and secretly bemoaning his fate and hers. Oothoon and Bromion therefore remain "bound back to back" in the barren relationship of slavery, while Theotormon, failing as a lover, sits "weeping upon the threshold." The rest of the poem consists of their three-sided soliloquy. Oothoon argues that she is still pure in that she can still bring her lover flowers of joy, moments of gratified desire; but he cannot act because he accepts Bromion's definition of her as a sinner.

Interpretation of the story on this level is sometimes blurred by failure

[12] *London Chronicle,* Feb. 2, 1792. Against the argument that it was simply strategic to concentrate first on abolition of the trade, consider the fact that as soon as the Slave Trade Bill was passed, in 1807, the Society dissolved. Slavery itself, and consequently the trade, continued to exist.

[13] In *V.D.A.* pl. 9, Theotormon is flaying himself with a three-thonged scourge, while Oothoon runs by unaided.

[14] See Stedman, I, 206.

to distinguish Oothoon's offer of herself to Theotormon from her rape by Bromion. The flower-picking is mistaken for a symbol of the rape, and her later argument is mistaken for defense of an "affair" with Bromion. But in Blake's plot-source, Macpherson's *Oithona,* where the heroine is similarly raped in her lover's absence, the lover returning does what obviously Theotormon ought to do, considers her still faithful and goes to battle at once in her defense, against great odds.[15] Oothoon's argument is not that she likes Bromion or slavery but that she refuses to accept the status of a fallen woman: only if her lover lets Bromion's name-calling intimidate him will she be "a whore indeed" (line 170). She is not asking merely for toleration but for love.

The allegorical level, indicated by Oothoon's designation as "the soft soul of America" (line 3) must not be neglected. Bromion's signet brands not simply a woman but "Thy soft American plains," and Bromion is no simple rapist but the slaver whose claim to "thy north & south" is based on his possession in both North and South America of African slaves: "Stampt with my signet . . . the swarthy children of the sun" (lines 20-21). When the soul of America goes "seeking flowers to comfort her" she is looking for a further blossoming of the revolutionary spirit (compare the Preludium of Blake's *America*), and when she finds a "bright Marygold" in the "dewy bed" of "the vales of Leutha," she is apparently taking note of the Negro insurrections in Santo Domingo in the Caribbean around which the debate in Parliament raged: "Bromion rent her with his thunders."[16] The first risings did not succeed, but the flower or

---

[15] Were Oothoon and Theotormon married before the story begins? Critics differ. Bromion's "Now thou maist marry" suggests they were not; Theotormon's jealousy of "the adulterate pair" suggests they were. What matters is that the affair was not consummated. Oothoon welcomes the "experience" that Thel shrank from, but her lover does not.

[16] *V.D.A.* 4-15, 170. In the abolition debates attention was focussed on this eruption of "democratic principles" in the West Indies. The fact that London merchant firms held investments in Santo Domingo in the then large sum of £300,000 "helps to explain why the British government in [1793-1798] sacrificed more than £4,000,000 in an effort to conquer the French colony and maintain or restore Negro slavery. It helps to explain also why Wilberforce's abolitionist program suffered a momentary eclipse." C. L. Lokke, "London Merchant Interest in the St. Domingue Plantations of the Émigrés, 1793-1798," *Am. Hist. Rev.,* XLIII (1938), 795-802. Leutha's Vale appears to be Blake's place-name for the French colony, Leutha being the Queen of France. In *Fayette* the Queen is one whose smile spreads pestilence. In *Europe* Leutha is "the sweet smiling pestilence," a "silken Queen" who has "many daughters" (colonies?), and in a phrase which recalls Paine's remark she is called the "luring bird of Eden." In the "Thiralatha" fragment (K211) the fading of "The British Colonies" is compared to the dying of a dream, perhaps of French colonialism, which has left "obscured traces in the Vale of Leutha." After the West Indies docks were located in the Isle of Dogs, Blake took to calling it the Isle of Leutha's Dogs. *Jerusalem* 31. Leutha's Vale is "dewy" perhaps because it lies in the dewy bed of the Caribbean.

nymph comforts "Oothoon the mild" both with her own "glow" and with the observation that the spirit of liberty is irrepressible: "Another flower shall spring, because the soul of sweet delight Can never pass away." On this level Theotormon, to whom Oothoon wings over the Atlantic in "exulting swift delight" expecting him to rejoice at the good news of another rising republic, acts like those English abolitionists who were embarrassed by the thunders of the Antijacobins.

Blake's acquaintance with the abolition debate is evident. The Bromions in Parliament cried that the Africans were "inured to the hot climate" of the plantations and therefore necessary for "labour under a vertical sun." Under Bromion's words Blake draws a picture, stretching across the page, of a Negro worker smitten into desperate horizontality, wilted like the heat-blasted vegetation among which he has been working with a pickaxe, and barely able to hold his face out of the dirt. The apologists also argued that Negroes understood only "firmness," were "contented and happy" and superstitious, and were now "habituated to the contemplation" of slavery. Bromion utters the same arguments: that "the swarthy children of the sun . . . are obedient, they resist not, they obey the scourge; Their daughters worship terrors and obey the violent" (lines 21-23).

In Parliament Lord Abingdon accused the "abettors" of abolition of promoting the new philosophy of leveling: "Look at the state of the colony of St. Domingo, and see what liberty and equality, see what the rights of man have done there." They have dried up the rivers of *commerce* and replaced them with "fountains of human blood." Moreover the levelers are prophesying that "all being equal, blacks and whites, French and English [*sic*], wolves and lambs, shall all, 'merry companions every one,' promiscuously pig together; engendering . . . a new species of man as the product of this new philosophy."

It is this sort of argument that Blake's Oothoon turns right side up again. For, as Abingdon put it, "what does the abolition of the slave trade mean more or less in effect, than liberty and equality?" Wilberforce joined Burke in a committee for the relief of emigrant royalist priests partly, as he admitted, "to do away French citizenship"—for the French had misinterpreted his liberalism and named him an honorary French citizen along with Paine and Priestley! Yet this demonstration did not prevent Burke from attacking the Abolition Bill as "a shred of the accursed web of Jacobinism." Blake's Theotormon is tangled in the suspicion that his own desires are part of an accursed web.

The argument of Oothoon is triplex, as she herself is. Stedman's emblematical picture treats Europe, Africa, and America as three separate women: Blake makes them into one. He can do this because Oothoon is not a person but a "soul." Pictured in chains she is the female slave, but she does not have the black skin and tight ringlets of the Africa of the emblem. Only in the picture of the exhausted worker is the Negro slave directly represented. Allowing for difference in mediums, Oothoon is the American Indian of the emblem, with the same loose black hair, sad mouth, and angular limbs. See especially the illustration of the title-page, where she runs along the trough of a green wave pursued by the mistaken God of slavery.

Yet her skin is not the copper color of the engraved America either, but theoretically "snowy" white, according to the text. "I am pure," she cries "because the night is gone that clos'd me in its deadly black." [17] Speaking as America she means that the night of oppressive chivalry is gone with the dawn of freedom. As Africa she means that the time is gone when people's vision was limited to their five senses and they could see only her dark skin and not her inward purity.

Blake had explained this symbolism in his *Little Black Boy*:

> My mother bore me in the southern wild,
> And I am black, but O! my soul is white.
> White as an angel is the English child:
> But I am black as if bereav'd of light.

To avoid a chauvinistic interpretation Blake explained that any skin color is a cloud that cannot obscure the essential brotherhood of man in a fully enlightened society, such as Heaven. "These black bodies and this sunburnt face," said the little black boy, are "but a cloud." If the Negro is to be free of his black cloud, the little English boy must be likewise free from his "white cloud," which is equally opaque. "When I from black and he from white cloud free," I will "be like him and he will then love me." In the second illustrated page of this Song of Innocence the black boy appears as light-skinned as the English boy—or as Oothoon.[18]

Oothoon's reason for letting the vultures prey upon "her soft snowy limbs" is to let Theotormon, who is an adult version of the English child, *see* that beneath the skin her "pure transparent breast" really reflects the same human "image" as his—that her color is morally that of "the clear spring, mudded with feet of beasts," which again "grows pure & smiles"

---

[17] *V.D.A.* 35, 51-52. Blake usually employed brown inks in printing *V.D.A.* though sometimes he chose pink, purple, or yellow. In contrast, *Europe* and *America* are usually printed in green, blue, or black.

[18] Not quite true for all copies. In at least one a slight tint has been given to the black boy in heaven; but the contrast with the solid color of the first page is still pronounced.

(line 42). As Africa she is urging the London citizen to ignore color differences. As America she is urging British law-makers to rescue her from the muddy feet of the slaver. As a woman enslaved by Marriage Act morality, she is imploring her lover to rise above accusations of adultery.

Beyond arguing her essential purity, she indicates by several analogies that there is something especially beautiful about dark skin and (she suggests both points at once) about pregnancy. Consider the dark skin of worm-ripened fruit, which is "sweetest"; or the darkness of "the soul prey'd on by woe"; or

> The new wash'd lamb ting'd with the village smoke & the bright swan
> By the red earth of our immortal river: I bathe my wings,
> And I am white and pure to hover round Theotormons breast.
>
> (lines 78-81)

It is the soul rather than the body of the slave that is "inured," in being richer in experience. The black boy already loves the English boy and is thus better prepared than he to "bear the heat" of God's presence.

And still we have not done with the complexity of Blake's symbolism, for in one illustration, on the page of the "Argument," Oothoon appears not as an American Indian but as the European woman of the emblem. Or rather in this illustration the Stedman influence is supplanted by that of a French neo-classical painter and engraver, Vien. Here the focus is on the buying and selling of woman's love, and Blake is reversing Vien's picture (based on a Roman original) of a procuress offering "loves" for sale in a basket: *La Marchande d'Amours.* Oothoon kneels in the same posture as that of the love-merchant, and her hair is knotted at the back of her head in a similar fashion. But whereas Vien's procuress holds one of her cupids by his wings like a captive bird, Oothoon keeps her hands to herself and lightly "kisses the joy as it flies," springing not from a basket but from the stem of a marigold.

In the most general sense the soaring joys which Oothoon offers her lover are sparks of Promethean fire or winged thoughts calculated to widen his brow. In her effort to prod him to cross the threshold of indecision—"I cry arise O Theotormon for the village dog Barks at the breaking day"—Oothoon insists that the revolutionary dawn is at hand and overdue and that the corn is ripe. But this "citizen of London" does not look up. He is not at all sure "what is the night or day"; he is nearly deaf to the cries of slaves and blind to visions of a new day: he cannot arise. The springs of rebellion are as obscure to him as those of moral purity. "Tell me what is a thought," he pleads, "and upon what mountains Wave shadows of discontent? and in what houses dwell the wretched" (lines 84-

88). But he fears that the new philosophy may carry his thought to a "remote land" (America) or may bring "poison from the desart wilds" rather than "dews and honey and balm" (lines 89-97). And he grows silent when Bromion shakes the cavern with rhetorical questions, just as the Abolitionists were silenced in 1793 by the clamor of Antijacobinism.

Bromion's arguments and those of the apologists of slavery are of the same order: Dare anyone question that subordination must be maintained? Has anyone even in this land of liberty and poverty yet heard of any way to maintain order without the fear of punishment? Are not war and slavery the basis of our Empire? Is not sorrow intended for the poor, joy for the rich? Is not fear of Hell necessary to keep the laborious poor from pursuing "eternal life"? (lines 105-110)

III

If war and subordination are the basis of Empire, peace and equality must be the ground of that condition in which "The Whole Business of Man Is The Arts & All Things Common," as Blake would reiterate thirty years later in his Laocoön inscriptions. Oothoon, in a series of elliptical counter-questions to those of Bromion and Theotormon, makes a number of glancing observations on the connection of scarcity and inequality which are not immediately clear but become so when we consult the analogous but more plainly worded agrarian definitions of Mary Wollstonecraft in her early *Vindication of the Rights of Men* (1790). There, for example, the Blakean axiom that "virtue can only flourish among equals" is linked to an economic proposal for the division of large estates into small farms, and we may recall that one of Blake's myths of the fall, from Urthona to Los, implies that man was and must again become earthowner. "In what gardens do joys grow?" asks Theotormon, dimly aware of a lost Paradise, "and upon what mountains Wave shadows of discontent?" (lines 95-97). In the *Vindication* the answer is that the polished vices of the rich and the "tremendous mountain of woe" oppressing the poor both depend upon economic inequality, without which England will be a garden more inviting than Eden, with "springs of joy" murmuring on every side and every man "contented to be the friend of man" (pp. 140-49).

Oothoon has similar notions. Surveying the delights of the rich and the woes of the poor, she contrasts the ideal form of human relations—in which each joy is "holy, eternal, infinite" and no one's joy absorbs another's—with the actual relations, in which the rich, both patron ("giver of gifts") and merchant, have "delights" while the poor, both industrious citizen and husbandman, have "pains." Since it is specious to call that joy which hinders and brings tears to others, she makes the point that the "joys" of the oppressor are really "tears." In a world of hindering and hindered it is a mockery for a Bromion to speak of joy and sorrow and "one law"—as if the tyrant could understand the feelings of the patriot: "Does he who contemns poverty [i.e., who views the poor with contempt], and he who turns with abhorrence From usury: feel the same passion, or are they moved alike?" (*V.D.A.* 115-124). Burke writing scornfully of "the swinish multitude," for instance, is hardly moved by the same indignation that moves Paine or Wollstonecraft to condemn monopolists and forestallers.

Oothoon comes finally to the two classes of men whose functions in the service of tyranny give them the most perverse views of human happiness, the recruiting officer and the tithing priest. The function of the priest is to supply the economic and ideological base of the whole superstructure of Empire from fortresses to marriage laws, and Oothoon outlines this process in her questions:

> With what sense does the parson claim the labour of the farmer?
> What are his nets & gins & traps, & how does he surround him
> With cold floods of abstraction, and with forests of solitude,
> To build him castles and high spires, where kings & priests may dwell.
>
> (lines 128-31)

The same process is alluded to in *America* (lines 85-120) when Paine and other Patriots are said to shelter the grain and the "fatness of the earth" from priest and prince who wish to subvert useful labor (plow and spade) to the building of fortresses (wall and moat) and who would bring "the stubbed oak to overgrow the hills." In both passages the issue is whether the land shall be used for peaceful farms or for castled "forests of solitude," an issue raised in Wollstonecraft's questions (p. 140): "Why cannot the large estates be divided into small farms? Why are huge forests still allowed to stretch out with idle pomp and all the indolence of Eastern grandeur?"

It is against such domination by "the idle" that the Patriots of *America* stand "with their foreheads rear'd toward the east." According to Paine, in the second part of *The Rights of Man*, "the government of the sword revolved from East to West" but a new government founded on a system of universal peace was "now revolving from West to East, by a stronger impulse . . ." Blake wrote in his notebook:

> The sword sung on the barren heath
> The sickle in the fruitful field.

> The sword he sung a song of death
> But could not make the sickle yield.
>   (*N*. 105)

This image of the sword on the heath brings us around to Oothoon's description of the man who drums to war, the other of the two agents of tyranny whose occupations make "different the world to them" and "different their eye and ear!"

> How different far the fat fed hireling with hollow drum,
> Who buys whole corn fields into wastes, and sings upon the heath!
>   (*V.D.A.* 125-26)

His function is like that of Sennacherib, King of Assyria, who laid waste fortified cities and dismayed the inhabitants "as grain blasted before it is grown." [19] Literally he brings the flames and trampling of battle to the fields of corn and makes his camp indifferently on field or barren heath. Cognate passages in *The Four Zoas* make the picture clear. Horses "trample the corn fields in boastful neighings" when they have been compelled to "leave the plow" and become cavalry horses. Officers of mountainous girth thrive on the ruin of peaceful husbandry:

> Let us refuse the Plow & Spade, the heavy Roller & spiked
> Harrow; burn all these Corn fields: throw down all these fences!
> Fatten'd on Human blood & drunk with wine of life is better far
> Than all these labours of the harvest & the vintage.[20]

In short, the fat hireling is Blake's Falstaff, the eternal recruiting sergeant who leads men from the plow and musters "mortal men" for the slaughter.

The imagery is, for us, puzzlingly telescoped. "Buys" is misleading, for the hireling is not buyer but bought; it is the king hiring him who "buys" cornfields into wastes, purchasing war instead of peace as well as refusing to transform his forested estates into fruitful farms. But these ideas were familiar enough to Blake's contemporaries, who would hardly have made the modern critic's mistake of supposing that Oothoon is opposing enclosures (in the 1790s these were undertaken to create, not destroy, cornfields)—or even at the moment talking about them. She is dwelling on the direct effect of war on food, obviously agreeing wih the pamphleteers who argued that the continental war, by interfering with imports, devastating grain areas, and requisitioning grain to feed non-productive soldiers, was the cause of scarce bread and high prices. In an age when Luxury was still a sin and every fat man was a living comment on the inequi-

---

[19] 2 Kings 19:25-26.
[20] *F.Z.* viia.199-201 (K328); ii.128-31 (K262).

table distribution of a meager food supply, Blake shared the popular belief that the drone or waster *was* the wolf at the door. In the famine year 1795 his *Song of Los* directly indicts the war-making King as the villain whose policy calls "for Famine from the heath" (the heath being the place where soldiers were trained to war).

Oothoon's questions, like those of Enion later in *The Four Zoas,* hint at answers but remain unanswered short of a Last Judgment; but they define the crisis of humanity in soul-searching terms.

States of Being:
The Four Zoas

by Harold Bloom

> Few poets of the highest class have chosen to exhibit the beauty of
> their conceptions in its naked truth and splendour; and it is doubt-
> ful whether the alloy of costume, habit, &c., be not necessary to
> temper this planetary music for mortal ears.
>   —Shelley, *A Defence of Poetry*

The difficulty of Blake's major poems, which has caused impatient
readers to call them failures, is the difficulty of the beauty of Blake's conceptions in its naked truth and splendor. Frye, the most Blakean com-
mentator on Blake we are likely to get, says of these poems that "they are
difficult because it was impossible to make them simpler."

The motto of *The Four Zoas,* from Ephesians, characterizes the tone of
the work:

> For our contention is not with the blood and the flesh, but with domin-
> ion, with authority, with the blind world-rulers of this life, with the spirit
> of evil in things heavenly.

The Zoas, the Four Mighty Ones who are in every Man, are now the
blind world rulers of this life, and their fallen status makes them also the
spirit of evil in things heavenly, for when united they had formed "the
Universal Brotherhood of Eden." How they came to fall, the manner of
their present warfare, and the ways in which they must regenerate form
the subject of the poem.

The first and greatest problem presented by *The Four Zoas* is that it is
neither complete in itself nor even one poem, but rather at least two poems intermingled, with many late additions and corrections in the manuscript. We cannot even date its versions confidently, except to say that
Blake began it in 1795 and finally abandoned it in 1804. Yet he gave the

manuscript to his disciple, the painter Linnell, just before he died, apparently in the hope that it would be preserved, so we cannot assume that Blake was altogether willing to see the poem die. In its first version the epic was entitled *Vala,* or the *Death and Judgement of the Ancient Man,* a *Dream of Nine Nights.* The hypothetical text of *Vala* was edited from the manuscript by H. M. Margoliouth, and can now be read and studied more or less in its own right. Here I will give a brief description of the second version, *The Four Zoas,* subtitled *The Torments of Love & Jealousy in the Death and Judgement of Albion the Ancient Man.* Though harder to hold together than *Vala, The Four Zoas* is much the richer poem, with an ampler rhetoric than the relatively chastened *Milton* or the somewhat astringent *Jerusalem.* It may even be that as Blake's poems become more widely read and accurately studied, our response to them will follow the now familiar pattern of response to Dante, where youth seems to prefer the *Inferno,* middle age the *Purgatorio,* and later years the *Paradiso.* The spectacular *Four Zoas,* with its dazzling *Night the Ninth, Being the Last Judgment,* is the most energetic and inventive of Blake's poems, while the rewards of *Milton* and *Jerusalem* become progressively subtler. The rhetorical movement is from the urgency of "The stars consum'd like a lamp blown out" to the quiet clairvoyance of "All Human Forms identified, even Tree, Metal, Earth & Stone." In action, the poems progress toward ever deeper internalization, until at last we can never forget that "all deities reside in the human breast."

The account of the fall, in Blake's more comprehensive version, begins not with Urizen but "with Tharmas, Parent power, dark'ning in the West," and lamenting the loss of his Emanations. Tharmas, in Eternity, was the particular representative of unity, man's attribute of the power of harmony between love, intellect, and imagination. Man's unified sense of taste and touch, which still come together in sexual experience, is in the domain of Tharmas. The origins of the name "Tharmas" are obscure, but this is really just as well, as it is usually misleading to interpret one of Blake's creatures by its name's supposed etymology. The names are arbitrary, but the functions and qualities are not. Blake's entire purpose in breaking with names like Venus and Apollo was to eliminate irrelevant associations, and we serve him badly by the more irrelevant of our pedantries.

Tharmas is the unfallen link between the potential and the actual, what man wants and what he can get. Before the fall into division, every desire is carried over into realization by Tharmas. As Albion, or primal Man, was all Imagination for Blake, Tharmas must therefore be what Wallace Stevens means by "a figure of capable imagination." Urizen was the firm outline of imagination, Urthona (who becomes Los in fallen time) its shaping spirit, and Luvah (who becomes Orc) the passion that imparted desire to the forming and shaping inventiveness of Man. When the human ceased to be divine, and our world came into being, then Tharmas necessarily fell first, which is the story of Night I of *The Four Zoas.*

Fall for Tharmas means separation from his outer female aspect, Enion, who becomes the earth mother of the generative world, and who resembles the fearful Earth, mother of Prometheus, in Shelley's lyrical drama. The poem's action begins with a pathetic dialogue of misunderstanding between Tharmas and Enion. Innocence has been lost, for Tharmas was the presiding genius of Beulah, where the Zoas rested in renovating passion, and where a fresh tide of life never ceased to pulsate. Split off from his emanation, Tharmas has lost Beulah and is in danger of becoming a shadow or spectral self of his shepherd's reality. He is now the western or Atlantic ocean to Enion's isolated British earth, and so Blake reminds us again of the myth of destroyed Atlantis, and the great deluge that overwhelmed it. Tharmas was, in a sense, Thel's river of Adona, the life of the Gardens of Adonis. When the other Zoas split the unity of Albion, Tharmas raged until he became an oceanic flood, which drowned out the married land and produced what and where we are.

The separated Enion, as a female will, both desired Tharmas and yet in him "found Sin & cannot return." His eloquent lament refuses reunion on her analytical and self-righteous terms:

> "Why wilt thou Examine every little fibre of my soul,
> Spreading them out before the Sun like stalks of flax to dry?
> The infant Joy is beautiful, but its anatomy
> Horrible, Ghast & Deadly: nought shalt thou find in it
> But Death, Despair & Everlasting brooding Melancholy.
>
> "Thou wilt go mad with horror if thou dost Examine thus
> Every moment of my secret hours. Yea, I know
> That I have sinn'd, & that my Emanations are become harlots.
> I am already distracted at their deeds, & if I look
> Upon them more, Despair will bring self-murder on my soul.
> O Enion! thou art thyself a root growing in hell,
> Tho' thus heavenly beautiful to draw me to Destruction."

Enion weaves the garment of phenomenal nature, until she has perfected a cycle or "Circle of Destiny" which is the monument and tombstone of her separation from Tharmas. The Daughters of Beulah, Blake's Muses, are terrified by the chaos their deity has become, and reject the now completed Circle of human destiny:

> The Circle of Destiny complete, they gave to it a Space,
> And nam'd the Space Ulro, & brooded over it in care & love.
> They said: "The Spectre is in every man insane & most
> Deform'd. Thro' the three heavens descending in fury & fire,
> We meet it with our songs & loving blandishments & give
> To it a form of vegetation. But this Spectre of Tharmas
> Is Eternal Death. What shall we do? O God, pity & help!"
> So spoke they, & clos'd the Gate of the tongue in trembling fear.

To close the Gate of the tongue is to restrict the natural entrance into Beulah, and limits the imaginative possibilities of human sexual experience. Enion now becomes "a bright wonder, Nature, Half Woman & half Spectre." From her intercourse with the raging Spectre of Tharmas she brings forth the weeping infants of the *Songs of Experience,* now identified as Los and Enitharmon, time and space, restricted imagination and confining form. These infants soon become fierce, reject their mother, and wander through the painful world of Experience.

Meanwhile, Blake's narrative goes back to the events that caused the ruin of Tharmas. The fall of man is no longer viewed as the fault of Urizen alone, but of Luvah as well, and so the contraries of reason and energy are equally capable of selfish plotting against the full life of man. Luvah, like Phaethon, seizes the chariot of the sun, which belongs to Urizen, Prince of Light. Yet desire cannot usurp reason without disaster, even in Blake, and Luvah's desertion of moon for sun is Albion's fall into a self-righteousness of emotional pride, a glorification of the heart's impulses at the expense of man's other legitimate powers.

The remaining Zoa, Urthona, is working at his anvil, preparing spades and colters for the heavenly plowing, when he feels the effects of the strife between Eternals. In this crisis of imagination, the inventive faculty experiences a failure in nerve, in which Enitharmon, his emanation, flees from him to the comforting Tharmas. In a first act of possessiveness, "Enion in jealous fear / Murder'd her, & hid her in her bosom." Left a spectre, Urthona also collapses into Enion, from whose form he is to reappear in the world below as the prophetic and poetic principle, Los.

Albion's emanation is Jerusalem. Blake said that he knew no other Christianity "than the liberty both of body and mind to exercise the divine arts of imagination," and Jerusalem is identified by him as this "liberty," which is in every man insofar as he possesses the Inner Light of the Protestant tradition. Night I closes with the darkening of this Light, as Jerusalem is "scatter'd into the indefinite," and man falls "downwards & outwards" into chaos.

Night II centers on the fall of Luvah and his emanation Vala, who be-

comes the deceptive beauty of nature after she has won primacy over
Albion. The wandering children of Experience, Los and Enitharmon,
whom we now know to be only foster children of Tharmas and Enion,
rehearse in song the story of Luvah's fall. The complexity of Blake's art
has largely escaped notice here. As Enitharmon and Los repeat the fall
in song, they enact the torments of love and jealousy between themselves
as well, and their nuptial song recapitulates both the terror of their own
ambiguous passion and the strife of Eternity. Their tribulations are the
direct consequence of Urthona's self-separating fear and doubt in Night I
of the poem.

As Los and Enitharmon torment one another, they become the proper
prey of Urizen, who descends as god of this world and offers the quarrel-
ing children dominion over the realm of the emotions, and the right of
judgment upon Luvah and Vala. They accept, and so lose their last heritage of Innocence, the refusal to judge or be judged. Their powerful
Nuptial Song places the blame for the fall entirely upon the emotional
life, and so prepares them for a marriage of mutual envy and jealousy, a
Urizenic compact between two grim children determined to perform
again the cruelties and deceptions that disintegrated Eternity. As this
dreadful union is celebrated, Enion wanders in chaos, lamenting the triumph of fallen morality to which she has contributed. At this point she
is the Earth of the introductory poems of the *Songs of Experience*.

Hearing the voice of the wailing earth mother, the sick-unto-death
Albion rises "upon his Couch of Death" and calls Urizen to take the
scepter of control, so as to impose some order upon chaos. It was at this
point that the poem *Vala* seems to have commenced.

Urizen now becomes "the great Work master," a demiurge who will
build the Mundane Shell of present-day reality around the Rock of
Albion. While Urizen prepared his instruments of measurement and re-
striction, the poem moves its focus to the fall of Luvah, now melted down
by Vala in the Furnaces of affliction. Albion, like Urizen, has now equated
chaos and emotion, and so man is delivered to Urizenic religion, with its
hatred and repression of human sexual love. Such love is now self-divided
and tormented, with its emanative portion become a separate, mocking,
elusive creation. Inspired by the example of Vala, Enitharmon sings a
courtly love hymn that proclaims the triumph of the female will:

> "The joy of woman is the Death of her most best beloved
> Who dies for Love of her
> In torments of fierce jealousy & pangs of adoration:
> The Lover's night bears on my song,
> And the nine Spheres rejoice beneath my powerful controll."

Night II concludes with what may be the finest of Blake's Biblical chants, the lament of Enion. The context of this song is complex; all of the Zoas are now separated from their Emanations, but Enion has been separated the longest. As she contemplates the active errors of Vala and Enitharmon, and grieves over her own outcast fate, Enion also excites Ahania, the wife of Urizen, to an awareness of the fallen state. Enitharmon is an Eve figure who will become a courtly-love Queen of Heaven. Vala is the beauty of outward nature, becoming progressively more deceptive as history continues. Enion herself is only a wandering Demeter, but Ahania is a more crucial figure in Blake's myth. As in *The Book of Ahania,* Urizen's Emanation is a total form of intellectual desire, which must express itself as sexual in the fallen world. Most particularly, then, Ahania is precisely the "lov'd enthusiast, young Fancy," of Collins' *Ode on the Poetical Character,* who must participate in any of the mind's acts of creation, lest those acts become merely the hindrances of sterility.

In the lament of Enion we hear for the first time in *The Four Zoas* the true voice of Blake himself:

> "What is the price of Experience? do men buy it for a song,
> Or wisdom for a dance in the street? No! it is bought with the price
> Of all that a man hath—his house, his wife, his children.
> Wisdom is sold in the desolate market where none come to buy,
> And in the wither'd field where the farmer plows for bread in vain."

The burden of Enion's song is a thought that, as Frye observes, can lead only to madness or apocalypse, for the song is a culminating lament for lost innocence, organized about the idea that human pleasure is based on a wilful ignorance concerning the suffering of others. Enion first "taught pale artifice to spread his nets upon the morning," when she accused Tharmas of sin. Now she understands the experiential price of such self-righteousness, but she has purchased wisdom at the expense of her being. Blake himself, in a passionate undersong, reminds us of the prophet's fate. Wisdom can be sold only where none will come to buy, and will be sought only where no harvest can come:

"It is an easy thing to triumph in the summer's sun
And in the vintage, & to sing on the waggon loaded with corn.
It is an easy thing to talk of patience to the afflicted,
To speak the laws of prudence to the houseless wanderer,
To listen to the hungry raven's cry in wintry season,
When the red blood is fill'd with wine & with the marrow of lambs.

"It is an easy thing to laugh at wrathful elements;
To hear the dog howl at the wintry door, the ox in the slaughter house moan;

To see a god on every wind & a blessing on every blast;
To hear sounds of love in the thunder storm that destroys our enemies' house,
To rejoice in the blight that covers his field, & the sickness that cuts off his children,
While our olive & vine sing & laugh round our door, & our children bring fruits & flowers.

"Then the groan & the dolor are quite forgotten, & the slave grinding at the mill,
And the captive in chains, & the poor in the prison, & the soldier in the field,
When the shatter'd bone hath laid him groaning among the happier dead.

It is an easy thing to rejoice in the tents of prosperity—
Thus could I sing, & thus rejoice; but it is not so with me."

The vision of Innocence is based upon ignorance, and the joy of right-eousness upon the prosperity of an untried Job. Enion's warning, which forever ends Ahania's rest, preludes the blindness of Urizen in Night III, where the fall of Urizen and Ahania leads to a reappearance of Tharmas, a second deluge. Night III is dominated by images of light and darkness, as we would expect in a Book of Urizen. The King of Light looks upon futurity, "dark'ning present joy." He beholds a reborn Luvah, in the shape of the rebel Orc, "that Prophetic boy," who will be "born of the dark Ocean" that Tharmas has become. In anticipated revenge, Urizen curses the passional life of man, asking that it die "a dark & furious death" in the loins of Los before that shaper can bring it forth as an articulated antagonist. Ahania remonstrates with the now Satanic Urizen:

"O Prince! the Eternal One hath set thee leader of his hosts.
Leave all futurity to him; resume thy fields of Light.
Why didst thou listen to the voice of Luvah that dread morn,
To give the immortal steeds of light to his deceitful hands,
No longer now obedient to thy will? thou art compell'd
To forge the curbs of iron & brass, to build the iron mangers,
To feed them with intoxication from the wine presses of Luvah,
Till the Divine Vision & Fruition is quite obliterated.
They call thy lions to the fields of blood; they rouze thy tygers
Out of the halls of justice, till these dens thy wisdom fram'd,
Golden & beautiful, but O how unlike those sweet fields of bliss
Where liberty was justice, & eternal science was mercy!"

The appeal leads to her expulsion, as Urizen suddenly sees her as an-other Vala, prophesying for him the fallen fate of Luvah:

He siez'd her by the hair
And threw her from the steps of ice that froze around his throne,

> Saying: "Art thou also become like Vala? Thus I cast thee out!
> Shall the feminine indolent bliss, the indulgent self of weariness,
> The passive idle sleep, the enormous night & darkness of Death,
> Set herself up to give her laws to the active masculine virtue?"

The fear of lapsing into passivity has begun to dominate Urizen. But to cast out one's desire is to become only the shadow of desire, and a Spectre must fall. Urizen crashes down, and his world of imposed reason and order with him. Noah's flood has come, and Tharmas with it as an instinctive principle of chaos, where once he was the spirit of unity. Emerging from the Smoke of Urizen, Tharmas stands on the affrighted Ocean:

> Crying: "Fury in my limbs! destruction in my bones & marrow!
> My skull riven into filaments, my eyes into sea jellies
> Floating upon the tide, wander bubbling & bubbling;
> Uttering my lamentations & begetting little monsters
> Who sit mocking upon the little pebbles of the tide
> In all my rivers & on dried shells that the fish
> Have quite forsaken! O fool! fool! to lose my sweetest bliss!
> Where are thou, Enion? ah! too near to cunning, too far off,
> And yet too near! Dash'd down, I send thee into distant darkness,
> Far as my strength can hurl thee: wander there, & laugh & play
> Among the frozen arrows; they will tear thy tender flesh.
> Fall off afar from Tharmas! come not too near my strong fury!
> Scream, & fall off, & laugh at Tharmas, lovely summer beauty,
> Till winter rends thee into Shivers, as thou hast rended me!"

One wonders how the voice of chaos could be better rendered. As always in his epics, Blake's rhetoric is wonderfully appropriate for each character, and in every context. Tharmas can barely articulate his watery longings, nor can he separate his desire for Enion from his wish to punish her in revenge. The confusions of fallen instinct are matched by the violent fluctuations of Tharmas' bellowing, as his voice thunders, sobs, and bursts over the ocean of space and time.

Night III climaxes in a desperate dialogue of misunderstandings and despairs. Enion, blind and bent by age, plunges into the cold billows in terror at Tharmas' mixed curses and entreaties, and she withers away in the cold waves of despair. Action and image are fused, as is characteristic of Blake's epic style. Enion asks to be only "a little showery form" near her "lovèd Terror," and she dissolves into a tear even as she utters her prayer. Too late, Tharmas recoils from his fierce rage into her semblance. He becomes a thundercloud dissolving in tears, hoping thus to join her.

But she is "vanished from the wat'ry eyes of Tharmas," and her wandering place at the verge of non-existence is taken by Ahania.

Night IV is a night of raging flood, as the despairing Tharmas pursues his lost "lineaments of ungratified desire." Luvah and Urizen, who actively caused Tharmas to fall, are now without power. The Spectre of Tharmas makes his instinctual attempt to find a way out of his own inchoate rage. He commands Los to "rebuild this Universe beneath my indignant power," but as "a Universe of Death & Decay." Los is now in much the same position that he held in *The Book of Urizen,* for he must hammer form out of chaos, and set both a Limit of Opacity (Satan) and a Limit of Contraction (Adam) beyond which man and the universe cannot fall. The fate of the poetic visionary as he performs this grim task is to take on the fallen form of what he beholds, to become what he is doing. Night V opens with a frightening metamorphic dance of destruction, as the creative imagination falls over into contraction. This, for Blake, is the true fall of man:

> Infected, Mad, he danc'd on his mountains high & dark as heaven.
> Now fix'd into one stedfast bulk, his features Stonify:
> From his mouth curses, & from his eyes sparks of blighting.
> Beside the anvil cold he danc'd with the hammer of Urthona
> Terrific. Pale, Entharmon, stretch'd on the dreary earth,
> Felt her immortal limbs freeze, stiffening, pale, inflexible.
> His feet shrink with'ring from the deep, shrinking & withering;
> And Entharmon shrunk up, all their fibres with'ring beneath;
> As plants, wither'd by winter, leaves & stems & roots decaying,
> Melt into thin air, while the seed, driv'n by the furious wind,
> Rests on the distant Mountain's top.

Night V recapitulates the story of the birth and binding of Orc from *The Book of Urizen,* with the difference that the bound babe of *Urizen* or "The Mental Traveller" is now understood to be a reborn Luvah, one of a series of such reincarnations which will culminate in the birth of Jesus. Urizen begins to explore his dens, as before, in Night VI, which largely follows chapter eight of *The Book of Urizen,* down to the creation of the Web of Religion. Toward the end of Night VI the exploring Urizen hears the howling of the bound Orc, redoubles his immortal efforts, and is about to have Orc at his mercy when he encounters Tharmas and a dreadful figure called the Spectre of Urthona:

>   & full before his path,
> Striding across the narrow vale, the Shadow of Urthona,
> A Spectre Vast, appear'd, whose feet & legs, with iron scalèd,
> Stamp'd the hard rock, expectant of the unknown wanderer

Whom he had seen wand'ring his nether world when distant far,
And watch'd his swift approach. Collected, dark, the Spectre stood.
Beside him Tharmas stay'd his flight & stood in stern defiance,
Communing with the Spectre who rejoic'd along the Vale.
Round his loins a girdle glow'd with many colour'd fires;
In his hand a knotted club whose knots like mountains frown'd,
Desart among the Stars, them withering with its ridges cold.
Black scales of iron arm the dread visage; iron spikes instead
Of hair shoot from his orbèd scull; his glowing eyes
Burn like two furnaces.

Faced by this double protector of man's imprisoned life force, Urizen
retires into his Web, which moves out to prepare his path before him,
and causes Tharmas and the Spectre of Urthona to flee. Their flight and
the descent of Urizen down to the Caves of Orc begin Night VII of the
poem, but this is a second Night VII. In 1799-1800 Blake seems to have
discarded his first version of Night VII, and to have created a second that
redetermined the shape of his poem. One influential critic, Margoliouth,
reads this revision as a major change in Blake's mind, even calling it a
"conversion" to a "new acceptance of Christianity." As Margoliouth concludes his useful book by saying that Blake "has much in common with
St. Paul," his fanciful account of a conversion was clearly part of a rather
personal pattern-making. Whatever Blake was, he believed to the end that
"Energy is the only life, and is from the Body," which is antithetical to
the dualism of St. Paul. Yet there is a crisis in Night VII of *The Four
Zoas*, and it is possible that some crisis in Blake's inner life is involved.
Erdman finds a double crisis embedded in the *Zoas* manuscript, the first
being the Peace of Amiens (first announced, autumn 1801) and the second
a renewal of war between France and England in the spring of 1803. This
may be, but the problematical Spectre of Urthona seems to have more to
do with problems of poetic incarnation than with the external warfare
that undoubtedly provides the basis for Blake's historical allegory.

If one reads *The Four Zoas* as a Freudian allegory, it would seem clear
that Urizen was a kind of superego, Tharmas an id, with Luvah-Orc rising from him as libido; but Los, the fourth Zoa, is hardly a representation
of the Freudian ego. His dark brother, the dread Spectre of Urthona, is
closer to a function that meets external reality and reacts to it by mediat-
ing between prevailing conceptions of it and instinctual drives. Blake
believed finally with the speculative psychologist Meister Eckhart that
"you are what you will to be," and his mature idea of Los identifies the
fallen shaper-in-fire with the active poetic will. Urizen is defied momen-
tarily by ego and id, the Spectre and Tharmas, but both yield to the Net

of Religion, and the bound energies of libido become vulnerable to the arts of the superego. Los has no part in this scene, which is deterministic and clearly indisputable as an act of psychic cartography.

Urizen proclaims that he has descended to view Orc out of pity, but the fiery youth rejects his advances. As Urizen sits brooding over Orc, the Tree of Mystery springs up around him. Though Orc continues to resist, he is forced into the cycle of Mystery, to become at length what he beholds. Urizen suddenly realizes that the terrible being in front of him is a reappearance of his brother Luvah, with whom he plotted to bring about the fall. Despising Urizen's light, Orc turns it into flaming fire, and in the fury of his hatred "begins to Organize a Serpent body." As the serpent, Orc goes up the mysterious tree and so represents a state of nature giving itself up to mystery, and the religion of Urizen.

The remainder of the revised Night VII deals with the crisis of the visionary will in Los. Beneath the tree of Mystery are Los and Enitharmon, absent from the poem since their binding of Orc in Night V. Enitharmon, in the shadow of the tree, puts on the Mystery of the possessive female will, and becomes the Shadow of Enitharmon, the "yardstick space" of the material world, as Frye calls her. The Spectre of Urthona, in his manifestation as the "clock time" that governs the ego, comes to embrace her. He has a clear idea of his own nature:

> Thou knowest that the Spectre is in Every Man insane, brutish,
> Deform'd; that I am thus a ravening devouring lust, continually
> Craving & devouring: but my Eyes are always upon thee, O lovely
> Delusion, & I cannot crave for any thing but thee. Not so
> The spectres of the Dead, for I am as the Spectre of the Living.
> For till these terrors, planted round the Gates of Eternal life,
> Are driven away & annihilated, we can never repass the Gates.

He takes her, knowing her for a "lovely delusion," hoping somehow that this act of possession will help him back into Eternity. But the product of dead time and dead space is "a wonder horrible," and the ego begets upon nature the image of a shadowy female, who in Night VIII is to be identified with Vala. The parents of this concentration of Mystery and Delusion have courted one another with a story that is the most sinister version of the fall of Albion. In taking Luvah's emanation, Vala, as his mistress and thus giving primacy to passive emotion, Man only prepared the way for his fall. The new element is that Urizen was born of that seduction, and finally conspired with Luvah to a joint revenge upon Man. That revenge attains its most ironic consequence in the dark event that has just taken place. The conspiracy of Urizen and Luvah led to the division of Urthona, which division in turn led to the fall of Tharmas. But the fall of one god is the collapse of all, and Luvah and Urizen followed Tharmas into the abyss. The falling Tharmas contained the divided components of Urthona, and we have summarized the complex story from that point on.

Everything that is material and negative culminates in Night VII with the birth of the Shadowy Female, which also climaxes the Orc cycle, as the serpent in the tree above the new Female is a final debased form of human energy and desire. But meanwhile another embrace leads to an apocalyptic prospect. Ego and will, clock and imaginative time, embrace in mutual forgiveness:

> Los embrac'd the Spectre, first as a brother,
> Then as another Self, astonish'd, humanizing & in tears

After a struggle, Enitharmon is reconciled to the work of creation that Los and the Spectre can perform together. Los summarizes the value of these labors:

> Stern desire
> I feel to fabricate embodied semblances in which the dead
> May live before us in our palaces & in our gardens of labour,
> Which, now open'd within the Center, we behold spread abroad,
> To form a world of sacrifice of brothers & sons & daughters
> To comfort Orc in his dire sufferings. Look, my fires enlume afresh,
> Before my face ascending with delight as in ancient times.

The palaces are of a City of Art, a New Jerusalem that Blake calls Golgonooza (evidently an anagram for New Golgotha, to replace the scene of the Crucifixion). The Center cannot hold, but opens this world into the firmness of Eternity, rather than into the Vacuum of Ulro, where things fall apart to no definite end. The new creation that provides bodies for the impending Resurrection is intended as a comfort for Orc, the desire now at the end of its suffering endurance.

Night VII is more of a textual tangle than my description would suggest, but the remainder of the poem is very clear. Night VIII records the events, positive and negative, that carry the world to the verge of apocalypse. A saving remnant of Eternity meets in council and takes on the shape of One Man, Jesus. Los has fixed the limit of sensual Contraction as Adam, man in his present form, so the fall can go no further. The limit of opaque matter, of Opacity, has been fixed by Los as the Selfhood, now called Satan or the Accuser. As he can be in no worse condition, Albion begins to wake upon his rock. A conflict for the specters of this world begins between Los and Enitharmon, on the side of vision, and "the Shadowy female's sweet delusive cruelty." Jesus descends and puts on the robes of Luvah, thus consenting to be the last of the crucified vegetative gods in the Orc cycle. That cycle burns itself out in fierce wars, against which Los labors incessantly to build up his City of enduring imaginative forms. Vala seeks a reborn Luvah as Adonis to her Venus, but her quest becomes only another part of the Direful Web of Religion, of a nature unable to save itself and unwilling to be saved by a renovated Human.

The long labors of Los and Enitharmon climax in a reappearance of Albion's emanation, Jerusalem, "a City, yet a Woman," who carries within herself the image of lost Innocence, the Lamb of God. In a last blood sacrifice of natural religion, the Lamb suffers the dual fate of Jesus and Prometheus, crucified on the dead tree of Mystery, and bound down to the rock of matter. The advent of Jesus is the start of the final Orc cycle, and though it ends in the irony of Jesus going up the dead tree to be worshipped as Jehovah, it also causes error to culminate in a new Babylon, identified by Blake with the Deism of his own day:

> For God put it into their heart to fulfill all his will.

> The Ashes of Mystery began to animate; they call'd it Deism
> And Natural Religion; as of old, so now anew began
> Babylon again in Infancy, Call'd Natural Religion.

Something of the force of Blake's hatred of Deism has been lost with time. If we understand Deism only as a rejection of supernatural revelation, or as an exaltation of an indifferent and withdrawn God, we will think Blake to have been merely obsessed. To Blake, Deism was everything in his world that hindered humanization and then justified such hindrance by an appeal to reason, nature, or morality. We would not call our culture a Deist one today, but the relevance of Blake's passion and protest is a constant, as the thing, if not the name, survives.

The scheme of the Zoas had failed Blake's imagination, not because it explained too little, but because it explained so much as to be a determinism. It could account for the genesis of horrors, but itself becomes a machinery of apocalypse, not a human form of renewal. Night IX is the Last Judgment, and by itself is a uniquely powerful and complete poem. Read as the last section of *The Four Zoas,* it lacks all necessity. We can understand where it is going, but we rightly wonder where it comes from. Its dialectic is purely emotional and not imaginative, though its execution is a triumph of imagination. In a terrified reaction to the death of the Lamb, Los does what we might expect a liberated Orc to do: he stretches out his hands and attacks the starry heavens of Urizen:

> his right hand, branching out in fibrous strength,
> Siez'd the Sun; His left hand like dark roots cover'd the Moon

And tore them down, cracking the heavens across from immense to immense.
Then fell the fires of Eternity, with loud & shrill
Sound of Loud Trumpet thundering along from heaven to heaven,
A mighty sound articulate: "Awake, ye dead, & come
To Judgment, from the four winds! Awake, & Come away!"
Folding like scrolls of the Enormous volume of Heaven & Earth,
With thunderous noise & dreadful shakings, rocking to & fro,
The heavens are shaken, & the Earth removèd from its place,
The foundations of the Eternal hills discover'd.

Revelation uncovers reality, but first the unreal vanishes in destruction:

> The tree of Mystery went up in folding flames.
> Blood issu'd out in mighty volumes, pouring in whirlpools fierce
> From out the flood gates of the Sky. The Gates are burst; down pour
> The torrents black upon the Earth; the blood pours down incessant.
> Kings in their palaces lie drown'd; shepherds, their flocks, their tents,
> Roll down the mountains in black torrents. Cities, Villages,
> High spires & Castles, drown'd in the black deluge; shoal on shoal
> Float the dead carcases of Men & Beasts driven to & fro on waves
> Of foaming blood beneath the black incessant Sky, till all
> Mystery's tyrants are cut off & not one left on Earth.

Albion, bowing his head over the consuming Universe, cries out against the "war within my members" but in a very different spirit from the cry of St. Paul. He summons Urizen, warning him that the "deceit so detestable" of Urizenic religion is past forgiveness. In a tremendous (and inexplicable) effort of will, Urizen reassumes the human:

> Then Go, O dark futurity! I will cast thee forth from these
> Heavens of my brain, nor will I look upon futurity more.
> I cast futurity away, & turn my back upon that void
> Which I have made: for lo, futurity is in this moment.

The effect of these lines depends upon *The Book of Urizen* as well as upon *The Four Zoas*. The fall of Urizen was from the beginning based upon his failure to see that "futurity is in this moment," in the timelessness of imaginative choice. Alive again in the moment, he rises again into the heavens in radiant youth, to be rejoined there by Ahania. Yet she seems to die, in excess of joy, but sleeps again until the final spring shall revive her. First comes a final cycle of plowing and sowing (the work of Urizen) in which the seeds of life are planted for a last time. Orc having burned up in the fires of judgment, Luvah and Vala return to where they belong, and the reign of what D. H. Lawrence called "sex in the head" is over:

                                             Return, O Love, in peace
Into your place, the place of seed, not in the brain or heart.
If Gods combine against Man, Setting their dominion above
The Human form Divine, Thrown down from their high Station
In the Eternal heavens of Human Imagination, buried beneath
In dark Oblivion with incessant pangs ages on ages
In enmity & war first weaken'd; then in stern repentance
They must renew their brightness, & their disorganiz'd functions
Again reorganize, till they resume the image of the human,
Co-operating in the bliss of Man, obeying his Will,
Servants to the infinite & Eternal of the Human form.

These lines summarize the themes of the epic. Luvah and Vala, Tharmas and Enion, are reborn into Beulah, to the accompaniment of Blake's
most rapturous hymns of innocence; nervous, intense and vivid, and
unique in literature as effective projections of paradise.

The last harvest begins with Urizen threshing out all nations, and with
"the stars thresh'd from their husks." Tharmas wields the winnowing fan,
until Luvah begins the fearful but necessary labor of the "Wine-press,"
and the vintage is trampled out. Urthona appears as the crippled heavenly smith of tradition, "limping from his fall," but able now to lean
upon Tharmas. The two most primal Zoas, restored as imagination and
intuition unhindered by negations, take on the task of loading "the wag-
gons of heaven," and take away "the wine of ages with solemn songs and
joy." The climax is in the fires that will not singe a sleeve:

        How is it we have walk'd thro' fires, & yet are not consum'd?
        How is it that all things are chang'd, even as in ancient time?

It is continuously inventive and beautiful, but Blake came to trust it
less and less. The Last Judgment, he began to sense, was not so dramatic,
and hardly so external a phenomenon. By 1804, at the latest, he had de-
cided to put *The Four Zoas* aside forever, and to transfer his vision to the
struggle within himself. A Last Judgment, as he came to understand, began within each man, and not in the outer cosmos:

        Whenever any Individual Rejects Error & Embraces Truth,
        A last Judgment passes upon that Individual.

The brief epic *Milton* (1800-08) shows an individual poet-prophet, Milton, rejecting Error in Eternity, and descending to earth again to embrace
Truth, thus passing a Last Judgment upon himself. When Milton enters
Blake, to be joined with him, a Last Judgment is passed upon Blake as
well, and an approach is made to an apocalypse shaped by the imagination out of strength as well as need, and without the necessity of natural
fear.

Poetry and Design in William Blake

by *Northrop Frye*

The ability to paint and the ability to write have often belonged to the same person; but it is rare to find them equally developed. Most people so gifted have been either writers who have made a hobby of painting, like D. H. Lawrence, or painters who have made a hobby of writing, like Wyndham Lewis. When the two are combined, one usually predominates. It is not uncommon for poets who can draw to illustrate their poems, like Edward Lear; nor is it uncommon for painters who can write to provide inscriptions to their paintings, like Rossetti. In a world as specialized as ours, concentration on one gift and a rigorous subordination of all others is practically a moral principle. Mr. Eliot uses the word "schizophrenia" even about the attempt to write both poetry and philosophy. Blake, it is clear, had a different attitude, and the reasons for his different attitude are of some interest.

Besides being a poet and painter, Blake was a professional engraver and a tireless and versatile experimenter in a great variety of media. He was an artisan or craftsman who was an expert in an important minor art as well as two major ones. His political sympathies were anarchist and revolutionary. The combination of talents and outlook reminds us of William Morris, and as the French Revolution wore on into Napoleonic imperialism, Blake came more and more to anticipate Morris in his view of the social function of art. Like Morris, he felt that revolutionary action would only go from one kind of slavery to another unless it were directed toward the goal of a free and equal working society. Like Morris, he believed that real work and creative activity were the same thing, and that as long as society supported a class of parasites, work for the great majority of people would be perverted into drudgery. And so, like Morris, he came to feel that the essential revolutionary act was in the revolt of the creative artist who is also a manufacturer, in the original sense of one

"Poetry and Design in William Blake" by Northrop Frye. From *The Journal of Aesthetics and Art Criticism*, X, 1 (September 1951), 35-42.
Reprinted by permission of the editor of *The Journal of Aesthetics and Art Criticism.*

who works with his hands instead of with automata. And as the tendency
of a class-ridden society is to produce expensive luxuries for the rich and
shoddy ugliness for the poor, the true manufacturer should present his
work as cheaply and as independently of commerce and patronage alike
as possible.

The creative producer, then, has to imitate, on a necessarily limited
scale, the mass-producing methods of commerce. Also, a revolutionary
break with both patronage and commercial exploitation is only possible
if some revolutionary new method of production is discovered. Blake
made at least three attempts to develop his own means of production.
First, and most important to students of literature, was his discovery of
the engraving process which he used for most of his poems. It is clear
that Blake expected this process to be more efficient and less laborious
than it was: he expected, in short, that it would make him independent of
publishers as well as of patrons, so that he could achieve personal independence as both poet and painter at a single blow. A character in his
early satire, *An Island in the Moon,* speaks of printing off two thousand
copies of engraved works in three volumes folio, and selling them for
£100 apiece. Next came an attempt at large-scale reproduction of prints
by means of a millboard, but the millboard proved too fragile for more
than a few copies, and the variety of results it produced was too unpre-
dictable. He was still dependent on patrons and connoisseurs to do the
work he wanted to do, and on publishers' commissions to keep himself
alive the rest of the time. Finally Blake turned to another idea on a much
bigger scale: he thought he might gain government support for the arts
if he could start a revival of fresco-painting on the walls of public build-
ings. The chief commercial disadvantage of fresco, Blake thought, was
that the original painting had to remain as long as the wall it was painted
on did, and he proposed that frescoes should be painted, not directly on
the plaster, but on canvas stretched over the plaster, so that they could
be taken off and changed. After he had worked out what he thought was
a practicable method of painting such "portable frescoes," he held the one
exhibition of his life in 1809, to introduce it to the public. The fate of
this exhibition is well known, though it is seldom realized that its primary
object was to advertise, not Blake, but a new instrument of production
that would initiate a social revolution.

It is natural that Blake, whose main source of income was illustrating
books, should at first think of his own poems as constructed on the same
principle as the illustrated book, an alternation of text and design. In
the passage from *An Island in the Moon* already quoted, he speaks of
making every other plate a high finished print. An early prophecy called

Tiriel survives in a manuscript and a group of twelve separate illustrations, about the same number of plates that would be needed for the text. Fortunately for us, however, Blake began his experiments with aphorisms and lyrics which took only a single plate apiece, and so hit very early on a form in which text and design are simultaneously present and contrapuntally related. From the start Blake avoids all devices that would tend to obscure either text or design at the expense of the other. In illuminated books we often find what we may call the tradition of hieroglyphic, in which the verbal sign itself becomes a picture, such as the ornamental capitals of medieval manuscripts or the tortuous decorations of the Book of Kells. There is nothing of this in Blake: occasionally the shoots and tendrils of the design are entangled with the longer letters of the text, but that is all. The words are left alone to do their own work. The only exception I can think of is the heading to *The Book of Los,* where Urizen is shown wrapped up in a net inside the letter O of "Los," and even this is intended as a joke.

More surprising than the independence of the words from the design is the independence of the design from the words. Blake's age, after all, was the age of the pictorial Slough of Despond known as "historical painting," in which the painter was praised for his grasp of archaeology and the history of costume and for the number of literary points he could make. Again, the *Songs of Innocence and Experience* are in the direct tradition of the emblem-books: they are by far the finest emblem-books in English literature. But the typical emblem is a literary idea to begin with: its design takes its form, not from pictorial laws, but from the demands of the verbal commentary, and it is allegorical in a way that Blake's lyrics never are. In Blake the poem does not point to the picture, as it regularly does in the emblem. On the other hand, the design is not, like most illustrations, an attempt to simplify the verbal meaning. The *Songs of Innocence* are not difficult poems to read, and one might expect them to be made even easier, at least for children, by being put into a picture-book. Perhaps even Blake expected this. But when we contemplate the great spiral sweep that encircles "The Divine Image," or the passionate red flower that explodes over "Infant Joy," or the marching horizontal lines of "Holy Thursday," we can see that, so far from simplifying the text, the design has added a new dimension of subtlety and power.

In the earliest prophecies, *The Book of Thel* and *Visions of the Daughters of Albion,* text and design approach one another rather tentatively. In *Thel* the design is always at the bottom or the top of the page, but in the *Visions* the text is occasionally broken in the middle, and an important step has been taken toward the free interpenetration of the two which belongs to Blake's mature period. In the early prophecies there is often an unequal balance between the amount Blake has to say in each of the two arts. Thus *The Marriage of Heaven and Hell* is in literature one of Blake's best known and most explicit works, but for that very reason it is less successful pictorially. The text predominates too much, and what design there is follows the text closely and obviously. So much so, in fact, that some of the marginal decorations become a rather irritating form of punctuation. Thus on Plate 11 the words "whatever their enlarged & numerous senses could percieve" are followed by a little drawing of a bird; the words "thus began Priesthood" are followed by a black serpentine spiral, and the words "at length they pronounc'd that the Gods had order'd such things" are followed by tiny kneeling figures. On the other hand, *The Book of Urizen* is pictorially one of Blake's greatest works: here there is no plate without a major design on it, and there are ten plates without text. Blake here seems to be trying to forget about the poem, which with its short lines sits awkwardly on the plate in double columns. It is clear that there were pictorial as well as poetic reasons for the long seven-beat line of Blake's prophecies.

The finest of the earlier prophecies, as far as the balance between verbal and pictorial elements is concerned, are undoubtedly the "continent" poems, *America, Europe,* and *The Song of Los,* the last of these divided into two parts called "Africa" and "Asia." After 1795 Blake began to meditate a prophecy of epic proportions, and between then and 1800 he undertook two colossal projects which enabled him to work out the archetypes of his verbal and pictorial systems respectively, on an epic scale. Each of these was a dream of nine nights: one was the great unfinished poem, *The Four Zoas,* which never reached the engraving process, but was left in a manuscript full of extraordinary sketches; the other was his illustrated edition of Young's *Night Thoughts.* The fascination that Young's poem clearly had for Blake was not due to Young so much as to the fact that Young's poem was based, like Blake's own symbolism, on the Bible. Throughout Blake's illustrations we can see how he infallibly goes to the Biblical archetype which gives what point and direction there is to Young's narrative. It was from his work on Young that Blake gained a coordinated vision of the leviathan, the four "Zoas" of Ezekiel, the Great Whore with her beast, and the other essential elements of his later symbolism. The final fruits of his effort were the two great poems *Milton* and *Jerusalem,* in fifty and one hundred plates respectively, after which Blake turned his main attention away from poetry.

It is difficult to convey adequately the sense of the uniqueness of Blake's achievement in these engraved poems. In the Preface to *Jerusalem*

Blake speaks with pride of having developed a free and unfettered verse, but he hardly seems to notice that he had at the same time perfected a far more difficult and radical form of mixed art, for which there is hardly a parallel in the history of modern culture. The union of musical and poetic ideas in a Wagner opera is a remote analogy; but the poetry is not independent of the music in Wagner as it is of the painting in Blake. Blake seems to have worked on his text and his pictorial ideas simultaneously: this is clear from the manuscript of *The Four Zoas,* where the pencil sketches in the margins indicate that Blake did not think in terms of a poem to be written first and decorated afterward, but, from the beginning, in terms of a narrative sequence of plates.

Blake felt that his conception of outline was one which held all the arts together, and his engraving technique does a great deal to prove his case. The stamped designs produced by a relief etching on metal, in which the details stand out from surrounding blank space, give us something of the three-dimensional quality of sculpture. On the other hand, the tremendous energy of Blake's drawings with their swirling human figures makes them of particular interest to dancers and students of ballet, even if more sedentary observers merely find them out of proportion. About the color it is more difficult to speak. After reading what Blake has to say about the subordinating of color to outline in painting, we are not surprised to find that there is no fixed color symbolism in the designs: every copy is colored differently. At the same time, as he developed confidence and scope, he began to move toward the luminous splendors of the golden city that was the end of his vision. "A word fitly spoken," says the Book of Proverbs, "is like apples of gold in pictures of silver." Such ideas were entirely unbefitting to Blake's station in life. The text of the only surviving colored copy of *Jerusalem* is in a strong orange which looks like a poor man's substitute for the golden letters he doubtless dreamed of.

The designs play a great variety of roles in relation to the words, besides that of direct illustration. The natural symbols lend themselves admirably to pictorial metamorphosis, and the process is simplified by the fact that the symbols of experience are often direct parodies of those of innocence. Vines with grapes, ears of wheat, and a profusion of green leaves sprout from the tree of life; brambles, thorns, thistles, dead trees, and tangles of roots belong to the tree of mystery. In Plate 75 of *Jerusalem* a row of angels, with haloes around their bodies, make a line of intersecting circles, the "wheels within wheels" of Ezekiel's vision. At the bottom of the page the same rhythm is picked up and parodied by a picture of Rahab and Tirzah caught in the rolling coils of serpents.

I have spoken of the analogy between Wagner and Blake, and some of

Blake's pictorial symbols incorporate ideas in a way that reminds one of Wagner's technique of the leitmotif. Thus it is one of Blake's doctrines that we see the sky as a huge concave vault because we see it with eyes that are imprisoned in a concave vault of bone. The title page of *The Book of Urizen* depicts Urizen himself, the fallen reason of man, and it therefore endeavors to give a concentrated impression of befuddled stupidity. The picture is built up in a series of rounded arches. Urizen sits crouching in the foetus posture that Blake regularly uses for mental cowardice, and two great knees loom out of the foreground. His skull and bushy eyebrows are above; behind his head are the two tables of the law, each with a rounded top; behind them is the arch of a cave, the traditional symbol since Plato of blinded vision, and over the cave droops a dismal willow branch, an imp of the tree of mystery.

Occasionally, though rarely, the design comments ironically on the text, if an ironic touch in the text permits it. Thus the ninth plate of *America* contains the speech of the terrified reactionary angel of Albion denouncing the rebellious Orc as "Blasphemous Demon, Antichrist, hater of Dignities," and so on. The design shows a graceful spreading tree with birds of paradise sitting on its branches; underneath is a ram and some children asleep, sunk in the profound peace of the state of innocence. A much more frequent type of comment, and one which also is sometimes ironic, is a pictorial reference or quotation, generally to the Bible. *The Marriage of Heaven and Hell* concludes with a portrait of Nebuchadnezzar going on all fours. Nebuchadnezzar is not mentioned in the text, but the prophecy deals with the overthrow of senile tyranny, and Nebuchadnezzar, the tyrant of Babylon who becomes a monstrous animal, first cousin to behemoth and leviathan, is for Blake a central symbol of the kind of thing he is attacking. The great picture of Albion before the cross of Christ, which concludes the third part of *Jerusalem,* is a more familiar example. It is more common, however, to have the designs focus and sharpen the verbal symbolism. Thus the poem *Europe,* if we had only the text, would seem an almost perversely intellectualized treatment of the theme of tyranny and superstition. It is when we look at the plates depicting famine, war, and pestilence that we realize how acutely aware of human misery Blake always is.

In the longer poems there is, of course, a good deal of syncopation between design and narrative. At the bottom of Plate 8 of *Jerusalem* is a female figure harnessed to the moon: the symbol is not mentioned in the text until Plate 63. The effect of such devices is to bind the whole poem together tightly in a single unit of meaning. And here, perhaps, we come closest to the center of the aesthetic problem that Blake's achievement raises. The words of a poem form rhythms which approach those of music at one boundary of literature, and form patterns which approach those of painting at the other boundary. To the rhythmical movement of poetry we may give the general name of narrative; the pattern we may call the meaning or significance. The Renaissance maxim *ut pictura poesis* thus refers primarily to the integrity of meaning which is built up in a poem out of a pattern of interlocking images. When Spenser begins the last canto of the Legend of Temperance with the words "Now gins the goodly frame of Temperance fairly to rise," he means that, in addition to the narrative, a unified structure of meaning has been built up which can be apprehended simultaneously, like a painting, or, to follow Spenser's image, like a building. Such a passage shows the principle of *ut pictura poesis* in action.

When we think of "meaning" we usually think of something to be expressed in general propositions. But the units of poetry are images rather than ideas, and a poem's total meaning is therefore a total image, a single visualizable picture. Not many rhetorical critics pursue their image-linking to this ultimate point. They usually remain close to the texture of the poem, engaged in the detailed study of the poetic equivalents of the technique of brush and palette knife. The critic who can only express meaning in terms of propositions has to stop his interpretation of the poem at the point of fitting it into the background of a history of ideas.

But it is possible to go further, and it is only when literary critics stand back far enough to see the imagery as one pattern that they are in a position to solve the problems of structure, of genre, and of archetype. The meaning of, for instance, Spenser's *Mutabilitie Cantoes* is not the conflict of being and becoming, which is only an aspect of its content. Its meaning is the total structure of its imagery, and this structure is a spherical, luminous, ordered background with a dark mass thrusting up defiantly in the central foreground: the same structural archetype that we find at the opening of *The Book of Job*. The propositional content of Blake's *Europe* could be expressed somewhat as follows: the root of evil and suffering is the fallen nature of man; this fallen nature is a part of physical nature; hence the basis of superstition and tyranny is the deification of physical nature; this deification has polluted Western culture from the sky-gods of Greece and Rome to the gravitational universe of Newton. But its poetic meaning, its total image, is given us by Blake himself in his frontispiece to the poem, the famous picture of the Ancient of Days, the bearded god whose sharp cruel compasses etch the circumference of the human skull and of the spherical universe which is its objective shadow.

Blake's prophecies are in the tradition of the Christian epic, and the

meaning or total image of the Christian epic is the apocalypse, the vision
of reality separated into its eternal constituents of heaven and hell. At
the time that he was completing his epic prophecies, Blake was preoccupied by the pictorial vision of the Last Judgement. He has left us the
magnificent picture reproduced as Plate 7 of Darrell Figgis's book on
Blake's paintings, and an elaborate commentary for a still larger design of
which nothing else remains. After this, Blake tended to make the picture
the unit of a new kind of non-verbal narrative, and so turned from poetry
to the sequences of his Milton, Bunyan, Dante, and Job illustrations.

The only complete edition of Blake's engraved prophecies is in the
third volume of *The Works of William Blake* edited by Ellis and Yeats
and published by Bernard Quaritch in 1893. This edition was a heroic
publishing effort, and it showed the true spirit of scholarship, as it must
have lost a great deal of money. But it is increasingly difficult to obtain,
and the reproductions, which are in black and white and done from litho-
graphs, a rather greasy medium that failed to interest Blake himself, are
not very satisfactory, to put it mildly. There are passable color reproductions of the lyrics and a few of the shorter prophecies, but so far as I
know there has been no good edition, with or without color, of *America,
Europe, Milton,* or *Jerusalem.* There are even editions of the lyrics which
have been illustrated by other people. For one reason or another, many
literary students of Blake have only the vaguest notion of what sort of
pictorial basis underlies his poetry. A good many foolish ideas about
Blake have resulted from staring at the naked text. The notion that he
was an automatic writer is perhaps the most absurd of these; the notion
that his prophecies offer only the dry bones of a vision that died within
him runs it a close second. We spoke at the beginning of the specialized
nature of modern culture; and a man who possesses so much interest for
students of religion, philosophy, history, politics, poetry, and painting
will be chopped by his critics into as many pieces as Osiris. It is all the
more necessary to correct the tendency to identify blinkered vision with
directed vision by trying to expose oneself to the whole impact of Blake
at once.

The First Illuminated Books

by Anthony Blunt

During the years 1789 to 1798 Blake's creative energies as a visual artist found expression in a new medium, engraving, which he had hitherto used almost entirely for reproducing the works of other artists, and in a new field, the illustration of his own works.[1] The first year of the period, 1789, is marked by the production of the *Songs of Innocence* . . . and the *Book of Thel* . . . , in which Blake launched on the world in complete and mature form his new method of illuminated printing.

It is true that he had made two preliminary experiments in the technique in pamphlets entitled *There Is No Natural Religion* and *All Religions are One,* both probably engraved in 1788,[2] but these are little more than variants of the type of emblem-book familiar since the sixteenth century and popularized in England by the often reprinted volume of Quarles.

In the *Songs* and *Thel* Blake creates something entirely new and personal in the way of book production. There was, of course, nothing basically novel in attempting to combine text and illustration in a single finely designed page, since this had been one of the aims sought by printers since the invention of the art, though it would probably be hard to find examples in which both text and illustration were the product of a single mind. Blake's actual method of achieving his effect, however, is fundamentally original in that he fused color and line more completely

"The First Illuminated Books" by Anthony Blunt. From *The Art of William Blake* (New York: Columbia University Press, 1959), Chapter Four. Copyright © 1959 by Columbia University Press.

Reprinted by permission of the author and the publisher.

[1] During these years he produced no water colors of importance, and the magnificent series of designs made in 1795, though in a mixed medium, are fundamentally variants of a type of engraving.

[2] The exact dates of these booklets are not known. They must have been engraved before the much more competently executed *Songs* but after 1787, for Blake said that his method of relief-engraving was revealed to him by his dead brother, Robert, who appeared to him in a dream. Blake's statements of this kind may sometimes have been fanciful, but in this case it must imply that the idea came to him after his brother's death, which took place in 1787.

than ever before and produced something of the brilliance of the painted pages in a medieval manuscript. In fact, his method can be defined as an attempt to recapture the effect of a medieval page, but in a technique which admits of reproduction.

The technique that he invented for this purpose was so curious that it needs detailed description.[3] Blake first took an ordinary copper etching plate. On this he drew the outlines of his decorative design in a varnish resistant to acid. The effect of this was that, when the plate was immersed in the acid, the unprotected parts were bitten away, leaving the parts painted out in varnish in relief. This is roughly an inverted form of the ordinary process of etching, or a transference of the process of wood engraving to a copper plate. It has the advantage over etching that the plate can be printed without the high pressure of a proper etching press, but it involves great technical difficulties because normally, with deep biting, the acid tends to undercut the ridge of copper protected by the varnish, and with Blake's process, where thin lines are left in relief, they could be almost entirely destroyed by this process. If, however, nitric acid is used instead of the usual sulphuric, it tends to bite more or less vertically and the undercutting is avoided.

With the text a further difficulty occurs. If it were painted in with varnish, like the designs, it would have to be done backward. Blake's solution seems to have been to write the text in varnish on a piece of paper which had previously been covered with gum arabic. The copper plate was then heated and laid on the paper, and the writing transferred under pressure. The paper was then removed and the writing was found to be clearly imprinted in reverse in varnish on the plate, so that the text could be bitten in exactly the same way as the decoration.[4]

Once the plate was bitten, the inking remained a considerable problem. If the ink was applied with an ordinary gelatine roller, it inevitably sank into the greater part of the area which should have remained clean, so that the result of printing in this way would have been a text written in black, surrounded by a thin white line, with the rest of the field black. This effect can be avoided by inking an unengraved plate and then transferring the ink from this plate under not very high pressure to the raised surface of the engraved plate. This not only keeps the whites clean,

---

[3] The exact method was not known till S. W. Hayter, Joan Miro, and Ruthven Todd made a series of experiments which led to their being able to repeat exactly the effects produced by Blake. These experiments are recorded by Hayter in *New Ways of Gravure* (London, 1949), pp. 85ff., and by Todd in *Print Collector's Quarterly*, XXIX (1948), 25ff.

[4] In fact, the text was undoubtedly transferred first, as the pressure of transfer might otherwise have disturbed the decorative parts.

but produces that mottled effect which is so characteristic of the pages in the printed books.[5]

This printing was usually done in a single color—black, bluish green, or golden brown—though on very rare occasions Blake varied the color from one part of the plate to the other, an effect which was made possible by his peculiar process of inking. The pull was then finished off in water colors, with the result that, though in the printed outline all copies of a particular plate are more or less identical, each acquires an individual character from the coloring. Further, since Blake kept the plates of his books and often printed and colored copies many years after he had originally engraved the plates, different copies can vary to a very striking degree. In the case of the *Songs of Innocence,* for instance, the early copies are simply colored in rather light tones, a single wash sufficing for any one figure or decorative element,[6] whereas later versions are often treated in the richer and deeper colors which Blake preferred in his last years and are worked up in small touches, a technique which he never used in his early days.

The plates in the *Songs of Innocence* vary considerably in character and in quality, an argument in favor of the view that the engraving of the whole book probably took a considerable time and may well have been started before 1789, the date on the title page. In some pages the figure composition is conceived as a unit separate from the text and occupies the top or bottom of the page. These plates are probably the earliest to be engraved. They are close in general pattern to Blake's emblem-books of 1788; the figures are most conventional in style, and they include many which differ little from those to be found in the illustrations of a contemporary artist such as Stothard. Additional support for this view is provided by the fact that they include three poems which appear in Blake's satire *An Island in the Moon,* which was probably written about 1787.[7] Even in these more conventional plates, however, there are details which are truly Blakean. The figures in the second plate of "The Ecchoing Green," for instance, are depicted in contemporary dress, but

[5] Only a fragment of one of Blake's original plates survives (in the Lessing Rosenwald Collection), but it shows that he took great pains to burnish the part of the plate bitten away by the acid, which is in fact as smooth and as even as a clean etching plate. This process would reduce the chance of ink catching on a ridge in the bitten areas.

[6] In the Rosenwald copy of "The Blossom" Blake used a single tone of green, almost exactly like that to be found in certain early French manuscripts (e.g., Lectionary of St. Martial of the tenth century in the Bibliothèque Nationale, MS Lat. 5901).

[7] "The Little Boy Lost," "Nurse's Song," and "Holy Thursday." A fourth, "Laughing Song," illustrated in the same style, is first found written on the flyleaf of the *Poetical Sketches* and is, therefore, also probably early.

they have an ethereal quality and a long swinging movement which is
unlike any of Blake's contemporaries; in the "Laughing Song" the idiom
is more neoclassical, but the movement is equally personal; and the
frieze-like train of children in "Holy Thursday" has a naïve rigidity
which no one else at Blake's time would have risked. And in all these
plates we see the delicate, curvilinear forms of flowers, leaves, or vine
tendrils which were to be so typical of Blake's best illumination.

In a second group of plates the fusion of text and decoration is more
complete. "The Shepherd" reminds one in many ways of Stothard,
particularly of his engravings to Marmontel, but the fantastic forms of
the trees and the wanton repetition in the silhouettes of the sheep are
typical of Blake; and here the scene painted in the lower half of the page
strays up to the top and begins to enclose the text of the poem. In certain
other cases the unity is achieved in a different manner. In the plate of the
Introduction, "Piping down the valleys wild," the text is enclosed in a
border composed of branches interwoven to form a series of oval panels,
a device clearly taken from certain types of medieval manuscripts in
which a series of scenes are enclosed in panels knit together by an interlacing design.[8]

The perfect fusion of text and decoration is to be seen in three plates
which must be the last of the book in time of engraving: "The Blossom,"
"Infant Joy," and "The Divine Image." Here the flame-like forms of the
plants and flowers envelop the text completely and carry on the spirit
of the poem so perfectly that it is impossible to separate the forms of the
decoration from the ideas of the lyric. Here at least Blake has created a
type of illuminated page for which no parallel can be found except in the
finest manuscripts of the later Middle Ages.

Equally accomplished in its complete unity, though in a somewhat
different idiom, is the title page of the *Songs* . . . which shows a
mother teaching two children to read, seated under a tree, the branches
of which are entwined round the words of the title. What is novel here
is the form of script used for the word *Songs,* the letters of which turn
into leaf-forms or support tiny figures, in a manner which was to be
widely employed in the nineteenth century but which was certainly rare,
and probably unique, at the time of the publication of the *Songs.*[9]

The *Book of Thel* represents the same state in the evolution of Blake's
art as an illustrator. The figure of Thel herself is still a Stothard type,

---

[8] The closest parallel is to be found in a Tree of Jesse in a thirteenth century
English manuscript in Sir John Soane's Museum.
[9] It was frequently used by Romantic illustrators, such as Grandville and Doré, and
later by Kate Greenaway and the draughtsmen of *Punch.*

and, except in one case, text and illustrations are fairly sharply separated from each other. The one exception is the title page, on which the words of the title, burgeoning into leaves and flowers like those of the *Songs*, are surrounded by a tree, almost Chinese in its delicacy, while the lower part of the page is filled with flowers like those of "Infant Joy," out of which spring tiny, fairy-like figures.

The ethereal lightness and flowing beauty of the forms used in the illuminations to *Thel* and the *Songs of Innocence* are the direct reflection of the tone of the poems and of Blake's state of mind at this stage in his career. Throughout his life his philosophy was based on a variant of the belief, common among mystics, that before his birth man exists in a perfect and infinite existence, and that his arrival into this world is a kind of fall from the infinite to the finite. In youth, however, memories of his previous state remain with man, till they are gradually crushed by education and the imposition of rules and conventions. At the time of the *Songs of Innocence* Blake was still conscious of his direct contact with the infinite, and living the imaginative life in its full and almost undisturbed peace. His material life was not without its difficulties, and he was not unaware of the political and social problems which existed in the world;[10] but he had not yet been embittered by them, and his faith in a solution to them was still unimpaired. In *Thel* the problem of the fall from the infinite to the finite is the principal theme, and the hesitancy of the soul to enter into the material world is described with a certain melancholy; but the emphasis is still on the possibilities of contact with the infinite rather than on the limitations of the finite, and the tone is one of relative optimism. It is, therefore, natural that in this happy early stage of his career Blake should use for the decoration of his poems the undulating forms of flames or plants and colors which, though simple, are fresh and gay.

This happy phase did not last, and with the beginning of the French Revolution Blake's thought takes on a more serious tone. In its initial stages, however, the Revolution was for Blake a symbol of liberation from the old order. It stood for the destruction of tyranny and superstition, and Blake was among those who devoutly prayed that a similar movement of freedom might visit England.

The degree to which he was personally acquainted with the leading radicals of his day, such as Godwin, Holcroft, and Paine, has been exaggerated,[11] but there is no question that he sympathised with their ideas,

---

[10] David Erdman has shown in his *Blake: Prophet against Empire* that there is more political awareness in Blake's early works than is generally supposed.

[11] It has been more exactly defined by Mr. Erdman (*ibid.*, pp. 139-47).

since these are reflected in the two works which follow the *Songs of In-nocence* and *Thel: The French Revolution* and *The Marriage of Heaven and Hell*. The first of these does not directly concern us here, since it was the one work which Blake planned to print and publish in the ordinary way, through the well-known radical bookseller Joseph Johnson, and not by his method of illuminated engraving;[12] but it is of importance in setting forth the story of the first years of the French Revolution in a manner which shows clearly that Blake was at this date a convinced Jacobin. *The Marriage of Heaven and Hell* was engraved by Blake's nor-mal process, and though it is not one of the most successful examples of his illumination, it contains his most moving and fervent declaration of revolutionary faith. Nowhere did he state with such poetic enthusiasm his faith in energy as a means of bursting through the bonds of conven-tion, false morality, and reason—already for him a negative faculty and the antithesis of imagination—and so enabling man to reestablish contact with the world of eternity and infinity which is his natural lot, but from which he is cut off by the limitations of the material universe. A few of the Proverbs of Hell in the *Marriage* are enough to give the flavor of the whole work:

The road of excess leads to the palace of wisdom.
He who desires but acts not breeds pestilence.
Prisons are built with stones of Law, Brothels with bricks of Religion.
The cistern contains: the fountain overflows.
The tygers of wrath are wiser than the horses of instruction.
As the caterpillar chooses the fairest leaves to lay her eggs on, so the priest lays
    his curse on the fairest joys.
Exuberance is Beauty.
Enough! or Too much.

The spirit of these violent sayings comes out in the contrast between the two illustrations at the beginning and end of the last section of the book. The first shows the figure of a naked youth from which emanate rays of light, the symbol of man in his free and imaginative state; the second shows a crude and almost grotesque figure of Nebuchadnezzar in his madness, the image of man in his lowest state of degradation, when he has allowed his imagination to be killed by materialism and rationalism. Blake was later to take up this figure again and to make of it one of his most striking designs.

That revolutionary energy which is the central theme of the *Marriage* infuses life into the title page of the book. The forms are still curvi-

---

[12] In fact, it never appeared and is known only from a proof copy.

linear, as in the decoration of the *Songs of Innocence* and *Thel,* but they now sweep across the page with a violence which is in marked contrast to the gaiety and lightness of the earlier decoration. The tone is more somber than before, but the title page still expresses a conviction that energy will win the day and that man will become free.[13]

The themes treated in *The Marriage of Heaven and Hell* are taken up and expanded in three works produced in 1793. The *Visions of the Daughters of Albion* is a protest against the frustrations caused by conventional rules of sexual morality and an attack on the institution of marriage itself on the grounds that sexual relations should be based on emotion and impulse and not bound by rules. *The Gates of Paradise* embodies the same protest in the form of emblems, and adds certain doctrines which were later to become of great importance in Blake's thought: the idea that mutual forgiveness of sins is the only source of true happiness; and the contrast between Christ's doctrine of love in the New Testament and the restrictive law of Moses in the Old. *America* deals with the first stage of the revolutionary movement in which Blake had believed so passionately, but was written at the moment when he was beginning to be disillusioned with its second phase. It differs, however, from *The French Revolution* in that it is no longer a straight narrative of events but is written partly in terms of the allegorical figures which Blake was beginning to evolve, so that Washington and Tom Paine appear in alternation with Urthona and Orc.

The little emblem-cuts of *The Gates of Paradise* are of no great moment, but the *Visions* and *America* mark the transition between the energy of the *Marriage* and the gloom of the later Lambeth books. The title page and the first plate of the *Visions* have the vitality of the *Marriage,* and even something of the lightness of *Thel,* but the tone soon changes to the grimness of [certain of] the crouching figures . . . , or the horror of the page representing Oothoon and Bromion chained back to back while Theotormon crouches in despair behind them, a group which symbolizes primarily the frustrating effects of the marriage tie. In *America*

---

[13] There is some doubt about the exact date of the *Marriage.* In one copy page 3 is dated 1790, and in others internal evidence points to this date; but some authorities have been inclined to take it as the beginning rather than the end of the composition (see Keynes, *Blake's Illuminated Books,* p. 35) and to maintain that it was mainly written at a date nearer 1793. For myself I find this hard to believe. By that time Blake's faith in the French Revolution was greatly shaken, and in the three books printed in that year his interests seem to be quite different. At most I should be prepared to believe that the *Marriage* might have been completed in 1791, about the same time as *The French Revolution,* which is in a sense its counterpart, setting forth the actual events of a revolution which, Blake still hoped, would turn into reality the principles outlined in the *Marriage.*

the tone is gloomier. One plate shows at the top an eagle about to devour the corpse of a woman and at the bottom the body of a drowned man being eaten by fishes. This atmosphere is relieved only by the occasional appearance of the naked youth who figures in *The Marriage of Heaven and Hell,* and by the delicate page on which two children lie asleep beside a huge woolly ram under one of those weeping Chinese trees which Blake had already used in the title page of *Thel.*

The most beautiful visual expression of this stage in Blake's development is to be found in the *Songs of Experience,* finished in 1794 but probably written and even engraved during the two or three previous years. In many cases the themes provide exact parallels with those of the *Songs of Innocence,* but in a different and more somber mood—"The Tyger" instead of "The Lamb," "The Sick Rose" instead of "The Blossom," "Infant Sorrow" instead of "Infant Joy"—and the same is true of the illustrations. The title page of *Experience* sums up the later mood as completely as that of *Innocence* typifies the earlier. Two dead bodies, an aged man and a woman, laid out on a bier, form the central motive, while two younger mourning figures move round them. The gay, curved forms of *Innocence* are replaced by severe horizontals in the dead figures, which are laid out like the effigies on a Gothic tomb, and the lower half of the page is completed by the simple rectilinear pattern of the architectural background. Even the script chosen for the words of the title reflects the change of tone: unadorned roman capitals, as opposed to the fantastic vegetable-curls of the earlier letters. The contrast between the decoration of "The Sick Rose" and "Infant Joy" is equally telling. Plant forms are still used, but now they are the angular and almost clumsy lines of a rose branch armed with grotesquely large thorns, arranged like the teeth of a saw. The rotting rose itself is as different as can be imagined from the life-giving flower in "Infant Joy." Even when Blake repeats a device used in the earlier book it takes on a quite different character. "The School Boy," for instance, has in its right margin the interlacing design which Blake had used for the Introduction to *Innocence,* but, instead of flowing smoothly up the page, the branches are now jagged and interrupted, producing an effect as abrupt and staccato as the other was smooth and legato. If the greatest achievements of the earlier volume are to be found in the illustrations to the happiest poems, in the later the most moving are either those to savagely bitter poems like "The Poison Tree" or the solemn night of the Introduction. The "Contrary States of the Human Soul" are given as clear and complete expression in the decorative treatment of the pages as they are in the text of the poems.

The years 1793 and 1794 mark a crisis for Blake and the group of radicals with whom he was associated. The September Massacres in 1792, and the execution of the King and Queen in 1793, followed by the Terror, made those whose support for the Revolution was combined with humanitarianism gradually change their views. Further, the reaction of Pitt's government to the new development in France led to a violent repression of all radicalism in England and the disruption of the group. Some, like Paine, fled to France; others were brought to trial, and though Holcroft escaped conviction, many of his friends were less fortunate and were condemned to deportation.

The intellectual members of the group found various solutions to the disillusionment which they felt at the failure of the hopes they had placed in the Revolution and the breaking up of their movement. Mary Wollstonecraft devoted herself to propaganda against social evils and the battle for the rights of women, and Godwin spent the rest of his life in pure speculation and the creation of anarchist Utopias.

Blake's solution was in many ways similar to Godwin's. He forswore political activity and turned inward toward "mental strife," seeking a philosophical and religious solution to the problems of the universe rather than aiming at the immediate improvement of man's state on earth. He gave his most moving expression to this recantation of his belief in revolutionary activity in "The Grey Monk," written some years later:

> But vain the Sword & vain the Bow,
> They never can work War's overthrow.
> The Hermit's Prayer & the Widow's tear
> Alone can free the world from fear.
>
> For a Tear is an Intellectual Thing.
> And a Sigh is the Sword of an Angel King,
> And the bitter groan of the Martyr's woe
> Is an Arrow from the Almightie's Bow.

But this solution was not to be found all in a moment, and for the next five or six years Blake was to be plunged into a despair from which he only slowly emerged after 1800, as he gradually discovered a final, mystical solution to his problems.

The poems which he produced during these years, called the Lambeth Books from his new place of residence, are the darkest and gloomiest in the whole range of his work, both in their text and their illustration. Blake's bitter awareness of the evil of the world led him to a dualist belief which insisted on the existence of an original force of evil, which he called Urizen (from the Greek ὁρίζειν, "to fix a limit") and identified with the Jehovah of the Old Testament in opposition to the Jesus of the New Testament, whom he identified with the force of good. This basic opposition he extended by adding to Urizen-Jehovah the attributes of reason, restraint, and law, as opposed to imagination, freedom, and love for one's neighbor, which he associated with Christ. The theme of the Lambeth Books is the struggle between reason and imagination, and in this phase of his career Blake tends to take a pessimistic view of the outcome of the struggle and prefers to paint the horrors of man's state when in the control of rationalism and materialism rather than dwell on the possibilities of recovering his freedom through the proper exercise of the imagination.

In form the Lambeth Books differ from Blake's earlier illuminated works in that the illustrations play a great part. On the pages which contain the text of the poems the proportion of decoration is on the whole greater than previously, and each book contains a number of plates which have no text at all. In fact one could say that, whereas the earlier books consist of text in the expression of Blake's ideas, and some of the full-page plates embody ideas which are not completely worked out in the poems themselves, . . . although the Lambeth Books contain some of Blake's least successful plates, the finest of them, such as "The Ancient of Days" from *Europe* . . . , or certain pages from *Urizen,* represent his art at its most splendid, and are far nobler expressions of his ideas than the turgid and repetitive poems.

The earliest of these works is probably *Europe*. It contains two plates, "Plague" and "Famine," which are unique among the illustrations to Blake's Prophetic Books in that the artist has chosen to depict his subject in contemporary dress and setting, almost as if he had been illustrating Mary Wollstonecraft's stories. But, generally speaking, the plates to the Lambeth Books are somber and allusive like the poems themselves. The serpent of materialism, which had appeared in smaller form in *The Marriage of Heaven and Hell,* sprawls menacingly across the title page to *Europe.* In one plate of *Urizen* we see the evil deity sunk in the waters of materialism, while on another Los, his antagonist and the embodiment of the Poetic Genius, howls amid the flames in which Urizen has imprisoned him. A third plate shows the embryo created by Urizen as a skeleton curled up as if in the womb, and the impression of horror is carried on through every page of the book. Some are really terrifying; some are grotesque; and some are on the very brink of the comic through their exaggeration; but all carry a certain conviction, and the best are deeply moving.

The other three Lambeth Books, *The Song of Los, The Book of Los,* and *The Book of Ahania,* all engraved in 1795, add little to what Blake had achieved in the illuminations to *Europe* and *Urizen,* and the most splendid plate of these years is the frontispiece to *Europe,* "The Ancient of Days," which we have already considered from a different point of view. It remains one of Blake's most impressive statements of what was for him at this time the central theme: the view of the creation as an evil act, and of the creator, Jehovah-Urizen, as the principle of evil, compelling man to live the bounded and restrained life of reason as opposed to the free life of the imagination. The compasses, which the colossal figure holds down onto the black emptiness below him, symbolize for Blake not the imposition of order on chaos, but the reduction of the infinite to the finite.

The ideas expressed in the frontispiece to *Europe* were expanded by Blake in a series of designs executed in 1795, which were bought ten years later by Blake's friend and patron, Thomas Butts, and of which the most important are now in the Tate Gallery. These designs, which are on a larger scale than Blake's works of the early 1790s, were executed in a special medium invented by the artist which bears some relation to his method of book illumination but is basically a variant of monotype. They were produced as follows. Blake would draw the outline in black on a piece of millboard, probably adding a certain amount of internal modeling and other details but all in one color. This he would print off under quite low pressure on a piece of paper. Then he would color the whole of his millboard to complete the design and again print this on top of the black outline already made. The result produced a mottled effect like that of some of the printed books, but far richer. The resulting design was touched up in water color, though this plays a far smaller part than it does in the printed books. It is usually stated on the authority of Tatham that these prints were made in oil colors, but, given Blake's well-known hatred of oil paint, this is intrinsically improbable, and experiment has shown that the effects can be produced with egg tempera.

There are good reasons for supposing that these color prints were planned by Blake as a single series. They were all produced in a very short period of time, and they are more or less identical in format and technique. Moreover, all the subjects can be shown to bear on themes connected with Blake's interpretation of the early history of the world as it is set forth in the Lambeth Books. The first in the series is the print of "God Creating Adam." [14] This is Blake's version of the creation of man as an evil act, and God is Jehovah-Urizen, like the figure on the title page of *Europe.* His "creation" of man consists in reducing him from the

---

[14] This is usually called the "Elohim Creating Adam," but on the only occasion when Blake refers to the print he gives it the simpler title "God Creating Adam."

life of infinity to the restricted and finite life of this world, which is symbolized by the serpent wound round the leg of Adam, the regular symbol
in Blake for materialism.

The next three prints deal with the Fall and its immediate consequences. The subject of "Satan Exulting over Eve," though very rare, is
self-explanatory, and the lost print of "God Judging Adam," mentioned
by Blake in a letter,[15] dealt with a moment preliminary to the expulsion
from Eden, a theme more traditional in European painting.

Next comes another very rare biblical subject, "Lamech and his Two
Wives." As told in the fourth chapter of Genesis the story is almost unintelligible, but the one point that emerges clearly, the fact that Lamech
killed a man, is evidently Blake's central theme and, like "The Death of
Abel," which Blake later treated in tempera and water color, symbolizes
death as one of the consequences of the Fall.

Another result of the Fall, sickness and suffering, is the theme of "The
Lazar House," though in this case Blake has turned to Milton rather than
to the Bible itself. In the eleventh book of *Paradise Lost* Michael shows
to Adam the consequences of his action, first death in the story of Cain
and Abel, then sickness and suffering in the celebrated description of the
Lazar House.

Another print not taken directly from the Bible seems to develop a
parallel theme. This is the composition of "Hecate." This print is usually
said to illustrate either *Macbeth* (Act III, scene 5, or Act IV, scene 1) or
Puck's last speech in *A Midsummer Night's Dream*, but in fact it bears
very little resemblance to either description, except for the fact that in
Puck's speech she is referred to as "triple Hecate" and is so depicted by
Blake. In the print she is surrounded by evil-looking creatures—a donkey,
eating thistle leaves with serrated edges like bat's wings (always a symbol
of evil with Blake), an owl, and an animal of which only the head is visible but which looks like some enormous lizard—while over her head hovers a still more alarming creature with a devilish face and bat's wings.
Hecate herself has her hand on an open book. She seems in fact to be depicted as the goddess of necromancy, a function which she regularly per-
formed in antiquity.[16] In this case the print would represent superstition,

---

[15] *Letters of William Blake,* ed. Keynes, p. 150.

[16] Blake's views on magic and miracles are set forth in one of his marginal notes to
Bishop Watson's *Apology,* written in 1798, three years after the "Hecate" was made,
and it is possible that in the "Hecate" he is attacking what he considered the false
conception of a miracle, asserted by Watson and "the priests" as "an arbitrary act of
the agent upon an unbelieving patient," an idea which he contrasted with Christ's
conception of a miracle as something based on faith.

another aspect of the domination of Urizen, in this case through the priesthood of established religion.

If this interpretation is correct, the "Newton" and the "Nebuchadnezzar" would form a sort of trilogy with "Hecate." Newton is a character regularly quoted by Blake, together with Locke, as the exponent of Urizen's religion of reason on earth. The figure of Newton is shown seated at the bottom of the sea and holding the compasses, both details which relate the figure to Urizen, one to his appearance on the frontispiece to *Europe,* the other to the plate in *Urizen* which shows him submerged in the waters of materialism. "Nebuchadnezzar" symbolizes the further stage of man's degradation. "Newton" shows him abandoning imagination in favor of reason only; in "Nebuchadnezzar" reason has vanished and man has submitted himself wholly to the dictates of the senses.[17]

The print called "Pity" is more allusive. It illustrates very precisely the lines in *Macbeth*:

> And pity, like a naked new-born babe,
> Striding the blast, or heaven's cherubin, hors'd
> Upon the sightless Couriers of the air,
> Shall blow the horrid deed in every eye,
> That tears shall drown the wind.

It may be connected with Enitharmon, one of the figures in Blake's private mythology, who is identified with pity and the female principle. Enitharmon came into existence at one of the stages in the division of the united fourfold man, which mark the Fall of man from his infinite existence. She was driven off by Los and became his emanation. According to Blake she dominated one early phase of history of mankind and so would fit into the series telling this story.

In "Ruth" Blake comes back to the Bible but is probably still dealing with the same theme. The story of Ruth refusing to leave her mother-in-law Naomi, while Orpah returns to Moab, is an obvious illustration for the theme of pity, and since the story is entirely enacted by women, it would fit well with Blake's identification of pity with the female principle.

The relation of the "Elijah" to the whole group is slightly different. For Blake the prophets of the Old Testament were, like the poets of later

[17] The "Nebuchadnezzar" is evidently intended as an exact pendant to the "Newton," and the parallel probably extends to the settings. The background of the "Nebuchadnezzar" is not easy to decipher, but in *The Marriage of Heaven and Hell* he is shown against tree trunks, which would appropriately signify the vegetative universe, and the woven forms behind the king in the big print may well be leaves, which would have the same symbolism.

times, the embodiment of the imagination, and the story of Elijah's going up to heaven in the chariot of fire is an obvious symbol for the chariot of inspiration, and letting his mantle fall on Elisha is clearly intended to bring out the continuity of the poetic tradition. The tone of the composition, however, is one of gloom, and it must be taken to indicate the unhappy position of the poet in a world dominated by Jehovah-Urizen and a society governed by the restrictive rules of his servant Moses. There may be a hope implicit in this design, but it is overshadowed by the tragedy of the poet's existence, which is a clear reflection of Blake's own position at this time.

The last print is the most obscure. In a letter already quoted Blake simply calls it "Good and Evil Angels." It has been called "Los," "Enitharmon and Orc" (Orc being the son of Los and Enitharmon and the spirit of revolution) and this may possibly be correct, though if so, it is puzzling that Blake should have referred to it only by a simplified title when writing to Butts. But in any case it certainly represents one aspect of the tragedy of man under the old dispensation. The male figure on the left, flying outward against a background of flames, but chained by one foot and blind, must symbolize in some form energy or imagination restrained by reason. The design is a development of a crude illustration in *The Marriage of Heaven and Hell,* but there also its meaning is, unfortunately, obscure.

This series of prints must be regarded as the most magnificent expression of the ideas expounded by Blake in the Lambeth Books. They are far more impressive than any of the illustrations to the books themselves, for they have a grandeur and a simplicity which Blake hardly ever attained on the smaller scale of his copper plates—the one exception is the frontispiece to *Europe*—and a clarity of design which is rare in his work before this time. The effectiveness of the prints is partly due to the very simple scaffolding of the compositions: the repeated horizontals of "Pity" and "Satan Exulting over Eve," the semi-circle of the sun behind the "God Creating Adam," the quadrant of the chariot of fire in "Elijah," or the symmetry of the figure of Death in "The Lazar House." The monotony and emptiness which might result from the use of such simple methods are avoided by means of the great richness of texture produced by Blake's special technique and the elaboration of details within the main scaffolding. The result is a combination of intensity and control rare in Blake's work, and it could be argued that from a purely artistic point of view these are his most successful compositions.

At about the same time Blake made a series of small prints of great beauty, now in the British Museum, which were produced by a combination of the methods used in the printed books and the monotype process used for the big prints. These small prints are pulled from the metal plates of pages from the Lambeth Books, but from the illustrations only, without any text. They also differ from the corresponding plates in the books in that the full coloring was applied to the plate, as was the case in the big prints, so that the rich and mottled texture obtained by this method is used over the whole surface and not only for the outline, as is normally the case with the books themselves. The result is an effect of gem-like beauty never to be found in the books, and the pages of *Thel*, for instance, take on a quite new intensity of color. The colored print of "Glad Day" was made by the same process, but its gaiety and its more optimistic theme suggest that it was made later, probably after 1800, when Blake was beginning to emerge from the despondency of the Lambeth period.

During the 1790s Blake's procedure as a painter changed fundamentally. In the first half of the decade his finest work consisted of the illustrations to the pages of his books. As has already been said, these take on an increasing importance till in the later Lambeth Books they frequently occupy the whole page to the exclusion of the text. In the color print series of 1795 he goes a step further and produces for the first time a series of compositions which are not related to any text, but which form the continuous exposition of a philosophical theme. From this time onward Blake was to make increasingly frequent use of this method, though the color prints of 1795 are in one respect unique. The other series of drawings, paintings, water colors, or engravings always illustrate a particular work—the Bible or one of the poets whom Blake admired; but in the 1795 set he seems to have chosen themes from various . . . sources—the Bible, Milton, Shakespeare, and English history—all of which were adaptable to the particular philosophical theme that interested him at that moment.

William Blake Rejects the Enlightenment

by Jean H. Hagstrum

William Blake, the first English Romantic, was born in 1757, the year in which Emanuel Swedenborg said the last judgment took place. Although Blake himself was never able to regard that fact as merely coincidental, his interpreter is more interested in observing that in the year of his birth neoclassic culture was still flourishing. Six months after the day on which Blake was born, Johnson began publishing the *Idler,* that attractive monument to witty common sense, and two years later he wrote *Rasselas,* that great embodiment of moral pessimism and philosophical wisdom.

Blake must never be regarded as a cultural orphan, living out his days in solitary anger, hostile to the society in which he was bred. He was deeply involved even in what he rejected. The man who mounted the fiercest, longest, and most effective attack [ever made] on the neoclassical and enlightened establishment . . . always revealed the marks of his origin in the age of Johnson. In an outburst of youthful impudence, he mockingly portrayed the Great Cham as winking and blinking like a bat in daylight,[1] but his Chaucer criticism shows the clear impress of Dr. Johnson's view of general nature. Though he regarded Reynolds as a hireling painter, he ringingly agreed with the President's attack on the fashionable picturesque—"So Says Sir Joshua, and So say I!" [2]—and finds the most unforgivable fact about the academician that he admired Blake's heroes for the wrong reasons. Blake's artistic pantheon is in fact more like than unlike official neoclassical taste—a taste represented, say, by the French Academy. Both placed Raphael and the high Renaissance at or near the top. Both preferred line to color, Rome and Florence to Venice, Italy to the Low Countries. Blake, a kind of salty and angry Dufresnoy, consid-

"William Blake Rejects the Enlightenment" by Jean H. Hagstrum. From *Studies on Voltaire and the Eighteenth Century.*
Reprinted by permission of the author and Institut et Musée Voltaire.

[1] *An Island in the Moon* (circa 1784-1785) in *The Complete Writings of William Blake,* ed. Geoffrey Keynes (London 1957), p. 54 (hereafter referred to as *CW*).
[2] Letter to Butts, November 22, 1802, *CW,* p. 814.

ered Rembrandt a maker of blots and blurs, called Jan Steen a boor, and retched at "the Venetian and Flemish ooze." [3]

Such similarities between Blake and the culture he attacked are not merely fortuitous. They are signs that what he rejected in one of the mightiest efforts of his imagination had in fact invaded the deepest recesses of his being.

I. Blake's Attack on Neoclassical Psychology and Aesthetics (to 1788)

Blake laid the foundations of his attack on the Enlightenment as a very young man—long before his first works of composite art appeared in 1788. The earliest and most obvious impulse to that attack arose from Blake's commitment to the literary school of the Wartons, the so-called pre-romantic writers of the English eighteenth century. Blake's juvenilia display a pre-romantic love of Gothic horror, of poetic melancholy, of ballad forms, and of Elizabethan song. The author of *Poetical Sketches* had obviously been impressed by the medievalism of Chatterton, the rhythms of Macpherson, and the blank-verse sonorities of Young. From Thomson Blake had learned the art of natural personification and from Collins the art of allegorical personification; and Gray's *Bard* must early have become one of the most potent influences on the younger poet's genius—a work he later pointed to as an example of the intellectual vision to which the sister art of painting should aspire.[4]

To the English pre-romantics Blake remained loyal until his death. As an old man he acknowledged a closer affinity to Macpherson and Chatterton than to Wordsworth and Byron, past whose prime his long life extended.[5] The influence of Thomson, Young, and their fellows was early united with the eccentric but powerful impact of Fuseli, fresh from Zurich and from Breitinger and Bodmer, whose own attacks on the Enlightenment were inspired by the very poets that first inspired Blake. Collins and Gray, Thomson and Young put Blake in touch with the giants of English literature—Shakespeare and Spenser, whom he early imitated and later illustrated, and above all Milton, whose literary example was the most potent Blake was ever to encounter.

Important though it was, the pre-romantic influence alone can explain neither the intensity nor the content of Blake's rejection of neoclassical

---

[3] Annotations to Reynolds (circa 1808), *CW*, p. 472; MS Notebook 1808-1811, *CW*, p. 547.
[4] *A Descriptive Catalogue* (1809), item no. IV, *CW*, p. 576.
[5] Annotations to Wordsworth (1820), *CW*, p. 783.

culture. Like Fuseli Blake must have found pre-romanticism too weak and conventional, too artificial and cloying for sustained nourishment. It was primarily literary and aesthetic, and Blake's vision was psychological, ethical, religious. The pre-romantics alone can never explain why Blake indignantly turned his back on romantic Hellenism and found romantic naturalism a Satanic blight that weakened and ultimately obliterated the life of the imagination.

Blake's earliest attack on the neoclassical establishment, made in the late seventies or early eighties, transcends the pre-romantic form that encloses it. A shadowy Collinsian allegory that does not quite succeed in forming a train of Spenserian personifications, the piece beginning "Then she bore pale desire" strikes a body blow at neoclassical ethics and psychology (*CW*, p. 42). The speaker, a devotee of Gray's kind of Melancholy, attacks Honour (the social respectability, one supposes, of Pope's Thalestris), Hate and Slander (the satires and journalistic polemics of both Swift and Grub Street), and Policy (the Baconian ethic that dominated the literary periodical, the coffee house, and the school). But the most memorable action—almost imperceptible in the riot of personification—is the dethronement by his own children of Father Reason, whose long beard and tyrannous habits must surely adumbrate Urizen. Young Blake has thus anticipated himself and unmistakably foreshadowed one of the central acts of his revolutionary and prophetic myth. In *The Gates of Paradise* of 1793, on a plate that bears as its motto the lament of David over Absalom, "My Son! My Son!" a young man stands poised to plunge a feathered spear in his father's breast. In Blake's mythology the meaning is that the red Orc of change is about to attack Urizen—revolutionary youth is about to destroy Aged Ignorance. On the sixteenth plate of *Milton* the heroic poet in a climactic action strides up to a venerable and enfeebled tyrant leaning on the tablets of legalistic religion and pulls him down from his stony seat as young men and women dance and sing in the scene above.

More precisely stated, though no more central to Blake's thought, is the psychological attack on empirical rationalism that Blake made unrelentingly in the aphorisms that constitute his first works of engraved art (1788).[6] The twenty-five or so tiny engravings—each containing a proverb and a spare but appropriate linear design—all either attack sensationist psychology or praise the liberating imagination and thus establish the most fundamental and irreconcilable polarities of Blake's thought—between the "Poetic or Prophetic character" and the "Philosophical & Experimental." Let there be no mistake about the seriousness and profundity

---

[6] "There is No Natural Religion" and "All Religions are One," *CW*, pp. 97-98.

of young Blake's attack. Hume had written, "But though our thought seems to possess this unbounded liberty, we shall find . . . that it is really confined within very narrow limits, and that all this creative power of the mind amounts to no more than the faculty of compounding, transposing, augmenting, or diminishing the materials afforded us by the senses and experience." [7] Blake wrote, "Man's perceptions are not bounded by organs of perception; he perceives more than sense (tho' ever so acute) can discover." Locke had said, "All those sublime thoughts which . . . reach as high as heaven itself take their rise and footing here: in all that great extent wherein the mind wanders, . . . it stirs not one jot beyond those ideas which sense or reflection have offered for its contemplation." [8] Blake said, "The desires & perceptions of many untaught by anything but organs of sense, must be limited to objects of sense. If it were not for the Poetic or Prophetic character the Philosophic & Experimental would soon be at the ratio of all things & stand still, unable to do other than repeat the same dull round over again."

Before he was thirty Blake had already come to recognize as his chief enemy that school of thought that engaged the deepest loyalties of both the English and the continental eighteenth century—what David Mallet called "the Baconian succession" [9] and Voltaire called "the new philosophy." Later Blake will form an unholy trinity of Bacon, Newton, and Locke, but now his chief villain seems to be Locke, whom he mentions only once but who, more than any one else, had created the hell of "meer nature," the inferno of being "shut up in corporeal desires." [10] Locke's epistemological chain, that links sense to nature, mind to sense, idea to mind, Blake was determined to break. As he himself said, science (the knowledge of the outside world) and intellect (the imagination that constitutes the only true man) are absolutely discrete and separate. Knowledge cannot teach us how to think any more than thought can teach us how or what to love. [11]

In his "mental fight" Blake engages the generals and only tilts with the lieutenants. He does now and then feint at Dryden, Pope, Chesterfield,

---

[7] "Of the origin of ideas," *Enquiry Concerning Human Understanding*, sect. II.

[8] *Ibid.*, II, i, 24.

[9] "A New life of the author", *Works of Bacon* (London 1741), I, li. Mallet calls Bacon "the father of the only valuable philosophy, that of fact and observation."

[10] Annotations to Swedenborg (circa 1788), *CW*, p. 93; Annotations to Lavater (circa 1788), *CW*, p. 74. "Corporeal" means, not sexual, which Blake regarded as energetic and wholesome, but merely physical or material.

[11] "Yet science cannot teach intellect. Much less can intellect teach Affection . . . science will not open intellect . . . they are discrete and not continuous" (Annotations to Swedenborg, *CW*, p. 93).

and Johnson—in a scurrilous doggerel, an insulting parody, or an angry ejaculation ("I hate scarce smiles: I love laughing").[12] Blake's real quarry are the philosophical creators of the enlightened establishment—its psychologists, scientists, and thinkers. In attacking Locke on the mind he shows a true instinct for the jugular, since Lockean psychology had insinuated itself into the work of virtually every neoclassical writer. In *A Tale of a Tub,* Swift in a bitter irony had called the memory the "grave" of things and had seemed to praise the imagination as "the womb of things" —whose "artificial mediums, false lights, refracted angles, varnish, and tinsel" minister to "the felicity and enjoyments of mortal men." Blake's life-long attack on the life-denying Daughters of Memory, without ever naming Swift, mocks his mockery. For Blake did in fact regard the memory as a grave and the imagination as a teeming, creating womb, from which spring the values that will save us all. Only the despicable "plagiary" works from the memory—the timid painter of paltry blots, the hireling of the establishment. The true artist possesses "that greatest of all blessings, a strong imagination"—the faculty that is religion, psychology, philosophy, ethics, and art all wrapped in one.[13]

II. *Revolution: The Decade of the Nineties*

A bad culture results from bad thought. If London's streets and London's river are "chartered" and if every face bears "marks of weakness, marks of woe," it is only because the manacles are "mind-forg'd"—because men are what their thinkers have made them. The last judgment is the casting out of bad thought by good thought, of bad art by good art; and it is prepared for by mental fight, in which the tear is an intellectual thing.

Blake had early characterized the philosophy of "demonstration by the Senses" as "Worldly Wisdom." [14] Such wisdom was not only worldly; it was official, established, and was bound to have profound artistic, political, and social consequences. A culture dominated by a passive psychology in which the mind is believed to accept data automatically from nature and then run them like water through the mill of the five senses is hardly calculated to produce visionaries, saints, or revolutionists. A society that believes, more or less officially, that the mind of its artists can do no more than reshuffle or recombine natural phenomena is one that inquires "not

---

[12] Annotations to Lavater, *CW,* p. 67; "Imitation of Pope" in MS Notebook 1808-1811, *CW,* p. 545; Public Address (circa 1810), *CW,* pp. 595-96.

[13] Remarks on Malkin's drawings (1805), *CW,* p. 439; Annotations to Reynolds, *CW,* p. 452, and passim.

[14] Annotations to Swedenborg (circa 1788), *CW,* p. 90.

whether a Man has Talents & Genius, but whether he is Passive & Polite & a Virtuous Ass & obedient to Noblemen's Opinions in Arts & Science." [15] Such a culture is incapable of creating greatness and is also tragically incapable of making itself capable. For inert psychology leads to inert personalities and lukewarm art. Locke had bound Englishmen to dead nature and imprisoned them in the cavern of their material bodies.

Even stronger than his indictment of Locke—at least more direct and overt in expression—was Blake's indictment of Bacon, whose philosophy, he said in 1808, "has Ruin'd England" (*CW*, p. 456). Blake as a revolutionary was deeply concerned with mending England's ruined state, and it is not surprising that toward the end of the revolutionary decade, two years or so before he went to his retreat at Felpham by the sea and some eight years after *The Marriage of Heaven and Hell* and *The French Revolution*, Blake wrote his annotations to Bacon's Essays (*CW*, pp. 396-410). The poet's indictment arises from profound hatred. Bacon was a hireling writer, guilty of "Contemptible Knavery & Folly," a Pilate who opposed Christ, a villain, a liar, a falsifier of values, an ugly embodiment of his own ugly prudential ethics, a man not really interested in the useful arts but only in himself. "His Business and Bosom was to be Lord Chancellor."

Blake's rage at the Man of Measured Merriment and at his large progeny—the elegant poetaster Hayley or the "creeping Jesus" of the established church, for example—was not merely personal and moral. It was also an intellectual indignation. Blake had early in life read the *Advancement of Learning* and would have agreed with Voltaire and most other thinkers of the age of reason that Bacon was the father of empirical philosophy. The legalistic, naturalistic, and utilitarian Bacon entered Blake's revolutionary myth as a Urizenic force that had to be destroyed, just as later he figured in the Christian epics as a Satanic figure that had to be melted down in the apocalyptic fires before he could be redeemed in the New Jerusalem. "Bacon calls Intellectual Arts Unmanly, Poetry, Painting, Music are in his opinion Useless & so they are for Kings & Wars & shall in the End Annihilate them" (*CW*, p. 407). The sense is uncertain, but Blake seems to say, not that kings will annihilate art, but that art will annihilate kings. Men of imagination like Blake and Paine will drive kings and their Baconian hirelings from their lairs and burn them root and branch—to the redemption of humanity. Revolution will destroy the "Philosophy of the Five Senses," which Urizen had delivered into the hands of Locke and Newton.

Bacon figures only indirectly in Blake's revolutionary myth. But New-

---

ton, on one occasion at least, is a *dramatis persona*. When, in the revolutionary prophecy *Europe* (XIII, 1-9), the red Orc of revolution seizes the "Trump of the last doom" but fails to blow it—an act that must refer to the frustration of revolutionary energy in France—a "mighty Spirit . . . nam'd Newton" seizes the trump and blows a mighty blast. Thereupon the myriads of angels who had been ready for a triumph fall like yellow leaves to the ground, seeking their graves in howling and lamentation. Newton's action is counter-revolutionary. The establishment has won a temporary victory.

For the revolutionary Blake all angels were "counter-revolutionary cads," and it was inevitable that in his inversion of all neoclassic value Blake should have transformed the divine Newton of English song and story to his own reprehensible "Sr. Isaac," another Urizenic oppressor of the human mind and spirit. "Art is the Tree of Life," and Newton was no artist. "Science is the Tree of Death," and Newton was, according to Voltaire, the greatest scientist mankind had ever produced.[16]

James Thomson praised Newton for having "untwisted all the shining robe of day," presenting to the charmed eye of the poet "the gorgeous train / Of parent colours"—and "infinite source / Of beauty, ever flushing, ever new." [17] But Blake treated Newton's colors with deep irony:

> That God is Colouring Newton does shew,
> And the devil is Black Outline, all of us know.[18]

Blake, the lover of line and denigrator of color, is obviously of the devil's party.

Voltaire said that Descartes was "the greatest geometrician of his age" but that "geometry leaves the mind where it finds it." [19] Blake made an even graver charge against Newton, whose fluxions (that is, the differential calculus) had weakened the authority of the line in art and helped to destroy human individuality. Newton's geometry subdivided the line— infinitely, to non-existence—dissolving it into the dots and points loved by the chiaroscuro colorists and tonalists, whom Blake loathed.[20] For

---

[16] *The Laocoön* (circa 1820), *CW*, p. 777.

[17] "A Poem to the Memory of Sir Isaac Newton" (1727), ll. 99, 101-2, 117-18.

[18] MS Notebook 1808-1811, *CW*, p. 554.

[19] *The Age of Louis XIV*, Chap. XXXI.

[20] "I know too well that a great majority of Englishmen are fond of The Indefinite which they Measure by Newton's Doctrine of the Fluxions of an Atom, A Thing that does not Exist. . . . For a line or a lineament is not formed by chance: a Line is a Line in its Minutest Subdivisions." Letter to Cumberland, April 12, 1827, *CW*, p. 878. Cp. Voltaire's comment on the line in Newton's geometry (*The Elements of . . . Newton's Philosophy* [London 1738], pp. 112-13). See also Martin K. Nurmi, "Blake's Ancient of Days and Motte's Frontispiece to Newton's *Principia*," in *The Divine Vision*, ed. Vivian de Sola Pinto (London 1957), pp. 208-10.

Blake the quarrel between the line artist like Dürer and Raphael and the colorists and tonalists like the Venetians or his fashionable contemporaries was not merely a conflict of styles. Chiaroscuro he called "that infernal machine" propelled by the hands of "Venetian and Flemish Demons" [21] to the destruction of true art and of human individuality. Because of Newton Englishmen love the "Indefinite" in art and reject the wiry, bounding line that creates true artistic character and have themselves become conventional, conformist, tame, and flat—"all Intermeasurable One by Another, Certainly a happy state of Agreement to which I for One do not Agree." [22]

In his first work of composite art, the stereotyped engravings of 1788 already referred to, Blake inscribed two sentences that can serve as an epigraph for his entire philosophy: "He who sees the Infinite in all things, sees God. He who sees the Ratio only, sees himself only." The first of these Blake illustrated again and again—as when his Apollo, Los, leaps into the sun, or his Poet bounds upward from the Earth, or his Risen Man lifts fallen and enslaved woman from the earth to carry her upward to the new Jerusalem. The second sentence ("He who sees the Ratio only, sees himself only") Blake also rendered often in line and word— but never more cogently than in two engravings that involve Newtonian values. Blake illustrates a phrase from Edward Young's *Night Thoughts*— "Ye searching, ye Newtonian Angels!"—by a female figure who kneels on the floor and stares at a triangle which she has drawn with her geometer's compass. . . . In a more famous work, the color print in the Tate gallery entitled "Newton," the scientist sits on a rock in the kind of stony and desolate landscape Blake elsewhere described as "the Barren Waste of Locke and Newton." [23] Although in some respects he resembles a Blakean hero, the young, blond, curly-headed nude does not aspire upward but bends his back in a geometrical curve, applies his compasses to a scroll on the ground to create a semi-circle in a triangle, and stares at the geometrical "ratio" he has made—and also, if Blake's full meaning is allowable here, at himself. "He who sees the Ratio only, sees himself only."

III. *Blake's Attack on Deism: The Period of the Great Epics*

Sometime before writing his two great epics, *Milton* and *Jerusalem*, Blake shifted the emphasis of his philosophy. Without ever destroying its

[21] *A Descriptive Catalogue*, item no. IX, *CW*, p. 582.
[22] Letter to Cumberland, April 12, 1827, *CW*, p. 878.
[23] *A Descriptive Catalogue*, item no. VI, *CW*, p. 581.

integrity, he altered its proportions. From being a revolutionary willing to unleash the tigers of wrath upon a decadent society, Blake became an unorthodox, undogmatic Christian, dedicated to the forgiveness of sin, the law of love, and the ways of peace. He transformed Satan from a healthy, energetic demon, capable of contributing to our salvation, to a youth of leering evil. Jehovah ceases to be an Old Testament tyrant and becomes a forgiving father. The revolutionists of America and France are replaced as guides and mentors by quietistic mystics: Madame Guyon, whose *Opuscules spirituels* were published in revolutionary Paris in 1790; Fénelon (not as author of the popular *Télémaque* but as the disciple and friend of Madame Guyon, who wrote the *Maxims of the Saints*); James Hervey, whose *Meditations Among the Tombs* Blake epitomized in one of his greatest works of Christian art; and Wesley and Whitefield, who, with the simple medieval monk, become representatives of free, uninstitutionalized Christianity. Blake's new loyalties may not be intellectually exciting—or even respectable—but they do not quite reveal the "utter indiscrimination" that Mr. Schorer has found.[24] Blake has returned to his earliest self—to Innocence, to the simple love of the lamb, to a nature impregnated with the spirit of Christ, and to the quiet ecstasy of the pastoral life.

Blake's Tolstoyan philosophy is never sentimental or flaccid. Although love has swallowed up violence, revolutionary energy and sexual impulse remain active, and the attack on aged evil and institutional repression continues unabated. Locke, Newton, and Bacon continue to be a triad of evil—attacked unrelentingly on page after page of the major prophecies. The psychology of the senses that had succeeded only in starving the senses; mathematical form that in depriving life of its exuberance had distorted its shape; general aesthetic law that weakens individuality and destroys Blake's "little ones"—the minute but holy life of nature— all these desiccating philosophies remain the object of Blake's withering anger.

To his pantheon of evil Blake has now added Voltaire and Rousseau, English deism and doubt, and the Greek and Roman classics. Rome now stands for war, Greece for stultifying mathematical form. The poet-painter, who had been under the spell of classicizing artists (his personal friends Cumberland and Flaxman), who had once said that he hoped to "revive the Greek workmanship," [25] and who had himself created under classical influence, now makes ancient civilization the symbol of violence, tyranny, state religion, rationalism, the loss of imagination, and the deg-

---

[24] *William Blake: The Politics of Vision* (New York 1959), p. 50.
[25] Letter to Cumberland, August 26, 1799, *CW*, p. 795.

radation of prophetic truth to priestcraft and allegory. "The Classics! It is the Classics & not the Goths nor Monks, that Desolate Europe with Wars." [26]

Everything that Blake came to say of the ancient classics he also came to say of what he regarded as their spiritual descendant—deism or natural religion, the faith of the European Enlightenment. Blake must always have disliked it, but during the revolutionary period he was willing to close an eye to its deficiencies, because so many of its adherents were attackers of the establishment and forerunners of revolution. Thus, ignoring Paine's religion—or lack of it—Blake put him on the side of Christ as an arouser of men to intellectual battle. He even compared Paine's achievement to the miracles of Jesus. "Is it a greater miracle to feed five thousand men with five loaves than to overthrow all the armies of Europe with a small pamphlet?" [27]

But though Blake had, in the decade of the nineties, made common cause with deists against the princes of the state and church, he now regards deism as an evil closely related to and fully as mischievous as established religion, the monarchy, Jewish legalism, and utilitarian ethics. "He never can be a Friend to the Human Race who is the preacher of Natural Morality or Natural Religion" (*Jerusalem,* plate 52). Blake was prepared to find in the deist all the Urizenic and Satanic traits he had always found in Locke, Bacon, and Newton. The deist was a flatterer, a proud tyrant, a Druid, a Greek, a Pharisee, a war-like perpetuator of the talonic law of revenge. It was inevitable that Voltaire and Rousseau—and also in less degree Gibbon and Paine—should now enter Blake's hierarchy of intellectual evil.

But it had not always been so. In Blake's vision of revolutionary France he had seen pale religious specters, weeping, shivering, driven out of their abbeys by Voltaire and Rousseau.[28] La Fayette, while still on the side of revolution and still a lover of human liberty, Blake saw as being inspired by the fiery cloud of Voltaire and the white cloud of Rousseau—Moses's pillar of fire by night and pillar of cloud by day transformed to revolutionary symbols. In the *Song of Los* (V) Voltaire and Rousseau, melting the Urizenic snows of Europe, are engaged in direct conflict with Urizen and his servants, Newton and Locke.

It must therefore have cost Blake a considerable expense of spirit to dethrone these French thinkers and place them in his inferno. Rousseau, probably through the translation of Fuseli, may have influenced Blake in

[26] "On Homer's Poetry" (circa 1820), *CW*, p. 778.
[27] Annotations to Watson (1798), *CW*, p. 391.
[28] *The French Revolution,* ll. 274-76.

America and *Tiriel* and in those features of his myth that are concerned
with luxury, agriculture, and the fall of man from natural innocence to
social experience.[29] But in *Jerusalem,* Blake's last prophecy, Rousseau is
viewed as a Pharisee, a hypocrite, a pretender to virtue, and one who,
whatever his theory of natural goodness in actual life, discovered only
evil in men and who in a long life found no friend. A kind of pseudo-
Christian, Rousseau's *Confessions* do not really confess, since the author
had no notion of real evil, true good, or the forgiveness of sin. The *Confessions* are a monument of apologetic self-pleading; they cloak the evil
of the heart.

Blake once said that "To defend the Bible in this year 1798 would
cost a man his life." [30] To have made a hero of Voltaire during the
revolution was also a danger to life and limb. For the old Son of the
Morning smelled of sulphur to pious Englishmen, and to the ruling
Tories looked like the veriest anti-Christ. When Blake was of the devil's
party, Voltaire's infernal wisdom was irresistible. The creator of Urizen
could hardly have been displeased by the Frenchman who exposed the
rack and wheel of the Inquisition and the murderous practices of the
Druids. Even the author of *Songs of Innocence* could make common
cause with the liberal thinker. Voltaire wrote in his *Treatise on Toler-
ance* (Chap. XXII): "What! call a Turk, a Jew and a Siamese, my brother?
Yes, of course; for are we not all children of the same father, and the
creatures of the same God?" One of Blake's finest lyrics proclaims that

> all must love the human form,
> In heathen, turk or jew.

In spite of the powerful affinities of the revolutionary decade, the
later Blake could hardly have avoided a break with his great French
contemporary. Voltaire's life and influence were in some respects anything but revolutionary. Blake's smiling, unctuous patron Hayley found
it possible to admire Voltaire—and Rousseau and Gibbon, too—without
altering his views. Voltaire himself, that prosperous heretic, consorted
with royalty, was flattered by the first two Georges, lived intimately with
the Prussian Frederick, flattered the age of Louis XIV, praised its rationalism, and lauded benevolent monarchy. The surly and impoverished
Englishman's republican blood must have boiled. And when he reflected
that Voltaire's deepest intellectual commitment was to deist and neoclassical England, that he regarded Bacon, Locke, and Newton as culture-

---

[29] David V. Erdman, *Blake: Prophet Against Empire* (Princeton 1954), pp. 118n, 399n,
229-30, 232.

[30] Annotations to Watson (1798), *CW*, p. 383.

heroes, that he was the world's greatest popularizer of the "new philosophy," and that to him Shakespeare was a barbarian, a fall from grace was inevitable.

Voltaire ends as a cold-hearted mocker; an ally of cruel virtue, war, glory; an enemy of prophecy, vision, and forgiveness. Blake throws in Voltaire's teeth the very epithets the Frenchman had himself hurled at the establishment. Blake calls him an intolerant "Inquisitor," a "Pharisee," and a "Hypocrite" who turns "a wracking wheel." [31]

IV. *Blake's Artistic Achievement*

Blake's rejection of enlightened Europe is expressed in poem, design, fiery epigram, and angry comments on the margins of books by Lavater, Swedenborg, Bishop Watson, Bacon, Reynolds. Though it is nowhere reasoned out, it is not therefore intellectually despicable. Quite the contrary, Blake's position has living nerve and muscle, that bind all its members together in organic unity. Even his altered views have a living bloom on them; they are natural growths, not unnatural or unsuccessful grafts.

But though Blake's rejection of the Enlightenment is conceptually firm and consistent, it is his artistic embodiment of meaning that ought to command the attention of the twentieth century. For even though we may reject Blake's rejection on philosophical grounds, his achievement as poet-painter is inescapable.

As one would expect, that achievement is both verbal and visual. The triumph in words comes at the climax of the epic *Milton* (plates 41-43), when the poet-hero, bearing the evils of neoclassical culture in his own body and being, moves to the climactic immolation. In action, dialogue, and tableau Milton the hero destroys this "thing," as Blake calls it, that has itself ruined his country and his people (XLVI, II-13)—

<blockquote>
this Newtonian Phantasm,
This Voltaire & Rousseau, this Hume & Gibbon & Bolingbroke,
This Natural Religion, this impossible absurdity.
</blockquote>

Blake's epic has its faults; but its climax persuades, as Milton enters death, strikes terror into the beholders, restores Blake and his wife to their high role, and causes all creatures to approach the "Great Harvest and Vintage of the Nations," when all social, philosophical, and artistic evil will be "annihilated away." The "Not Human" will be washed away—along with Rational Demonstration, the rotten rags of Memory,

<hr>

[31] "A Vision of the Last Judgment" (1810), *CW*, p. 615; Poems from the Notebook 1800-1803, *CW*, pp. 418, 420; *Jerusalem*, plate 52, *CW*, p. 682.

Bacon, Locke, & Newton, uninspired poetry and paltry rhymes, and the caterpillars of the church and state. The idiot questioner who has no answer, the despairing scientist, the imitator of nature's images drawn only from memory—all in fact who have built their faith on empirical demonstration—will be swallowed up in the fires of regeneration, and a new age of inspiration, imagination, and humanistic faith will arise out of the ashes of the neoclassical Phoenix.

Blake's other notable embodiment of the ideas discussed in the paper is the figure of Urizen, who haunts the words, borders, and designs of almost every Blakean page—from the adumbrations of him in the natural personifications of the juvenile poetry to the last sapphire-studded apocalypses. Urizen is vastly more than an allegorical personification of the faculty Reason. He is a natural force—storm, winter, snow, ice, water, rock, sand—natural death itself. He lies in a desolate landscape, his hand rests on a skull. He sits as a skeleton without flesh in the fire, he struggles in water, he emerges from a vegetable cave, he sits under blasted trees with a poisonous serpent, he weaves a frosty net. He is in part Blake's vision of Newtonian nature—cold, remote, mathematical, empty.

Urizen is also an active force. Dividing, partitioning, dropping the plummet line, applying Newton's compasses to the world, he creates abstract, mathematical forms. Like Locke, he shrinks the senses, narrows the perceptions, binds man to natural fact. Like Bacon he creates the laws of prudence and crucifies passion. He is the man neoclassical psychology and ethics have delivered into our hands—a passivity, a receptacle, a "soul-shuddering vacuum," an "abominable void," an "unknown, abstracted, brooding, secret" power of dark negation.

Urizen has Greek, Roman, and Hebrew as well as English blood in his veins. His face recalls the sightless, bearded classical statues of iron, warlike men, and the God of Sinai. He conveys powerful social meaning because, as a father-figure compounded of Zeus, Jehovah, and Dr. Johnson, he bears lineaments of traditional dignity, suggesting that the cruelty, ignorance, and repression he represents are perversions of the good. Fathers are good, but Urizen is an unnatural tyrant. Language is a great gift, but Urizen has perverted books and writing to repressive legal tablets. Religion is created by man's imagination and can produce freedom, but Urizen has rationalized it into the whip and wheel of church and state. It is the institutional Urizen who as primeval priest squats on a book bearing mystical letters, the tablets of the law at his back like stony wings. Tears of pious and conventional pity ooze from his compressed lids and drop into his frozen beard. He is that worst of all negations of living humanity—the human abstract that grows in the human brain and spreads over society.

This hoary being is more and other than a personification of the Enlightenment. But he will not achieve his full imaginative force unless we see that, besides being a symbol of social and political repression, he is also an intellectual tyrant, motivated by the *espirit de système*. He is the Geometer God of deism, the general nature of Reynolds and Locke, who sleeps the slumbers of abstraction.

He must have been conceived when Blake—"very Young," as he said when he was about fifty years old—first read the philosophers of the Enlightenment.[32] For it is Urizen who, weeping, delivers the Philosophy of the Five Senses into the hands of Newton and Locke.[33]

---

[32] Annotations to Reynolds, *CW*, p. 476.
[33] *The Song of Los*, IV, 16-17, *CW*, p. 246.

Blake and the Druids

by Peter F. Fisher

The context of Blake's treatment of Druidism was primarily his own particular vision of human history, but much of what he had to say was understandably connected with traditional sources and the theories of contemporary antiquarians. The theories of antiquarians such as Bryant, Davies, and Stukeley have received more attention, since they happen to be in the mainstream of scholarly research, and the traditional sources a good deal less. Of these traditional sources, references in classical authors have been noticed, but practically nothing has been said about that large body of folklore containing the remains of Welsh bardism. No one could deny that this material was a mixture of ancient tradition and later additions, but this very fact would have attracted Blake, and may have moved him to add another "moment" to the life of the bardic tradition with his "Welch Triades" at the beginning of his *Descriptive Catalogue* of 1809.[1] To establish the relationship between the traditional sources of Druidism and Blake's own use of the term in *Milton* and *Jerusalem* will involve considerable reference to some of the theories of the antiquarians, relevant statements in classical authors, and especially his conception of natural religion. For him history was the field of recurrent attempts to wake up human conscience, both individual and social. Each attempt was a new vision finally reduced by the dead weight of self-interest and misunderstanding to some system of accepted beliefs with its conventional morality and its sacrificial rites. Bardic tradition provided him with an apt symbol of what history was about and also with a convenient foil for his gospel of vision.

Blake did not actually mention the immediate source of this interest

"Blake and the Druids" by Peter F. Fisher. From *The Journal of English and Germanic Philology*, LVIII (1959), 589-612.

Reprinted by permission of the editor of *The Journal of English and Germanic Philology*.

[1] Northrop Frye, *Fearful Symmetry* (Princeton 1947), p. 173, refers to Blake's "triads" as imitations or adaptations in the fashion of the day. They certainly are not to be found in Williams' collection at the back of his *Poems, Lyrical and Pastoral* (London 1794, Vol. II).

in bardism, but some of the triads had been collected and translated by Edward Williams and were to be found as an appendix to a collection of his poems published in 1794. Williams called himself a "Bard according to the Rights and Institutes of the Bards of the Island of Britain," and claimed that his triads were translated from the Silurian or most ancient dialect.[2] The "triad" itself was said to be the most common of all aphoristical forms used by the bards, since it was constructed on the basis of certain fixed and unalterable principles where the connections of its parts were related to one another simply and concisely. The form was evidently used for oral instruction in that lore which the Druids refused to commit to writing.[3] These particular triads were selected from a manuscript collection by Llewelyn Sion, a Bard of Glamorgan, about 1560. Of this particular manuscript, Williams claimed to have a transcript, and the original collection was said to have been made from various manuscripts of great antiquity. To such a collection as that of Williams, Blake probably referred in his *Descriptive Catalogue* when he wrote of having "in his hands poems of the highest antiquity." [4]

Blake's attitude toward Druidism was likely influenced and, in many ways, perhaps formed by such fragments and the commentaries on them. He first saw Druidism as the "Patriarchal Religion" which, in its completed cycle, exemplified every aspect of an inspired, prophetic faith, and later, of a degenerate cult. Part of this outlook was taken from the antiquarians who, like Bryant and Davies, emphasized the civilization and learning of the ancient Britons and also an original unity of language, culture, and religion.[5]

There was understandably a great deal of accommodation to Christian belief in these traditions. The traditional chronology (*amseryddiaeth*) gave some support to antiquarian theory which was already trying to expand the scope of Genesis without actually contradicting it. Druidic chronology was divided into three main dispensations: from creation to the sixth century B.C. was the first; from the sixth century to the third century A.D., the second; and the third was the Christian. These contribu-

---

[2] Williams, I, xx: "The Silurian differs in many particulars from the Biblical dialect of modern writers. To attempt an investigation of the true sense of the very obscure term *Abred* would have required a longer dissertation than I had room for; and probably, my abilities would have failed me."

[3] *Ibid.*, II, 225. Cf. Caesar, *De Bello Gallico*, VI, xiii. Caesar also noted that the institution (disciplina) was said to have originated in Britain. See *Jerusalem*, II, 27, Pref., where Blake calls Albion the "Parent of the Druids."

[4] Blake, *Descriptive Catalogue*, No. V, "The Ancient Britons."

[5] *Ibid.*: "The Britons (say historians) were naked civilized men, learned, studious, abstruse in thought and contemplation; naked, simple, plain in their acts and manners; wiser than after-ages."

tions of Celtic enthusiasts and of the antiquarians confirmed Blake's conviction that all antiquities could be traced to one source—a prophetic and inspired faith.

> The antiquities of every Nation under Heaven, is no less sacred than that of the Jews. They are the same thing, as Jacob Bryant and all antiquaries have proved. . . . All had originally one language, and one religion: this was the religion of Jesus, the everlasting Gospel. Antiquity preaches the Gospel of Jesus.[6]

The kind of "Antiquity" to which Blake referred was a universal, "Druidic" antiquity where his own conception of genius and inspiration at first flourished and then suffered a decline.

Blake's identification of the original, universal culture with Druidism was supported by both Davies and Stukeley, but the traditional sources for it went back to bardic legends and classical authors. Davies cited Diogenes Laertius' opinion that the "philosophy of Greece originated in the Celtae." [7] Abaris, a priest of Apollo among the Druidic Hyperboreans, was said to have visited Pythagoras for the ostensible purpose of taking back to one of the northern temples the gold which he had collected. An actual exchange of doctrine was implied, and the most durable of the Greek philosophic schools whose founder had learned from Egyptian priests, Persian Magi, the Brahmans of India, and the initiates of Samothrace was also directly connected with British Druidism. The Pythagoreans emphasized this latter connection more than any of the others, for they said that Pythagoras himself was the incarnation of the Hyperborean Apollo, and inferred that the most Greek of Greek gods had originated in Britain. No wonder Blake called Greek philosophy "a remnant of Druidism." [8] Diodorus Siculus, out of Hecataeus and other

---

[6] *Ibid.:* "The British Antiquities are now in the Artist's hands; all his visionary contemplations, relating to his own country and its ancient glory, when it was, as it again shall be, the source of learning and inspiration." Milton, *Doctrine and Discipline of Divorce,* in *Works* (Columbia ed., New York 1932), III, 376, mentioned the Druids as those "by whom this Island was the Cathedrall of Philosophy to France."

[7] Edward Davies, *Celtic Researches* (London 1804), p. 184. Cf. *Mythology and Rites of the British Druids* (London 1809), sec. II, p. 123: "The mythology of the Britons was of a character somewhat more antique than that of the Greeks and Romans, as we find it in their best writers." Diogenes Laertius traced the beginnings of philosophy to related sources which included the Persian Magi, the Chaldeans, the Indian gymnosophists, and the Druids (*De Clarorum Philosophorum Vitis,* proemium). See also Pliny, *Historia Naturalis,* XVI, 95; XXIV, 62-63; XXIX, 12. Cf. Milton, *Areopagitica, Works* (Columbia ed.), IV, 339: "Writers of good antiquity, and ablest judgement have bin perswaded that e'n the school of Pythagoras, and the Persian wisdom took beginning from the old Philosophy of this Island."

[8] *Jerusalem,* III, 52, Pref. The story of Abaris is first recorded by Herodotus (*Historiae,* IV, 36); other references are Porphyry's life of Pythagoras and Iamblichus

sources, said that the Britons worshipped Apollo above all other gods, and that they had a special regard for the Greeks—particularly the Athenians and the Delians. Abaris was supposed to have renewed the ancient league of friendship with the Delians.

It is not surprising that these classical references to British Druidism were exploited to the full by the antiquarians who laboured with enthusiasm at the task of demonstrating Blake's own thesis: "All things Begin & End in Albion's Ancient Druid Rocky Shore." [9] That part of their work which included classical culture was buttressed by the evidence of ancient writers, but the link with Hebraic tradition required more ingenuity. Stukeley did not hesitate to claim that the Druids came to Britain as a Phoenician colony as soon as Tyre was founded, during the life of Abraham. They brought with them the customs and beliefs of the patriarchal religion and even the technical details of sacred architecture.

> I must prepare the reader for a right understanding of our Druid edifices, by informing him, that Stonehenge, and all other works of this nature in our island, are erected by the most ancient measure call'd a cubit, which we read of in the holy scripture and in ancient profane authors. I mean the same individual measure, call'd the Hebrew, Egyptian, Phoenician cubit; most probably deriv'd from Noah and Adam. 'Tis the same that the pyramids of Egypt and other of their works are projected upon; the same as that of Moses's tabernacle, Solomon's temple, &c., and we may reasonably pride ourselves in possessing these visible monuments of the old measure of the world.[10]

Davies went still further and quoted an ingenious friend of his who suggested that Menyw, the first man of the Druidic tradition, was identical with Menu (Manu) of the Indian Veda. He even extended the conjecture

---

(*De Pythagorica Vita*, xix, xxviii). Abaris was said to have traveled over the whole world, without food, carrying an arrow which he later showed Pythagoras. By means of this arrow, he claimed to have passed through inaccessible places and expelled pestilence from cities on the way. He lived in temples and was never seen to eat or drink. Davies, *Celtic Researches*, p. 183, connected the arrow with the wheat straw used by the Druids in the rites of Apollo and Diana, and also suggested that "arrow" (ὀϊστός) was a play on the word "think" (Ep. ὀΐω), so that what Abaris really conveyed was his doctrine. Stukeley, *Abury* (London 1743), pp. 96-97, even supposed the arrow to be some kind of instrument like a magnetic needle. See Diodorus Siculus, *Bibliotheca Historica*, II, 47. Finally, the encircling of the globe by Abaris could refer to the mystical journey of the soul around the Circle of Inchoätion (*abred*) before attaining the Circle of Felicity.

[9] *Jerusalem*, II, 27, Pref. *Milton*, I, 6, 25. The fact that Blake associated the "Religion of Jesus" with an original Druidism should surprise no one who has noticed Stukeley's title of "patriarchal Christianity" for the larger theme of his work (*Abury*, pp. i-ii),

[10] William Stukeley, *Stonehenge* (London 1740), p. 6. Cf. *A Descriptive Catalogue* &c., No. V: "The Ancient Britons." "Adam was a Druid, and Noah . . ."

to include Minos, king of Crete, who became one of the judges at the court of Pluto whose worship by the Druids of Gaul Caesar noticed. Both Menu and Minos, however, were finally made to refer to the patriarch Noah.[11]

Blake made use of all this in much the same spirit as Dante made use of Thomistic philosophy and the astronomy of Ptolemy. If he had been a Greek, he would have found the navel of the world at Delphi. For one who was never tired of emphasizing that the journey to Eden started from the ground under one's feet, and that the most visionary perspective included the geography of one's own country, antiquarian theory provided accommodating material. It was clear that Bryant and Davies concentrated on the more favorable aspects of Druidic culture—aspects which Blake used to establish his account of the fall of man and the impact of prophetic inspiration on the subsequent history of man's fallen societies. An indication of the relationship Druidism bore to the elaboration of this original pattern was to be found in *A Descriptive Catalogue* (particularly nos. IV and V) where Gray's bard, the last of the Druids, was placed beside a description of the last "Battle of King Arthur" (Albion) and the rout of his forces (disorganization of Albion's faculties, the "Zoas"). Here Blake was associating inspiration and the divine vision with Druidism. However, he later came to treat Druidism pejoratively— in the last two books of *Jerusalem*—as the degenerate effect of man's fallen historical destiny on original prophetic inspiration.[12] Druidism became the symbol of the outer husk of an earlier vision, and such a translation of the triads as that of Williams must have provided him with material for evaluating both husk and vision.

Williams himself was the zealous prophet of what he considered an expression of the true faith. He ridiculed Gray's *Bard* as an example of the literary confusion of a "savage Scandinavian Mythology" with British antiquities. The charge was obviously that of an enthusiastic purist who could see nothing but good in the Druidic tradition. It was perhaps be-

---

[11] Davies also claimed that Arthur was one of the titles of Noah to whose deification he attributed the development of pagan myth (*Mythology and Rites of the British Druids*, sec. III, p. 187). Blake's association of Arthur with Albion could be traced to Davies, along with Atlas, who is called a Hyperborean (cf. Hesiod, *Theogony*, 736). For the connection between Menu, Minos, and Druidism, see sec. III, p. 197. See also Caesar, *De Bello Gallico*, VI, xviii.

[12] Cf. Frye, p. 175; Joseph Wicksteed, *William Blake's* Jerusalem (London 1953), p. 57. This same ambivalent outlook (which is far from being equivocation) may be seen in his remarks on the antiquities of the Jews. On the one hand, he called the laws of the Jews "the basest & most oppressive of human codes" (*Annotations to Watson's* Apology for the Bible, p. 25), and on the other, spoke of the "Return of Israel" as a "Return to Mental Sacrifice & War" (*Jerusalem*, II, 27)—a return to the original prophetic religion of inner struggle and search.

cause of this that he resented the appropriation of ancient British lore by the "Gothic" revival. However, the tradition had itself undergone various changes which made it difficult to decide how much of an authentic original was to be found in the synopsis of Llewelyn Sion in the first place. The selections which Williams chose gave no evidence of the interest noticed by classical writers in the theology of a pantheon of gods. Caesar, for instance, described the Druids as interested in disputes concerning the power of the gods, and added that they paid particular honors to Mercury whom they considered the inventor of all arts. After Mercury, he went on to say, they worshipped Apollo, Mars, Jupiter, and Minerva like other nations. Strabo, the geographer, cited the authority of Artemidorus that in "an island close to Britain," presumably Ireland, Ceres and Proserpine were venerated with rites similar to those of Samothrace.[13] By calling himself, on his title page, "Bard according to the Rights and Institutes of the Bards of the Island of Britain," Williams might be said to lose the objectivity of the editor, and become an apologist for the triads he was translating.

Along with the polemic of the apologist and the voice of the prophetic bard, he also mixed the ardor of the republican revolutionary—a combination which would not prove unappealing to Blake. He spoke of his intention of going to America to escape the injustice of laws which were not "made equally for the poor as for the rich." Another motive is to ascertain the truth of an opinion, prevalent in Wales, on good authority, that there are still existing, in the interior parts of the American continent, the remains of a Welsh colony that went over there in the twelfth century under the conduct of Madoc, the son of Owen Gwynedd, Prince of Wales.[14] Southey's poem came as a later illustration of the legendary unity between Britain and America which formed part of the source for Blake's development of Albion as "Patriarch of the Atlantic." There was also his conception of a prehistoric "Atlantic continent"—the basis of both cultures—and he made use of the Atlantic ocean to represent

[13] Strabo, *Geographica*, IV, 4; Caesar, *De Bello Gallico*, VI, xiv-xvii. These references were also cited by Davies (sec. II, pp. 88-89). Williams (II, 202) admitted that his outline was what had been refined by Christianity "in which the Bards adopted nothing that was averse to their Ancient Theology, but rather confirmed the truth of it." Milton (*Mansus*, ll. 42-43) described the Druids as a race "busied with the holy rites of the gods (*sacris operata deorum*)."

[14] Williams, I, xii; II, 64n. The material for Southey's *Madoc* was taken from William Robertson's *History of America* published in 1777. Southey's story of a Celtic adventurer who founded a settlement in mythical "Aztlan"—the ancestral home of the Aztecs—and was finally made to fight for his life at the foot of the stone of sacrifice suggested the common origin of both Aztec and Druidic sacrificial rites. Blake spoke equally of the "reared Rocks of Albion's Sons" (*Jerusalem*, II, 43, 82) and the "Rocks of the Altars of Victims in Mexico" (*ibid.*, 7).

the flood which destroyed an original civilization of the world. To Blake, however, the "flood" was ultimately synonymous with the "fall." The real origin of cultivated life lay in his "Atlantic Mountains where Giants dwelt in Intellect"—the paradise state of Eden far beyond the "stony Druids" and the "Creation that groans, living on Death." [15] But while he made use of the materials of Celtic myth to communicate his own vision, Williams tried to accommodate the triads of Bardism to Christian doctrine.

Aside from ignoring any reference to those parts of the tradition which might be interpreted as polytheistic, Williams was faced with a conception of reincarnation which, in one form or another, held a central position in the Druidic system.

> I have in one passage mentioned a qualified sense in which the Christian Bards and Druids believed the Metempsychosis: this was, that the depraved soul of man passes in a state beyond the grave into progressive modes of existence corresponding with the nature of Earthly worms and brutes, into whom, in the literal sense, the Aboriginal or Patriarchal Druids believed it passed. Taliesin places this probationary, divestigating, or purifying Metempsychosis in the Hell of Christianity, whence the soul gradually rises again to Felicity, the way for it having been opened by Jesus Christ.[16]

Blake's outlook, expressed explicitly at the end of *Jerusalem*, that all lives, through the process of time, came to the realization of a full "Humanity" was in striking contrast to the Druidic conception of a ladder of ascent from the subhuman to the superhuman. This very ladder seemed to infer that man had been something else, and was about to become something else, and it tended to make man turn aside from the realization of his human existence. He was to find the source and order of life elsewhere—either beneath, in the forces of nature, or beyond, in the ideal of

---

[15] *Jerusalem*, II, 50, 1-7. See this fragment to the Countess of Egremont:

> My designs unchang'd remain.
> Time may rage but rage in vain.
> For above Time's troubled Fountains
> On the Great Atlantic Mountains,
> In my Golden House on high,
> There they Shine Eternally.

Cf. *Jerusalem*, II, 36, 38-398. G. M. Harper, "Blake's Neo-Platonic Interpretation of Plato's Atlantis Myth," *Journal of English and Germanic Philology*, LIV (January 1955), 72-79, traces this and other references to Thomas Taylor's commentaries on Plato.

[16] Williams, I, xx-xxi. He later claimed that the doctrine of metempsychosis most clearly vindicated divine justice (II, 194n). "It is sufficiently countenanced by many passages in the New Testament, and was believed by many of the Primitive Christians, and by the Essenes amongst the Jews." Cf. Job 33: 29-30; Malachi 4: 5; Matthew 11: 13-14; 17: 10-13; Mark 9: 11-13; John 9: 2-3.

divine perfection. Both routes distracted him from himself and the field of his actual experience. Blake saw in Druidism the prototype of all systematic theology which attempted to explain the paradoxes of spiritual life in the rational terms of fallen man and his world of nature.

Druidism, according to Blake, gradually degenerated into man's first attempt to let theory take the place of reality, and theorizing the place of realizing, so that the fallen condition became more comfortable and apparently more secure. He called the Indian systems of thought "Abstract Philosophy," and the systems of Pythagoras and Plato, "Abstract Law," to express the progressive reduction of inspired insight to some absolutely logical scheme.[17] The traditional theory of reincarnation, like the orthodox Christian doctrine of election and reprobation, provided an absolute rule of thumb for what was relative in actual human experience. Both were attempts to reduce insight beyond the fallen perspective to dogmatic form, and both left out the other side of the paradox which even ordinary experience suggested. What is given in experience is always unique, and at the same time, always a repetition of everything like it, but this does not necessarily mean that everything is predetermined once and for all or that everything is bound to repeat itself. The circle of recurrence was identity in motion, in process, so that the temporal cycle was, as Blake came to see it, the "analogy" of eternal identity. One of his definitions of character was what could be repeated with infinite variety but could neither be surpassed nor changed into something else,

> for we see the same characters repeated again and again, in animals, vegetables, minerals, and in men; nothing new occurs in identical existence; Accident ever varies, Substance can never suffer change nor decay.[18]

The truth underlying the reincarnation of character and that underlying the unique individuality of each character formed part of this visionary analogy which Blake tried to establish between time and eternity throughout his prophetic books. What was perceived as periodic and successive was seen from the temporal point of view, and what was perceived as

[17] *The Song of Los,* ll. 8-19.
[18] *A Descriptive Catalogue* &c., No. III. Needless to say, Blake nowhere gave any support to the change of human into animal existences implied by the literal interpretation of the Pythagorean tradition. Williams (II, 197) reflected the Druidic belief in subhuman and superhuman progressions, and spoke of a falling away from good and a return to it through "a succession of animal existences." Thomas Taylor in his translation of Proclus' *Theology of Plato* (London 1816, I, I n.) quoted that particular philosopher's commentary (V, 329D-E) on Plato's *Timaeus* (42B-C) with reference to human souls descending into brute animals, and concluded that the rational essence of man could by no means become the soul of a savage animal. "For a brutal nature is not a brutal body but a brutal life." See Blake's *Vision of the Last Judgment,* p. 79.

unique and simultaneous was seen from the eternal point of view. Both points of view coincide in the moment of vision when the paradox was resolved, and everything was seen to be eternal.[19]

The problem of presenting a unified vision of temporal periodicity had become clarified for Blake while writing what he finally called *The Four Zoas*. It was probably during this part of his life that he read Williams or encountered the bardic triads in some form. Whatever he found in them to disagree with, they must have struck him as authentic, in the same sense that he considered Macpherson and Chatterton authentic. He was not the least interested in documentary authenticity, but rather in the authentic original as it survived and was recreated continually in the human mind.[20] The authentic original of Druidism which developed systematically from the central notion of cyclical recurrence was deeply involved with Blake's theme of creation, redemption, and judgment in *The Four Zoas*. The writing of this work made clear a distinction he later used in *Milton* and *Jerusalem*—a distinction between inspired, prophetic religion which united temporal process and eternal identity in one vision and its recurring distillate, "Natural Religion," which abstracted temporal process and the wheel of becoming into a false kind of absolute identity expressed in the form of theological dogma. In these later works, he called the first the "Everlasting Gospel," and the second, "Druidism."

In *The Four Zoas*, he began with the conception of the cyclical pattern of natural necessity called the "Circle of Destiny"—in *Jerusalem*, "Divine Analogy"—and the problem of temporal recurrence dominated the work.[21] Like the Druids, he recognized the larger cycle which contained man's historical destiny from Adam to Luther and included what he later called the "Twenty-Seven Heavens" and their "Churches." He also recognized the lesser lunar cycle which contained man's individual destiny from birth to rebirth and included the phases of life outlined in "The Mental Traveller." Most important, however, was the constant interplay of life and death, joy and sorrow, pleasure and pain, the one contrary living off the other, yet never completely absorbing it. As in Swedenborg, Blake found in Druidism a deep-rooted tendency to eliminate one contrary in favor of the other and to regard this process as the moral triumph of good over evil.

---

[19] Cf. *The Laocoön Group:* "All that we See is Vision, from Generated Organs gone as soon as come, Permanent in The Imagination, Consider'd as Nothing by the Natural Man."

[20] *Annotations to Wordsworth's Poems*, pp. 364-65: "I Believe both Macpherson & Chatterton, that what they say is Ancient Is so." See also *Annotations to Watson's Apology for the Bible*, pp. 15-16: "As if Public Records were True! Impossible; for the facts are such as none but the actor could tell."

[21] *The Four Zoas*, I, 71-102; *Jerusalem*, II, 49, 56-59; IV, 85, 3-13.

All modes of existence which are necessarily as numerous as Divine Conception can make them, will forever remain in existence with no other change than that of being thoroughly divested of all their Evils, and continue eternally as beautiful varieties in the Creation, which without this numerosity of externalities would not possess perfect beauty.[22]

The moral judgment abhors a paradox, but it is only in paradox that the recurrent nature of life and its unique identity can both be understood. To fall short of this paradox is to become committed to the half-truths of formal logic and dogmatic theology where, to get a final answer, it is necessary to eliminate the contrary aspect of every problem.

The inability to sustain the paradox of the contraries was, in effect, a submission to the cloven fiction of two exhaustive alternatives to every problem—in this instance, that of recurrence and identity. Druidism which stood for a view of eternal identity in terms of temporal succession was typical of all natural religions according to Blake. On the other hand, the everlasting gospel was the vision of the circle of time contained by eternal identity as the substantial form underlying every possibility. Orthodox Christian doctrine had to come to accept as limited a view of the problem as Druidism, and Augustine's attack on the whole cyclical theory, which he attributed to the failure of logic to grasp the nature of infinity, could as easily be turned against his own doctrine of special creation and predestination.[23] On the level of accepted doctrine, Christianity obviously regarded the theory of cycles as a contradiction of the historical principle inherent in Scripture—the progressive disclosure of the spirit of truth. It also objected to the repetition of typical or characteristic individuals and events as contrary to the unique character of personal identity and historical situations.

As a professed Christian, Blake was careful to distinguish between the visionary significance of periodicity and the crass naturalism with which it was later interpreted by both the Druidic and classical traditions. But he continued to accept the notion of cyclical recurrence as one of the contraries involved in the relationship between identity and process. In *Jerusalem,* he clearly indicated that the "Circle of Destiny" of his *Four Zoas* was to be understood as an analogy which served to express the

---

[22] Williams, II, 202. Blake even spoke of suffering as necessary (H. Crabb Robinson, *Diary* [Boston 1869], p. 27). "There is suffering in heaven, for where there is the capacity of enjoyment, there is also the capacity of pain." The painless, effortless paradise of the faithful could only be pleasant, or even endurable, as an impossible dream. Cf. *Marriage of Heaven and Hell*: "Without Contraries is no progression. Attraction and Repulsion, Reason and Energy, Love and Hate, are necessary to Human existence."

[23] Augustine, *De Civitate Dei*, XII, 18-22; V, 9-10. The rejection of the theory of cycles (*circuitus temporum*) was an early characteristic of Christian thought (see Origen, *Contra Celsum*, IV, 68).

seer's visionary experience of the polarity of the unique and the periodic. He gave no indication of trying to reconcile these two contraries on the level of doctrine at all. It was probably not until *Milton* and *Jerusalem* that he finally succeeded in liberating himself from his own "Circle of Destiny," so that he saw it as "Divine Analogy."

Within the context of *The Four Zoas,* however, Blake described the attempt of man's natural reason to encompass the fallen world of space and time in terms of cyclical repetition. Urizen was the "Mental Traveller" who united the larger cycle of human history to the individual cycle of human life—one whose contrary was no longer a female counterpart but the earth's "bosom of clay" created in the void.

> When wearied, dead he fell, his limbs repos'd in the bosom of slime;
> As the seed falls from the sower's hand, so Urizen fell, & death
> Shut up his powers in oblivion; then as the seed shoots forth
> In pain & sorrow, so the slimy bed his limbs renew'd.
> At first an infant weakness; periods pass'd; he gather'd strength,
> But still in solitude he sat; then rising, threw his flight
> Onward, tho' falling, thro' the waste of night & ending in death
> And in another resurrection to sorrow & weary travel.[24]

In addition, Urizen was represented bearing with him his books which remained unconsumed after each periodic death and resurrection. The continuity of experience and a final "perfect recollection" was also emphasized by traditional Bardism:

> Man, on arriving at a state above Humanity, recovers the perfect recollection of all former modes of existence, and to eternity retains it.[25]

Blake never supposed that man could surpass his human identity, although he could realize it to an extent which included an eternal progression. There were references, however, to what Shelley might have called pre-existence and to "former modes of existence." In a letter to Flaxman, sent from Felpham on September 21, 1800, he wrote:

> I look back into the regions of Reminiscence & behold our ancient days before this Earth appear'd in its vegetated mortality to my mortal vegetated Eyes. I see our houses of Eternity which can never be separated, tho' our Mortal vehicles should stand at the remotest corners of heaven from each other.

---

[24] *The Four Zoas,* VI, 159-66. Urizen's fall, it will be noted, took the form of a spiral whirling in "unresistible revolutions" (l. 154).
[25] Williams, II, 198.

Crabb Robinson mentioned a sense in which Blake claimed to have been, or to have been with, Socrates.[26]

All these references tend to show that the Druids took their analogy from the cyclical order of nature and applied it to human destiny as a part of that order. Blake took his analogy from his own vision of human existence and applied it to the circle of time or what he meant by "nature." In other words, "nature" to the Druid and the Deist was the basic reality containing a scale of being including man, but to Blake, "nature" was the lowest degree in a scale of visionary perception which man himself contained. He came to see in Druidism the original of contemporary Deism with its remote, unapproachable Deity whose laws were to be found in the natural order. After the complimentary remarks of his *Descriptive Catalogue,* he made use of "Druidism" as the most perverse form the "Religion of Generation" could take to destroy human conscience in the person of Jerusalem.[27] In spite of Williams' denial of any connection between Druidism and natural religion and the antiquarians' praise of it as the religion of the patriarchs, Blake saw in its isolation of the Deity and its exaltation of him into the Supreme Moral Agent the root of the worst of all tyrannies—one based on the apparently reasonable and benevolent demands of the natural man's ideals. So interpreted, nature and natural laws became the "Stone of Trial" and the "Stone of Torture" to balance the scale of moral justice between good and evil for the human victim in this best of all possible worlds.

The victimization of man, in Blake's opinion, followed the immemorial pattern of the deterioration of religious discipline from internal effort to external pressure, and finally, to the kind of adjustment to social order and natural necessity required by the Deist. Such a deterioration was the inevitable result of virtue ceasing to mean "a man's leading propensity" and becoming a synonym for an acceptable pattern of behavior. Correction of behavior according to some pattern or code tended to become increasingly negative, and eventually culminated in the ritual murder of criminals in the name of moral virtue. Blake considered the whole process negative and therefore vicious, however necessary the expedient and however good the intention. Morality was a concession to the ways of this world and the natural man's substitute for conscience.

---

[26] Quoted by Alexander Gilchrist, *Life of William Blake* (Everyman ed., London 1942), p. 333.

[27] *Jerusalem,* I, 7, 63-64. Williams (II, 199) consistently referred Druidic doctrine to divine revelation. "Bardism always refers its origin to *Divine communications,* and never talked of, I know not what, *Religion of Nature.*"

While we are in the world of Mortality we Must Suffer. The Whole Creation Groans to be deliver'd; there will always be as many Hypocrites born
as Honest Men, & they will always have superior Power in Mortal Things.
You cannot have Liberty in this World without what you call Moral Virtue,
& you cannot have Moral Virtue without the Slavery of that half of the
Human Race who hate what you call Moral Virtue.[28]

Those who hated what was called moral virtue were those whose morality
took the inner form of conscience.

Conscience in those that have it is unequivocal. It is the voice of God. Our
judgment of right & wrong is Reason.[29]

As the abiding ethical principle, forgiveness of sins represented to Blake
the eternal process of regeneration as against the purely temporal process
of moral justification with its calculated balancing of ethical debits and
credits. Forgiveness of sins was the characteristic feature of the activity of
conscience, just as self-righteous condemnation tended to become the
negative activity of the moral judgment.

What finally reunited regenerate man (Albion) to his eternal sense of
values (Jerusalem) or his conscience was the recognition of the distinction
between the religion of generation represented as "Druidic" and the
religion of regeneration called the "Everlasting Gospel." It took Albion
from the beginning to the end of Jerusalem to see the difference between
them, and in the process, explore the depths of Ulro—"meer Nature or
Hell." The three states of Ulro were called "Creation, Redemption &
Judgment," [30] and they formed the infernal counterparts of those which
led on to eternal life: Generation, Beulah, and Eden. The difference between the kind of universal outlook implied by the infernal states and
that implied by the others was the difference between an outlook dedicated to outer conformity and one disciplined to inner fulfillment. The
three states of Ulro were three stages in the individual's relationship to

[28] *Vision of the Last Judgment*, pp. 92-95. "In Hell all is Self Righteousness; there is
no such thing there as Forgiveness of Sin; he who does Forgive Sin is Crucified as an
Abettor of Criminals, & he who performs Works of Mercy in Any shape whatever is
punish'd &, if possible, destroy'd, not thro' envy or Hatred or Malice, but thro' Self
Righteousness that thinks it does God Service, which God is Satan."

[29] *Annotations to Watson's* Apology for the Bible, p. 2. Blake's marginalia to this
particular book reflect his attitude to the pretensions of any *rationale* of morality. Cf.
p. 117: "The Gospel is Forgiveness of Sins & has No Moral Precepts; these belong to
Plato & Seneca & Nero." See also *Jerusalem*, III, 61, 17-27.

[30] *Jerusalem*, II, 36, 41-42. Reuben is called (ll. 23-24) the "Vegetative Man," and
Merlin is "his Immortal Imagination." "Ulro," probably an anagram of "rule" or
"ruler," is the natural state of "Single vision" (*Letter to Thomas Butts*, November 22,
1802) associated with Newton and mere spatial extension. See also Annotations to Swedenborg's *Divine Love and Wisdom*, pp. 195-96.

the ruler of this world conceived as the supreme moral agent and judge—a cosmic version of Orwell's Big Brother. The other three states, however, were stages in the individual's progressive realization of his "Human Existence." Generation was the state into which he was born and in which he dare not remain or he would consolidate in it and fall into Ulro. It was the state of nature as seen by the visionary imagination, just as Ulro was nature without vision. It was, in fact, human life seen as a living process within the circle of time—with its problems, contradictions, and constant change. Beulah was the state in which these problems and contradictions disappeared—"where Contrarieties are equally True."[31] It was the state where the individual had put to rest the natural "Selfhood" without having fully realized his "Human Existence"—a state significantly associated with the Quietists such as Fénelon and Teresa, rather than the prophets. Finally, there was Eden, the "land of life," where the "Human Existence" was fully realized, and time could be seen from the standpoint of eternity.

How, then, did Blake's "states" compare with the "circles" of Druidism found in Williams? For, according to the tradition of the Welsh Druids, there were three "Circles of existence."

> There are three Circles (or states) of existence: the *Circle of Infinity*, where there is nothing but God, of living or dead, and none but God can traverse; the *Circle of Inchoätion*, where all things are by Nature derived from Death; this circle has been traversed by man; and the *Circle of Felicity*, where all things spring from Life; this man shall traverse in Heaven.[32]

At first glance, the three circles of Druidism would seem to correspond to Blake's states: Generation, Beulah, and Eden, but the most notable features of his outlook were missing. First of all, there was no evident conviction that all existence must be seen as human to some degree, since man could not hope to understand anything from a viewpoint other than his own. Suddenly, struggle and search, the mental warfare of eternity, was understood as an unfavorable aspect of the lowest circle of existence

---

[31] *Milton*, II, 30, 1. For references to the states of existence, see D. J. Sloss and J. P. R. Wallis, *The Prophetic Writings of William Blake* (Oxford 1926), II, 134-37; 151-52; 162-63; 234-35.

[32] Willams, II, 241. "Infinity," Williams points out, is a translation of *Ceugant* which "in its etymological sense, signifies the *Circle of Vacuity;* in its metaphysical acceptation, here, it signifies the immense void beyond the bounds of the material Creation, into which none but the Deity can penetrate." Another translation would be "closing circumference," reminding one of Urizen's compasses. "Inchoätion" is a translation of *abred (ab*, "from," and *rhed,* a "course") which presumably referred to the transmigration of the soul. *Gwynfyd* (or *Gwynvyd*) meant the "white" world, and was usually translated the "Circle of Felicity."

—as belonging to death rather than life.[33] Finally, Blake's notion that man contained both creator and creature in himself, along with heaven and hell, was apparently avoided in favor of a disciplined resignation to an absolute code of imposed conditions.

Blake obviously thought that Druidism had come to sacrifice life to its conditions. Every "religion" was prone to take this degenerate form—a form which was usually expressed as a code of rules or laws. He therefore emphasized that the source of the good life lay in individual struggle and search rather than in conformity to an established set of regulations. But the God of the Welsh Triads would seem to be a Supreme Regulator like Plato's Divine Geometer and Priestley's Watchmaker—one for whom the correct conditions of life were more important than life itself.

> The three regulations of God towards giving existence to every thing: to annihilate the power of evil, to assist all that is good, and to make discrimination manifest, that it might be known what should and what should not be.[34]

The deification of conditions which included natural, social, and moral laws amounted to a deification of the nature of things seen by man's limited perceptions in his present degree of development. This meant that man fell from Generation into Ulro—the net of conditions which, when accepted as final, Blake called "Nature," "Natural Morality," and "Natural Religion." In opposition to the deification of life's conditions, he chose to deify human life itself, or rather, human existence, since he did not worship what man usually was, but what it was in him to be. "For everything that lives is Holy." He found it necessary to restore the priority of life over its functions, conditions, and especially its ideals. In the prophetic books, man's fallen state was attributed to the fact that his "Human Existence" was asleep, and his faculties and the conditions of his life had usurped control over him. To emphasize law at the expense of life would keep Albion asleep forever.

For Blake conscience was the actual criterion of moral rectitude, the living law as distinct from the law of the members which was the rule of temporal conditions. He did not suppose it possible to get rid of the outer law of nature and society, but he did object to giving this kind of legal sanction a dignity beyond immediate necessity. The very worst that could happen was to give such legal sanctions and conventions an absolute

---

[33] The static nature of the Circle of Infinity was in marked contrast to Blake's "Mental War" in eternity (*Jerusalem*, II, 43, 31-32).

> And the two Sources of Life in Eternity, Hunting and War,
> Are become the Sources of dark & bitter Death & corroding Hell.

[34] Williams, II, 240.

moral authority by basing them on a divine decree. By this means morality acquired a prerogative beyond conscience and tended to supersede and finally destroy it. As Blake put it, Jerusalem who was Albion's conscience was then "Offer'd up to Holiness" in the interests of "Natural Religion." [35] Druidism became the original example of the destruction of conscience in the name of morality and religion. The Druidic rite of human sacrifice was the central symptom of a disintegrating society where all sacrifice was regulated from without and the sacrificial victim was the scapegoat for society's ills. The sacrifice of the victim was a parody of self-sacrifice, just as the self-righteous virtue of the moralist was a parody of conscience. Blake thought of the "Patriarchal Religion" as one of self-sacrifice which later declined

> From willing sacrifice to Self, to sacrifice of (miscall'd) Enemies For Atonement.[36]

Sacrifice which was not self-sacrifice was both useless and criminal.

Bardic tradition, as Williams reported it, made every effort to justify the sacrificial rites of the Druids. The sacrifice of animals was considered a means of advancing them along the path of development.

> The sacrifice of animals, which were always those of the least ferocity of disposition, was a religious co-operation with Divine Benevolence, by raising such an animal up to the state of Humanity, and consequently expediting his progress towards Felicity; it was not to appease, we know not what, *Divine wrath,* a thing that cannot possibly exist; the idea of which is of all others, the most blasphemously disgraceful to the Deity.[37]

The sacrifice of human life, on the other hand, was regarded as a cooperative effort between the sacrificers and the victim, based on a doctrine of moral compensation.

> Man, having been guilty of crimes that are punishable by Death, must be so punished; and by giving himself up a voluntary victim to Death, being

---

[35] *Milton*, I, 19, 46-48:

> Come, bring with thee Jerusalem with songs on the Grecian Lyre!
> In Natural Religion, in experiments on Men
> Let her be Offer'd up to Holiness!

See also *Annotations to Watson's* Apology for the Bible, p. 3: "If Conscience is not a Criterion of Moral Rectitude, What is it?" Blake's conception of conscience or honesty was also involved with his attack on Locke's denial of innate ideas and the whole notion of a merely natural and experimental scheme of knowledge. Cf. Annotations to Reynolds's *Discourses*, p. 58: "The Man who says that we have No Innate Ideas must be a Fool & Knave, Having No Con-Science or Innate Science."

[36] *Jerusalem*, II, 28, 20-21. Compare Blake's reference to "Justice" and "Truth" in line 23 with Williams' sixteenth aphorism (II, 199).

[37] Williams, II, 199.

conscious of deserving it, does all that lies in his power to compensate for his crimes. . . .[38]

The notion of compensation and of a rule distinct from individual conscience tended to separate self-sacrifice from the moral judgment and allow the moralist to concentrate on the sacrifice of others. Blake noticed this tendency, and Druidism became the symbol of life as trial and experiment where the object of experiment was always another. He saw that the whole doctrine of moral compensation was too easily twisted by self-deceit into an excuse for vengeance in the name of the social order and into a cloak for personal jealousy.

Blake's symbol of "Druid Law" was used to uncover the negative effects of the scales of moral justice in the hands of Rahab, the goddess of Nature. In her was brought together the perverse poison of mutual accusation and judgment in the infested specter of fallen man's inner life.

> The Jealousies became Murderous, uniting together in Rahab
> A Religion of Chastity, forming a Commerce to sell Loves,
> With Moral Law an Equal Balance not going down with decision.
> Therefore the Male severe & cruel, fill'd with stern Revenge,
> Mutual Hate returns & mutual Deceit & mutual Fear.[39]

Blake made Druidism into a comprehensive symbol of all the perversities of fallen existence which were respectably hidden in the "Religion of Generation." What made Druidism the cult of the world from which all "worldly" religions came was its attempt to consolidate the original voice of the prophet into the fixed ritual and rule of the priest. The terms which had not been final for the seer became final in the name of an organized cult, and the conditions of life and worship were rendered invariable in the interests of an established clergy. This always produced, according to Blake, cruelty in the name of a benevolent concern for the victim's welfare, and he represented the human race in the person of

---

[38] *Ibid.*, p. 199. A later authority (J. Williams ab Ithel, *Barddas* [London 1862], I, lxix) referred to the doctrine of *eneidvaddeu* which placed the soul in a better state when, by the act of conscious atonement, it had compensated for its crimes.

[39] *Jerusalem*, III, 69, 33-37. Providentially, the temporal universe, according to Blake, was so constructed that error caused the least possible suffering to the sinner (II, 31, 30-34):

> I could not dare to take vengeance, for all things are so constructed
> And builded by the Divine hand that the sinner shall always escape,
> And he who takes vengeance alone is the criminal of Providence.
> If I should dare to lay my finger on a grain of sand
> In way of vengeance, I punish the already punished.

For the theme of revenge, see also III, 63, 39-41; 66, 38-39. Cf. *Annotations to Watson's* Apology for the Bible, p. 25.

Albion being sacrificed by his daughters in the temple of "Natural Religion." The "Divine Vision" was lost, and the human form of man's possibilities was altered, so that her perceptions were dissipated into the "Indefinite Becoming" of natural process.[40] Druidism became the composite symbol of fallen man's preoccupation with a natural security at the expense of a greater human adventure.

Blake treated the decline from the "Patriarchal Religion" to "Druidism" as fundamentally a degeneration in man's powers of perception, and hence, a falling off of his imaginative genius which integrated perception and was the root of his very existence. He had become less than himself— a mere wraith or "Spectre"—and in so doing, had ceased to think of the universe as the field of intelligent agency or as a "Cosmic Man." Humanity had become something in between God and nature—a something which partook of both but was neither. The original myth of the Cabalistic Adam Kadmon or "Grand Man," who was the archetypal principle of intelligent agency in the universe, had given way to the naturalistic view of man as merely a constituent factor in the cosmic process. Blake placed the roots of the former tradition in the "period" before Adam or in the state before the creation of the natural man. Speaking "to the Jews" in his preface to the second chapter of *Jerusalem*, he referred their ancestry to the patriarchs who were the first Druids.

> Your Ancestors derived their origin from Abraham, Heber, Shem and Noah, who were Druids, as the Druid Temples (which are the Patriarchal Pillars & Oak Groves) over the whole Earth witness to this day.
> You have a tradition, that Man anciently contain'd in his mighty limbs all things in Heaven & Earth: this you received from the Druids.[41]

The myth of the Giant Man was not developed in Williams' version of the triads, but instead, there was the conception of a gradual progression from the "lowest point of existence" to the state of felicity—a progression which stopped short of the circle of "Ceugant"—the eternal "Void" of the Deity. Blake objected to the disembodied Absolute or any nonhuman abstraction of Deity as the false vision of unattainable perfection, and he

---

[40] *Jerusalem*, III, 66, 1-56. The union, in Blake's use of imagery, between cruelty and a benevolent, even experimental, interest in the victim might be compared with Tacitus' charge (*Annals*, XIV, 30) that the Druids used prisoners for purposes of divination, "for they considered it lawful to offer the blood of captives on their altars, and to consult the gods by means of the nerves of men (*et hominum fibris consulere deos fas habebant*)." The same tendency prevailed in ecclesiastical Christianity. Cf. Notes Written on the Pages of *The Four Zoas*: "Christ's Crucifix shall be made an excuse for executing Criminals."

[41] *Jerusalem*, II, 27.

placed this "Central Void" in opposition to the "Divine Vision" of Christ.[42]

His conception of the Deity was certainly not, however, what is usually called "anthropomorphic"—the projection of fallen man's subjective idiosyncrasies. It was connected with the fact that the beginning and end of anything can never supersede its essential origin, and the ultimate extent of man's possibilities must be the fulfillment of his "Humanity." Luvah's statement concerning the human faculties applied to the whole question of human aspirations and ultimate aims: "Attempting to be more than Man We become less." [43] The attempt to surpass the balanced fulfillment of one's actual capabilities was characteristic of the perverse will of the natural man who wished to be superior to his neighbor and to all men. One of the main sources of unbalanced development, in Blake's opinion, lay in the primary use of the rational faculty to encompass man's present limitations of perception and on them establish the limits of the entire universe. This was precisely what Urizen was trying to do in the sixth Night of *The Four Zoas* when, like the typical eighteenth century philosopher, he sought the basis of his life by examining the limitations of his faculties. At the very commencement of his journey around the worlds of man's fallen faculties, he encountered Blake's version of the three fates, the threefold representation of Vala, Goddess of Nature. They wore the three colors of the three orders of Druidic priests, and repre-

---

[42] *Ibid.*, II, 30, 19-20. See Williams, II, 240-41: "All animated Beings are subject to three Necessities: a beginning in the Great Deep (lowest point of existence), Progression in the Circle of Inchoätion, and Plenitude in Heaven, or the Circle of Felicity; without these things nothing can possibly exist but God. Three things are necessary in the Circle of Inchoätion: the least of all animation, and thence the beginning; the materials of all things, and thence increase, which cannot take place in any other state; the Formation of all things out of the dead mass, hence discriminate individuality." The Druidic "Circles," however, appeared as the creations of a superhuman Deity for whom progression took place, while Blake's "states" were the creations of a "Divine Humanity" in whom progression was the realization of an individual existence. Cf. *Jerusalem*, II, 35, 9-10:

> In Me all Eternity
> Must pass thro' condemnation and awake beyond the Grave.

[43] *The Four Zoas*, IX, 709. Williams (II, 197) spoke of the accommodation of the Deity to the life of man. "Finite Beings can never comprehend Infinity; they cannot conceive anything of God, but as something external to themselves individually different, and, consequently, *finite*. The Deity for this reason, though in himself *infinite*, manifests himself to *finite* comprehensions as a *finite being*, as in the Person of Jesus Christ, &c." Cf. Annotations to Swedenborg's *Divine Love and Wisdom*, p. 24: "That there is but one Omnipotent, Uncreate & God I agree, but that there is but one Infinite I do not; for if all but God is not Infinite, they shall come to an End, which God forbid." See also p. 11: "Man can have no idea of anything great than Man, as a cup cannot contain more than its capaciousness. But God is a man, not because he is so perceiv'd by man, but because he is the creator of man."

sented respectively the presiding, attracting, and conducting powers reflected in natural process.[44] In this way, Druidism was connected with the
initial stages of man's fall from innocence through the birth of a rational
set of moral values based on a definitive system of nature.

Blake did not suppose, however, that the primitive Druids, whom he
had called "wiser than after-ages," were less than the "ancient Poets" who
had formed the basis of an original priesthood in his *Marriage of Heaven
and Hell*. In fact, the Bardic Triads gave the same priority to original
"genius" as he did. By "genius" he had meant the "true Man" from which
his outward form was derived and to which every intellectual and physical activity could ultimately be traced. It was the "whatness" in man, and
underlay the form of anything. Most important, the "Poetic Genius" was
the universal source of forms in the species and the individual. It was the
faculty which experienced, or what he called the "Imagination"—the
basic root of the total imagery of experience.[45] As the "Spirit of Prophecy," his conception of "genius" could be compared with what the Druids
had called *awen*. Although neoclassical terminology and poetic diction
clearly affected Williams' translation of the "Poetic Triades" or "Triades
of Song" (*Trioedd Cerdd*) there was much Blake could still appreciate:

> The three final intentions of Poetry: accumulation of Goodness; enlarge-
> ment of the Understanding; and what increases Delight.[46]

But this original emphasis on genius was finally corrupted, according to
tradition, along with the institutes of the Bards, by the Scots, Irish, Bret-
ons, and even the Germans. Bardism survived in its pure form only among
the Welsh.

Williams' attitude was ultimately sectarian, although his view that
Britain had been the original seat of the Patriarchal Religion was cer-

---

[44] *The Four Zoas*, VI, 8-19. This is a threefold representation of the "Daughters of
Albion" who dismember him (*Jerusalem*, III, 66, 17-34) and reduce his vision to that of
the corporeal senses. The "Eldest Woman" whose name is written on her forehead (l. 18)
obviously suggests the Babylon of Revelation (17:5). The three orders of Primitive
Bards, according to Williams (II, 230-31) were Bards, Ovates (or Euvates), and Druids.
The last of these was the chief, and it was the Druid (*Derwydd*) who dressed in white
as a symbol of truth and sanctity. The Ovate (*Ofydd*) wore green like the vegetation
of the earth, and the Bard (*Prifardd*), blue, the color of heaven. See also Edward Jones,
Musical and Poetical Relicks of the Welsh Bards (London 1794, 2nd ed.), pp. 2-9. Strabo,
Geographica, IV, 197, called the Bards chanters and poets, the ovates sacrificers and
physiologists, and the Druids moral philosophers.

[45] *All Religions are One*. Cf. Williams, II, 232: "Without three qualifications no one
can be a Bard: a poetical genius (*awen wrth gerdd*); the knowledge of Bardic institutes;
and irreproachable morals." The orders of the original Bards (p. 231) were determined
by genius (*awen*), exertion (*Ymgais*), and incident (*dichwain*).

[46] Williams, II, p. 256. For the corruption of Bardism see p. 248.

tainly shared by Blake. Neither one adopted the legend reported by Geoffrey of Monmouth, who claimed the authority of Taliesin, the celebrated bard of the fifth century, for the story of Trojan Brutus. Blake's use of Arthur, however, probably did come from the emphasis given him by the successors of Geoffrey, but his reference to the existence of genuine Bards in the fifth century could refer to Williams' mention of Meugant, Merlin, and Taliesin who were said to have lived around that time.[47] Apart from these references, his "Druidic" period covered all but the last quarter of the "Circle of Destiny" with its historical perspective stretching over six thousand years—beginning with Adam and ending with Luther. Original Druidism, indeed, began even before Adam and included the first two "Eyes" of God within the cycle of seven from Lucifer to Jesus.[48]

The "Twenty-seven Heavens & their Churches" provided Blake with his cyclical calendar of history graduated according to the separate attempts to reestablish communication between time and eternity. Within this context, Druidism stretched from Adam to Terah the father of Abraham who "was called to succeed the Druidical age, which began to turn allegoric and mental signification into corporeal command, whereby human sacrifice would have depopulated the earth." [49] The "Churches" and their respective "Heavens" were ways of ordering popular belief and social practice, but the "Eyes" of God were the ways God was "seen" or understood by each succeeding epoch. In *The Four Zoas,* the "Eyes" took the form of "Guards" sent to sacrifice themselves for Satan—Blake's symbol for the opacity of man's fallen perception. The Patriarchal Religion began with the first two—Lucifer and Molech—who were of the pre-Adamite age before the corporeal senses had become completely consolidated as fallen man's only avenues of perception. Between the Elohim who created Adam and Pachad whose name meant "fear" was Blake's "Druidical" age, succeeded by the worship of Jehovah by the "Church" of Abraham and the children of the promise.

Druidism as a symbol in the prophetic books began to be developed in the later additions to *The Four Zoas.* The sources which Blake actually mentioned were Milton and Jacob Bryant. If the internal evidence be considered sufficient to assume that he also knew something of Davies and

[47] *A Descriptive Catalogue* &c., No. V. Blake's reference to the "remains of those naked Heroes in the Welch Mountains" was connected with the reign of Arthur and the account of ancient British history given by Milton. Milton's evident belief in the accusations of the Romans (*History of Britain,* Book II, *Works,* Columbia ed., X, 51) made him call the Druids "Progenitors not to be glori'd in." See Williams, II, notes to 1-3; 5-7.

[48] *The Four Zoas,* VIII, 398-406; *Milton,* I, 13, 17-29; *Jerusalem,* III, 55, 30-33. For the twenty-seven heavens and their churches, see *Milton,* II, 37, 35-43; *Jerusalem,* III, 75, 10-22. Cf. Zechariah 9:10; Revelation 4:5.

[49] *A Descriptive Catalogue,* &c., No. V.

Stukeley, there is certainly as much to suggest that he had seen Williams' collection of "Welch Triades" or some such collection. The use he made of the triadic form to describe the last battle of Arthur significantly united the characteristics of the four human faculties or "Zoas" to the fall of his own Arthur who was the Giant Albion.

In the last Battle that Arthur fought, the most Beautiful was one
That return'd, and the most Strong another: with them also return'd
The most Ugly, and no other beside return'd from the bloody Field.

The most Beautiful, the Roman Warriors trembled before and worshipped:
The most Strong, they melted before him and dissolved in his presence;
The most Ugly they fled before with outcries and contortions of their Limbs.[50]

The reference, as he explained, was to the human faculties represented by the "Zoas": pathos or emotion (Luvah), sublimity or power (Tharmas), limitation or reason (Urizen), and vision or existence (Los) who was Arthur (Albion) himself. The battle was the "Intellectual Battle" mentioned at the beginning of *The Four Zoas*; it was the fall of the Giant Man, the Adam Kadmon of the Cabala, whose collapse from unity into diversity brought about the creation of the universe. For his Giant Man, Blake used the figure of Albion and the myth derived from the ancient Cabalistic tradition which he traced to the origins of Druidism.[51] He related the stories of Arthur to such a conception, and in the traditional death and promised return of the King, he saw the fall of man and his final redemption. Malory's own account of Arthur's epitaph suggested this same theme of death, transformation, and return.

Yet some men say in many parts of England that King Arthur is not dead, but had by the will of our Lord Jesu into another place; and men say that he shall come again, and he shall win the holy cross. I will not say it shall be so, but rather I will say, here in this world he changed his life. But many men say that there is written upon his tomb this verse: Hic jacet Arthurus Rex, quondam Rexque futurus.[52]

The statement that Arthur "changed his life" in "this world" contained Blake's notion of regeneration working in and through the entire cycle of birth and death.

[50] Sloss and Wallis, II, facing 302.
[51] *Jerusalem*, II, 27: "Albion was the Parent of the Druids, & in his Chaotic State of Sleep, Satan & Adam & the whole World was Created by the Elohim." In his *Descriptive Catalogue*, the "Triple Elohim" (cf. *Milton*, I, 13, 22) became the threefold life of man represented by the three Britons. The awakening of Arthur (Albion) "with tenfold splendor" probably refers to the ten *sephiroth* of the Cabalistic "Tree of Life" representing the full extent of what Blake called "Human Existence."
[52] Malory, *Morte d'Arthur*, XXI, vii.

However, his final treatment of Arthur in *Jerusalem* was typical of his treatment of Druidism as a whole. In the scornful speech of Vala, declaring the natural man's utter dependence on the "Female Will" of Mother Nature, she described both priest and king as the false front of the fallen "Worm" in his futile attempt to establish the natural analogy of an eternal society. Arthur became the symbol of the dream of imperial power which would prove an enforced imitation of the real communion of eternity.[53] He even became, in company with Satan and Cain, an infernal counterpart to the inspired ruler such as Moses or David and the states of existence they represented.[54] It was not that Blake condemned the effort to establish an analogy of eternal existence in time, for the whole of the temporal order was a "Divine Analogy." As he had said in *The Marriage of Heaven and Hell*, "Eternity is in love with the productions of time." But inspiration from eternity must remain the true basis of these productions, and the temporal order of things should not be made—in the spirit of the builders of Babel and their utopian successors—the basis and end of its own productions. "Eden" was the point where the productions of time and the life of eternity met. Blake claimed to be "an inhabitant of that happy country," and his professed aim was to unite the world of generation, through Eden, to its eternal source.

[53] *Jerusalem*, II, 64, 12-17. The use of Arthur by Blake suggests an association with Alexander whose legendary fame probably influenced Geoffrey of Monmouth's description of Arthur. See J. S. P. Tatlock, *The Legendary History of Britain* (Berkeley and Los Angeles 1950), p. 312. As a precedent for Arthur, Alexander's search for imperial hegemony would reflect the search of man for the universal community of an earthly paradise enforced and maintained by the sword. Blake associated this ideal of enforced political community with the ideal of "Moral Virtue"—the basic cause of war—and with its principal protagonists: "the Alexanders & Caesars, the Lewis's & Fredericks" (*Jerusalem*, III, 52). For Blake's association of Druidism with a society cut off from eternity, see *Jerusalem*, III, 66, 1-15.

[54] *Ibid.*, III, 73, 35-42.

Chronology of Important Dates

1757	Born (November 28), at 28 Broad Street, Golden Square, London. The house still stands.
1771	Apprenticed to James Basire, engraver.
1779-80	Studies at the Royal Academy for a few months. Beginning of his friendship with Fuseli.
1782	Marriage to Catherine Boucher.
1783	Publication of *Poetical Sketches,* his only book to be published in the ordinary way. The poems in it were written between 1768 and 1778.
1784	Goes into partnership with James Parker in a print-selling shop. Probable date of *An Island in the Moon.*
1787	Partnership dissolved and Blake moves to Poland Street. His younger brother Robert, to whom he was greatly attached, dies.
1788	Begins to develop his engraving process, and becomes interested in the Swedenborgian movement.
1789	*Songs of Innocence* and *Book of Thel* engraved.
1790	Probable date of the writing of *The Marriage of Heaven and Hell.*
1791	*The French Revolution,* Book I, printed as far as proof sheets by the left-wing publisher Joseph Johnson.
1793	*America* and *Visions of the Daughters of Albion* engraved.
1794	*Europe, Songs of Experience,* and *The Book of Urizen* engraved.
1795	*The Book of Los, The Book of Ahania,* and *The Songs of Los* engraved.
1796	Gets a commission to illustrate Young's *Night Thoughts,* for which he eventually made over five hundred designs.
1797	Probable date of beginning work on *Vala,* his first long poem, later called *The Four Zoas.*
1800	Accepts invitation from William Hayley to settle with him at Felpham in Sussex.
1803	Breaks with Hayley and returns to London.
1804	Acquitted at trial for sedition in Chichester as the result of a

fracas involving a soldier, John Scholfield, the previous August. *Milton* and *Jerusalem,* two long poems engraved in fifty and a hundred plates respectively, bear this date on their title-pages, but were probably completed some years later.

1805   Designs to Blair's *The Grave*; swindled by his dealer Cromek.

1809   First and only private exhibition of his work, for which he wrote *A Descriptive Catalogue.*

1818   Meets John Linnell and begins to emerge from obscurity.

1820   Woodcuts to Thornton's *Pastorals* (of Virgil).

1823-25   Work on the Job engravings.

1825-26   Work on illustrations to Dante.

1827   Dies, August 12.

1831   Death of his wife Catherine.

1863   *Life of William Blake, Pictor Ignotus,* by Alexander Gilchrist, who died in 1861, completed and published by Anne Gilchrist and the Rossetti brothers. Second edition 1880.

1868   Swinburne's critical essay on Blake published.

1893   Three-volume edition, including biography, commentary, and reproductions of the Prophecies published by E. J. Ellis and W. B. Yeats. *The Four Zoas* printed for the first time.

1924   *William Blake: His Philosophy and Symbols,* by S. Foster Damon. First major commentary.

1925   *The Writings of William Blake,* ed. Geoffrey (now Sir Geoffrey) Keynes. First complete standard edition.

1952   The Blake Trust in England begins, with *Jerusalem,* to issue a fine series of reproductions in color of the original works.

1957   Bicentenary of Blake's birth: commemorative lectures, articles, and exhibitions all over the world.

Notes on the Editor and the Contributors

HAZARD ADAMS, Chairman of the Department of English in the University of California at Irvine, has written on aesthetics and critical theory (*The Contexts of Poetry*, 1964) as well as on Blake. The selection in this book is an extract from *William Blake: A Reading of the Shorter Poems* (1963).

HAROLD BLOOM, of Yale University, has written on the English Romantic poets, including *Shelley's Mythmaking* (1959) and *The Visionary Company* (1961), from which this extract is taken, besides *Blake's Apocalypse* (1963). He also has provided the commentary for Erdman's edition (see below).

SIR ANTHONY BLUNT, Director of the Courtauld Institute in the University of London, is a well known authority on the history of art. This essay is from *The Art of William Blake* (1959), the Bampton Lectures in America, delivered at Columbia University.

IRENE H. CHAYES, formerly of the University of Maryland, has written extensively on the English Romantic poets.

DAVID V. ERDMAN, of the New York Public Library, is the author of *Blake: Prophet Against Empire* (1954), from which the essay in this book is taken, one of the most important commentaries on Blake, especially for Blake's reaction to the history and social developments of his time. He has also edited *The Poetry and Prose of William Blake* (1965), with textual notes.

PETER F. FISHER, drowned in a sailing accident in September 1960, was at the Royal Military College, Kingston, Ontario. His book on Blake, *The Valley of Vision* (1961), posthumously edited and published, is concerned mainly with intellectual and philosophical issues connected with Blake.

NORTHROP FRYE, Principal of Victoria College in the University of Toronto, is the author of *Fearful Symmetry: A Study of William Blake* (1947) and *Anatomy of Criticism* (1957).

ROBERT F. GLECKNER, Chairman of the Department of English in the University of California at Riverside, is the author of *The Piper and the Bard* (1959), a study of Blake's lyrical poetry.

JOHN E. GRANT, at the University of Iowa, has written many articles on Blake and related subjects.

JEAN F. HAGSTRUM, of Northwestern University, has written authoritative studies on the relation of poetry and painting in the eighteenth century, including *The Sister Arts* (1958) and *William Blake: Poet and Painter* (1964).

WILLIAM J. KEITH, of McMaster University, Hamilton, Ontario, is the author of a forthcoming study of Richard Jeffries.

MARTIN K. NURMI, of Kent State University, Ohio, is, with G. E. Bentley, Jr., author of a definitive *Blake Bibliography* (1964).

Selected Bibliography

The most generally used text of Blake is *The Poetry and Prose of William Blake,* ed. Sir Geoffrey Keynes (most recent ed. 1957). This text is modernized; an unmodernized one is provided by *The Poetry and Prose of William Blake,* ed. David V. Erdman (1965), which was not available to the contributors of this book, though some of them have preferred to leave their quotations unmodernized.

An account of Blake scholarship and criticism by the present editor, down to the end of 1956, appears in *The English Romantic Poets and Essayists,* ed. Houtchens, 1957. A new edition, with this essay revised and updated by Martin K. Nurmi, is due to appear soon.

In addition to the books listed in the notes on contributors and the chronology, the reader may consult *William Blake,* by H. M. Margoliouth (1950), a good general introduction; *A Man Without a Mask* (1943), by Jacob Bronowski; *William Blake: The Politics of Vision* (1946), by Mark Schorer; and *The Divine Vision* (1957), ed. de Sola Pinto. *From Sensibility to Romanticism* (1965), a Festschrift for Professor Frederick Pottle of Yale, contains three essays on Blake, two by contributors to this volume, which illustrate Blake criticism at its most contemporary.

Of reproductions of Blake's paintings and engravings, two collections, *The Paintings of William Blake* (1925), by Darrell Figgis, and *The Engraved Designs of William Blake* (1926), by Laurence Binyon are excellent, available in most large university libraries, and contain most of the designs referred to in this book.